# GERMANY AND THE EUROPEAN COMMUNITY

# GERMANY AND THE EUROPEAN COMMUNITY

## Beyond Hegemony and Containment?

Edited by Carl F. Lankowski

St. Martin's Press
New York

Chapter 2, "West German Labor and Europe '92," first appeared as "German Labor and Europe '92" in *Comparative Politics* 24 (January 1992) and is reprinted by permission of the publisher.



First published in the United States of America in 1993

Printed in the United States of America
ISBN 0-312-06035-1

Book design by Acme Art, Inc.

**Library of Congress Cataloging-in-Publication Data**

Germany and the European community : beyond hegemony and containment?
/ edited by Carl F. Lankowski.
p. cm.
Includes bibliographical references.
ISBN 0-312-06035-1
1. European Economic Community—Germany. I. Lankowski, Carl F., 1949- .
HC241.25.G3G465 1993
337.4043—dc20 93-4511
CIP

*This one is for Alex and Matt*

## CONTENTS

# ACKNOWLEDGMENTS

Germany and the European Community are involved in a process of parallel and combined metamorphosis. This situation provides both the rationale and the challenge for producing this volume. I am grateful for the assistance and inspiration of friends and colleagues in all phases of the project. But I am particularly indebted to the authors of this text. They responded to the challenge with work of exceptional quality.

Peter Katzenstein did his customarily brilliant job of dissecting early versions of the papers on a panel at the annual meetings of the American Political Science Association.

Andy Markovits encouraged the project in one way or another since we were graduate students together at Columbia. He has been an abiding inspiration.

Lily Gardner Feldman, director of research at the American Institute for Contemporary German Studies in Washington, has supported this book materially and intellectually, specifically and generally, by creating a stimulating setting for exploring ideas and analyzing events.

I benefited greatly from a study grant from the German Academic Exchange Service in the summer of 1991 to work on the text at the institute. I also appreciate the help of Jerry Livingston, Jack Janes, and Manfred Stassen, who have consistently provided a lively and enriching program at the Institute. Cornelia Danier rendered valuable service at the institute's library.

Special thanks are due to Peter Doyle, Director of Public Affairs at the EC Commission's Delegation in Washington, for doing so much to facilitate discussion about the European Community in the United States. Vlacia Vassikeri has been enormously helpful in finding EC documents.

Dave Brown, dean of the Washington Semester and World Capitals Program at the American University in Washington, kindly made resources available for the preparation of some of the manuscripts.

Joan Kloepfer has been a magnificent copy editor and a source of great comfort during the final stages of this project.

This volume could not have been conceived without the selfless and engaging assistance of German colleagues, friends, and acquaintances too numerous to list.

Simon Winder, my editor at St. Martin's, has provided just the right mix of motivation, interest, and involvement. I am also grateful for Laura Heymann's excellent technical support.

Needless to say, I claim sole responsibility for all remaining errors of omission and commission.

*Carl F. Lankowski*
Washington, February 1993

## CONTRIBUTORS

**CHRISTOPHER S. ALLEN** is associate professor of political science, University of Georgia, Athens.

**SIMON J. BULMER** is lecturer in government, University of Manchester, England.

**MICHAEL G. HUELSHOFF** is associate professor of political science, University of New Orleans.

**PAULETTE KURZER** is associate professor of politics, Babson College, Wellesley, Massachusetts.

**ROBERT LADRECH** is assistant professor of political science, St. Mary's College, Notre Dame, Indiana.

**CARL F. LANKOWSKI** is assistant professor in the Department of Comparative and Regional Studies, The American University, Washington, D.C.

**ANDREI S. MARKOVITS** is professor and chairman of the Department of Political Science, the University of California, Santa Cruz.

**ALEXANDER OTTO** graduated summa cum laude from Harvard College and is currently studying at the Harvard Business School.

**JAMES SPERLING** is associate professor of political science, the University of Akron, Akron, Ohio.

1

# Introduction

# Germany and the European Community: The Issues and the Stakes

Carl F. Lankowski

## THE GERMAN QUESTION IN THE EUROPEAN INTEGRATION PROJECT

According to a recent study, the future of the European Community (EC) depends on the ability of its policies and institutions to "dampen a rising hegemon's national aspirations so that they will remain acceptable to the less powerful states, without at the same time appearing too burdensome to the hegemon" (Keohane and Hoffmann 1991, p. 32). Insofar as they describe and analyze the configuration and exercise of German power in Europe in the midst of a major metamorphosis of the international system, the chapters in this volume respond to the agenda implied by this statement. The European Community plays a critically important role in connecting the long period of U.S.-Soviet bipolarity with the present, post–Cold War period. Major efforts at widening and deepening the project of regional integration have been launched just as its Cold War rationale has all but disappeared from the historical stage with the dissolution of the Soviet Union. That this renewed dynamism owes much to the desire of European states to gain influence over decision-making centers in newly unified Germany is no less important for being obvious.

Although this neorealist framework illuminates one important dimension of the German-EC relationship, the picture conveyed is necessarily partial. The neorealist approach would highlight the end of the Cold War as a defining moment in the evolution of this relationship, but the really important changes were initiated already prior to the 1989 political earthquake in Eastern Europe. Indeed, there is more continuity than change in German-EC relations than might have been predicted through preoccupation with interstate relations. That social and economic developments are equally important in establishing Germany's relationship with the EC is a major theme in the chapters in this volume.

## The Geopolitical Dimension

Serious proposals for European political unity in this century begin with Aristide Briand's 1930 overture to the League of Nations on behalf of a European Federal Union (Stirk 1989). Unfortunately, Briand's proposal was overtaken by the Great Depression. European political institutions were subsequently severely tarnished by fascism, and the European state system was eclipsed by the carnage of World War II. This "political collapse" paved the way for renewed efforts at regional organization that would provide a framework for peaceful cooperation and restoration of Europe's role on the world stage. The Congress of Europe, with representatives from sixteen countries, met at the Hague in May 1948, setting in motion a process that would produce the Council of Europe a year later. Providing for security, that is, dealing with the possible revival of a German threat, was part of this same project. Building on the 1947 Treaty of Dunkirk that it signed with France, Britain joined France and the Benelux countries in signing the Brussels Treaty in March 1948 (Robertson 1966).

The plan launched by French Foreign Minister Maurice Schuman for a supranational coal and steel community with Germany in May 1950 was influenced by America's policy of containing the Soviet Union. Launched in 1947, that policy of containment supported economic, then military revival of that part of Germany under the control of the Western occupying powers. The June 1948 currency reform that sealed the economic division between East and West and Germany's participation in the Organization for European Economic Cooperation set up to distribute Marshall aid were milestones in the reconstitution and eventual remilitarization of a West German state. By the same token, French leaders were in the forefront of those Europeans aiming to increase Europe's capacity to pursue its interests independent of the superpowers. In retrospect, the genius of the Schuman Plan lay in the fact that it corresponded to the double logic of containment as well as to the logic of European revival. The open-ended American presence in Germany facilitated the French gambit by lessening the risks of cooperation with Germany and simultaneously mobilized resources to be deployed in the deepening cold war (Diebold 1959; Hanrieder 1989; Marjolin 1989). This convergence of logics is repeated in the case of the European Defense Community (EDC), another French initiative designed to accommodate the raising of German military contingents that gained almost immediate American support (Schwartz 1991). But the French National Assembly decided against ratification of the treaty establishing the EDC.

France paid for this attempt to deny the logic of German revival with German rearmament in the framework of the North Atlantic Treaty Organization (NATO) on terms that promised much greater American interference in European affairs and much less direct French influence over the rearmament process. From this point of view, Germany's military revival, accomplished through prior integration into the refurbished and renamed Brussels Treaty Organization and henceforth known as the Western European Union (WEU), constituted a rearguard damage-limitation policy.

To make matters worse, exasperated by the Europeans' inability and/or unwillingness to meet the NATO force goals set at Lisbon in 1952, the Americans nuclearized the alliance and insisted on placing an American officer in command. This process coincided with the refusal of the U.S. government to aid French nuclear efforts in the interest of nonproliferation. Then, in October 1956, the U.S. government joined with the Soviet premier in condemning the joint Franco-British-Israeli operation to retake control of the Suez Canal and compelled them to end the action. Meanwhile, Soviet tanks crushed the rebellion raging in Hungary. Similar helplessness was displayed when the Berlin Wall was constructed in August 1961; when in October 1962 U.S. President John Kennedy and Soviet Chairman Nikita Khrushchev bargained over the heads of the Europeans about the fate of the world during the Cuban missile crisis; when the Soviets forced the return of political winter in Czechoslovakia by crushing the Prague Spring in August 1968; and when the American strategic nuclear forces were alerted during the Yom Kippur war in October 1973 to prevent Soviet intervention in the Middle East.

Konrad Adenauer's foreign policy was based on the premise that Europe was, indeed, caught between the superpowers (DePorte 1979). This acceptance of block logic may have reassured the French in one way, but it constantly threatened to nullify efforts at independent European positions.

In this light it is not difficult to find the geopolitical logic in the negotiations leading to the Treaty of Rome establishing the European Economic Community (EEC) and the European Atomic Energy Commission (EURATOM). Contrary to the hopes and expectations of the greatest enthusiasts of regional integration, however, it was not the sectoral format of EURATOM but rather the Common Market established by the EEC that gave that project its strongest push (Scheinman 1967). In any event, Germany's interest in EURATOM declined when it became apparent that that organization was not needed to serve as a basis for German nuclear aspirations in the civilian domain (Deubner 1979).

## The Economic and Social Dimension

In a keenly perceptive analysis, Donald Puchala (1990) shows that one of the main outcomes of the functional integration strategy embodied in the Treaty of Rome was the *increased power of the member states.* Increased trade produced greater wealth, which resulted, in turn, in state revenue growth to finance Europe's substantial entitlement programs and collective consumption demands. On balance, the ability to meet these needs *enhanced the legitimacy of the European state.* The logic of the 1987 Single European Act conforms to this pattern by mandating the removal of a vast array of nontariff barriers and granting the Community authority to act in new policy domains.

The dialectics of this process are of particular interest. Not all fiscal systems in EC-Europe benefited equally from trade liberalization. In fact, intra-EC regional disparities grew, despite the existence of some Community redistributive mechanisms (Holland 1976, 1980). Even though the country is a net contributor to the EC's social, regional, and agricultural support funds, in the aggregate, Germany has been the big winner, accounting for disproportionate shares of EC-manufactured exports both within the EC and externally. Until recently, Germany was at the same time responsible for a stable but disproportionately low share of manufacturing imports (May 1982; Cutler et al. 1989, chap. 1) Indeed, prior to 1989, in the context of effective industrial conflict resolution mechanisms, training programs, and the special status accorded its monetary institutions (Katzenstein 1987), Germany's export position became one of chronically large trade surpluses. German monetary authorities took advantage of this situation to maintain a hard currency, the effects of which feed back into price formation and competitiveness in the export sector. Armed with this systemic advantage,

Germany has been able to encourage the other EC member states to adopt macroeconomic policy targets in line with its own (Lankowski 1980, 1982).

In sum, far from functioning as a confining corset, the EC framework actually facilitated the pursuit of West Germany's interests prior to the events of 1989. These developments occurred within the Cold War framework in piecemeal, incremental fashion. The Single European Act is perhaps the best example of this pattern. Certainly this reform had important consequences for the overall development of the Community, but a primary reason for this lay in the fact that member states were becoming more heterogeneous with respect to regulatory regimes in health, safety, and the environment. And this, in turn, had more to do with the existence of social movements pushing a reform agenda than with the form and content of the act, which was quite modest.

The act consisted of four titles, only three of which were substantive. The first and third titles acknowledged practices in which the member states had already been engaged for over a decade, namely, foreign policy cooperation (EPC) and institutionalized summitry (the European Council). EMS was brought into the EEC framework in the middle title amending the EEC and launching the internal market program. Formally this title (II) did little more than restore Council operations to procedures that had been abandoned due to French protest in 1965, and then only in a restricted set of cases. New policy sectors were added that increased the scope of the Community's authority to act, but only by unanimity. The most important institutional change consisted in incremental upgrading of the European Parliament's capacity to intervene in the EC decision-making process, but this was more a matter of increasing the amplitude of its voice than it had to do with providing that body with traditional parliamentary authority.

## The Interaction of Geopolitical and Economic Forces

As long as Germany remained divided and the Cold War, bipolar block structure remained intact, France's status as an allied victor guaranteed it leverage over Germany in the EC. The amount of leverage was proportional to the level of adherence of German politicians to the promise of German reunification or any kind of direct relations with the German Democratic Republic. In other words, France was also a beneficiary of the block logic it had been simultaneously trying to escape. In launching his *Ostpolitik,* Chancellor Willy Brandt drew conclusions from the "enduring balance" between the superpowers (DePorte 1979). That logic placed clear limits on German relations with Eastern Europe in general and East Germany in particular. But from it the Social Democrat drew different conclusions from his Christian Democratic predecessor. Paradoxically, acknowledgement of the finality of the bipolar system that divided Germany signaled not only the possibility of pluralism within each camp, but also chances for increasing contacts and hope for eventual *rapprochement* between states on either side of the German-German border.

The patterns of EC institutional development in the 1970s showed that *Ostpolitik* could not be carried out without *Westpolitik*. The December 1969 EC summit meeting at The Hague launched an innovative period of EC institution building and program expansion that in many respects resembles the convocation of intergovernmental conferences in 1989 that eventuated in the Maastricht Treaty on European Union.

The Hague summit set in motion an effort to achieve a European Economic and Monetary Union (EMU) and launched the EC's experiment in foreign policy coordination, the European Political Cooperation (EPC). The French government already possessed a privileged line of communication to the German government. Their Treaty of Friendship and Cooperation of 1963 reaffirmed the central diplomatic fact of the West European regional integration process at the symbolic level and provided for frequent bilateral consultations that are aided by a system of issue-area working groups (Simonian 1985). The EPC provided an important channel for working out common EC positions without the Americans, in the multilateral phase of détente. According to the American envoy, the EC managed this to great effect during the negotiation of the Helsinki Accord, which set up the Conference on Security and Cooperation in Europe (CSCE) process (Maresca 1987). Any discussion forum from which the United States was excluded almost automatically increased the leverage of the French.

The central issue of the EMU project involved defining the strategy by which economies with different scores on macroeconomic indicators—rate of inflation, level of unemployment, external and internal debt, growth rate—could be induced to converge. While the French favored a regime that introduced monetary convergence at an early stage, the Germans preferred convergence of economic structures, which, it was hoped, would bring spending and debt ratios into line. Monetary union would be the "crowning achievement" of progress toward convergence in the "real" economy. There is evidence to suggest that Germany's political calculus included accommodation of the French position when that might not have been warranted on strictly economic grounds. In particular, during the "hot" phase of Chancellor Brandt's *Ostpolitik* in 1971-1972, when French support was particularly important—to placate both the vociferous domestic opposition and win over the skeptical Americans—the German government adhered to an exchange rate structure despite upward pressure on the mark and the recommendation of Karl Schiller, the very popular minister of economics and finance, to float or at least to revalue it. This action, strongly desired at the time by France, led to the minister's resignation (Lankowski 1980).

But as time went on, the more enduring pattern involved European adjustment to German economic and monetary priorities. Once again, French policy illustrates the process of EC institution building. Launched in March 1979, the European Monetary System (EMS) institutionalized a de facto Deutsche Mark zone that grew out of the monetary turbulence of the 1970s. Germany's abiding interest lay in maintaining the Common Market in the context of its generally austere monetary policy. This objective required exchange rate stability at least around a core of countries. France, Germany's largest trading partner, was its natural choice. Cooperation was facilitated by the decline in the value of the U.S. dollar associated with persistent and growing trade deficits. An independent European posture also derived from economically and politically based differences between Europe and America over relations with the Third World in light of the success of the Organization of Petroleum Exporting Countries (OPEC) as a commodity cartel. France's refusal to join the Kissinger-inspired countercartel of oil importers, French initiatives for North/South and Euro/Arab dialogues, and the negotiation of the EC's 1975 Lomé multilateral trade and aid accord comprised important corollaries to the convergence of Franco-German economic policies leading to the EMS. The neoliberal turn of French economic policy launched by the Valery Giscard d'Estaing–Raymond Barre team created the conditions for German support for the French currency and a vindication of its strategic orientation. With this in mind already in 1976, the German Social Democrats waged the federal election campaign with the slogan *Modell Deutschland.* Thus, "the EMS was arguably the first major act of German leadership in the history of the European Community" (Ludlow 1982, p. 290).

Despite the major shifts in the Franco-German political constellation, the continuity of the parameters for monetary cooperation in the 1980s is impressive. Once the socialists had taken over the reins of government in France, they did try to break out of the "Giscardian knot," pursuing a Keynesian reflation strategy from 1981 to 1983. Despite their attempts to neutralize anticipated capital flows, when faced with the foreign exchange turbulence associated with a policy that diverged so clearly from those of its EC partners, the government relented, making a fundamental decision to readopt German priorities: the internal market and economic convergence. By that time, the British government already had been moving toward resigned acceptance of increased powers for the European Parliament in return for concrete steps toward economic deregulation at the EC-level.

Neither the project of European revival advocated especially by the French nor America's containment policy were thought to be capable of functioning in the absence of German participation on terms that would be perceived as equal in Germany. In other words, it was thought that the revival of Europe required the revival of German economic and military might. As the preceding paragraphs demonstrate, however, at least on the economic side, once begun, the process took on a dynamic of its own. The French position is clarified by the insight that France has always acknowledged the legitimacy of German power. French governments have done everything they could to prevent a powerful Germany from loosening the ties that bind their countries together. How else to interpret the apparent paradox of fundamentally opposite anxieties driving France's European policy over the years? Was it not the specter of German *militarization* that both inspired the EDC and caused the National Assembly to refuse to ratify the treaty in the 1950s? And was it not the fear of German *pacifism* in the 1980s in the debate over the "modernization" of NATO theater nuclear weapons that led the Socialist French government to rebuke its sister party in Germany, embark on a rapprochement with NATO, and initiate tighter Franco-German military cooperation that included both an element of joint nuclear planning (for the Hades and Pluto missiles) and the symbolic Franco-German brigade? There is no paradox here, only different manifestations of France's abiding interest in embedding every exercise of German power in a decision-making framework in which France has a strong voice.

If implied in the French policy of European regional integration is the expectation that German power can be "mellowed" and/or diffused, its fundamental premise is that the European system will continue to be a system of states. There is room in this conception for pooling of sovereignty, but there is no question of adopting any policy that would undermine the cohesion of the French state. This position was made abundantly clear between June 1965 and January 1966 by the drama of France's boycott of the EC Council of Ministers over Commission proposals that would have conferred some independent budgetary authority to the European Parliament. The crisis occurred because under Council procedures, France could have been outvoted on the issue (Newhouse 1970). The impasse was *ritualized* by the understanding that any member state could require unanimity (or veto power for each state) in any matters it considered to be of vital national concern. And it was *partially resolved* by the decision-making procedures introduced in the Single European Act.

## CONTINUITY AND CHANGE AFTER 1989

In contrast to the incremental pattern of EC development prior to 1988, the situation since 1989 involves the parallel and combined metamorphosis of Germany and the EC. The Intergovernmental Conferences (IGCs) on Economic and Monetary Union and Political Union led to the Maastricht Treaty, which created the entirely new European Union, extended the span of EC authority, and significantly realigned the relationships between institutions in the EC system. For its part, the unification of Germany, although of more restricted geographic scope, is having dramatic and lasting ramifications for the nation's economy, society, and constitutional balance. Despite this, the relationship between Germany and the EC exhibits more continuity than change. In 1989-1990, in the context of President Mikhail Gorbachev's domestic reform program, the Soviet refusal to save neo-Stalinist regimes in Eastern Europe from collapse meant that the Cold War was over and the rationale for the strategy of containment had vanished. Suddenly NATO's mission had become unclear. The consequences for Germany were enormous.

It took almost three weeks for Chancellor Helmut Kohl to announce his government's posture toward the GDR after the Berlin Wall was breached on November 9, 1989. Kohl's was a cautious statement advocating cooperation, confederation, and federation in the undefined future. By this time, however, mass demonstrations had already begun to shift from advocating self-determination and reform of the GDR to unification with the West. Over the next ten weeks, as it became apparent that the economic situation in the GDR was untenable, and East Germans continued to pour relentlessly into the West, the government embraced unification wholeheartedly. Once committed to the project, the chancellor overrode his economic policy advisors, notably Bundesbank Chairman Karl-Otto Pöhl, in pressing forward with a plan for German economic, monetary, and social union to take effect on July 2, 1990, in preparation for full unification the following October. The increase in liquidity resulting from the one-to-one exchange rates caused the Bundesbank to peg rates at high levels, just as the European economy outside of Germany was entering a period of stagnation.

The French, supported by most other EC members, launched a diplomatic counteroffensive that emphasized acceleration of the pace of EC institutional development. Meeting in Dublin in June 1990, the EC heads of state and government formally launched not only the intergovernmental conference on economic and monetary union, but also an additional one on "Political Union." The transformations in Eastern Europe also prompted President François Mitterrand to push for the establishment of the EBRD (European Bank for

Reconstruction and Development), the first post–Cold War pan-European economic agency. The other major initiative was the stepping-up of Franco-German and West European military cooperation by way of elevating the joint brigade to a corps and the use of the Western European Union (WEU) in the Persian Gulf War. As in the case of the EDC from 1952 to 1954, there were some who had tired of the Franco-German embrace, a sentiment elegantly presented in the best-selling *La Grande Illusion,* a plea for a pan-European focus (Minc 1989). In the September 1992 French popular referendum, the Maastricht Treaty was affirmed by only two percentage points.

The Franco-German theme of the preceding paragraphs, dictated by the history of postwar Europe, highlights the enduring geostrategic dimension of EC policy. As the Germanys were more objects than subjects of international politics in the Europe of the 1950s, they were classical "penetrated states" (Hanrieder 1969). While there can be no doubt regarding the analytical power of placing the state at the center of the analysis, the analytical lens must be adjusted in line with evolving societal trends to maintain its accuracy. For a generation prior to the "*annus mirabilis*" of 1989, the historical structure of the Cold War was gradually being transformed from below. Attention to social forces and political culture will complicate the picture of Germany and the EC, but it pays dividends in clarifying the essential continuities of German-EC behavior before and after 1989.

The EMS story shows that West Germany had already influenced the trajectory of institutional development of the European Communities in the 1970s. At the same time, German society was being transformed from within by a burgeoning social movement sector. Taking seriously Chancellor Brandt's 1972 challenge to "dare more democracy," citizens organized thousands of grass-roots initiatives outside the political party framework. Germany's became the most densely populated and active social movement sector in Europe. The historical legacy of fascism and military defeat helped imbue the green project in West Germany with its characteristically tenacious countercultural, antisystemic outlook. Connected organizationally by way of various umbrella groups and green and alternative parties, most movement segments share a holistic, ecological ideology oriented toward transformation of the existing social order. Out of this movement sector came the Green Party, which got its start in local elections in 1977, following the first intense phase of antinuclear protest.

The Greens became a substantial political force in Germany, as the first new political party to enter the Bundestag since the early years of the Bonn republic. Thousands of Green municipal counselors and dozens of Green Landtag members were elected in every Land except the Saar, laying the basis for "red-green" governments in Hesse, Lower Saxony, and Berlin by 1989. From 1987 on, as Chancellor Kohl's political position showed signs of significant erosion, many prominent Green Party members anticipated the possibility of participating in the federal government with the Social Democrats.

It is worth recalling that the Greens' presence on the German national scene began with the election campaign for the first direct elections to the European Parliament in 1979. The elections provided an important occasion to stitch together three central themes at the heart of their emergent ideology and thereby to consolidate its identity as a agency of general systemic transformation. The conventional belief that economic growth is the best and even only solution of societal defects is rejected in favor of an ecological, solidaristic society of controlled and limited economic action. Nationalism is challenged by a vision of inclusive diversity based on protection for minorities, sub- or transnational regionalist identifications, and tolerance of a wider range of gender identities. And a remote and faceless technocracy is attacked from the point of view of alternative forms of political organization that feature decentralized, grass-roots, and plebiscitary participation and cooperative, consensual forms of decision-making. In short, the movements and their parliamentary tribunes took on both Germany and Europe together.

In the 1979 elections to the European Parliament, the fledgling green list scored 3.2 percent of the vote in Germany with 65.7 percent of those eligible to vote actually casting a ballot. This result was good enough to convince the leadership to organize as a regular party at the national level, although under the German 5 percent electoral floor it deprived the Greens of any representation in the Strasbourg Parliament. Seven Greens entered the European Parliament in 1984 on the strength of 8.2 percent of the German vote in an election in which 56.8 percent of those eligible turned out. In 1989 the figures improved to 8.4 percent on a 62.4 percent turnout rate.

However else they differed, governments of the EC member states had agreed on the basic aims and modalities of the Community. In reacting against the experience of economic nationalism and trade wars of the 1930s, the Common Market was conceived as an economic growth machine. As we have seen, the Germans considered themselves to be the vanguard of this policy orientation. It must be viewed as an irony, then, that the "new politics" of the social movements that challenged this very premise first emerged in Germany.

West Germany flourished along with all of Western Europe in the block structure. As its export-oriented economic performance improved in the European setting, Germany became EC Europe's center of gravity; Europe was being transformed by Germany. But Germany itself was transformed by the movements. In the European multiparty context, a party receiving the degree of electoral support claimed by the Greens could not safely be ignored either by the German government or the EC Commission. Even a conservative government was compelled to absorb the environmental message and begin to produce green policy initiatives. The greening of Germany produced powerful stimuli in the same dimension at the EC level.

## NETWORKS AND MECHANISMS IN GERMAN-EC RELATIONS

From one point of view, the issue of Germany's relation to the European Community resolves itself into a question about German responsiveness to other member states, as demonstrated by the case of France. An indicator of this interstate, geostrategic "French" framework is Germany's willingness to pool sovereignty by subjecting areas that are closest to the core of state power to joint decision-making procedures.

Nevertheless, Germany's relationship to the European Community can no longer be portrayed accurately in that dimension alone. Although the concept of hegemony stalks these chapters, it is meant to refer to a broader concept than the traditional definition—the deliberate use of influence by public authorities to advance a national interest by imposing their will on other states. Although that definition can be expected to illuminate the patterns of transactions between states, it is ill-equipped to track changes in the composition and orientation of nonstate entities. A more complex notion of hegemony that identifies the policy-making subject in a web of institutions, ideas, and material resources broader than the state facilitates the drawing of a more nuanced picture of the effects of regional integration (Cox 1981, 1983).

Another valuable indicator of the character of Germany's relationship with the EC will be the degree to which the state permits or even encourages the devolution of managerial control over significant resources to lower levels of government in the EC context or assigns competences to transnational bodies. This is partly a matter of creating networks that circumvent national decision-making centers. It also depends upon the willingness of economic and political agents to activate EC networks or adopt an EC frame of reference in the pursuit of their interests. This societal focus is an important part of the analytical work in the following chapters, since it can reveal the European idea as it is reworked by successive generations. Despite the dominance of the French *idiom* in the integration process, new collective identities are beginning to impose their agenda on Europe.

The volume opens by looking at the impact of the EC's internal market program. The internal market continues to be sold by the Commission to its public in terms of its aggregate effects. For Germany's part, given its dependence on exports to EC Europe, the German government has been a longtime advocate of internal market reform, due to very high export levels in important industrial sectors. Until now, relatively little has been known about how "1992" is actually affecting business strategies. In Chapter 1 Michael G. Huelshof explores the attitudes and perceptions of German manufacturers in different industrial segments toward the EC project. The relevant EC directives are being implemented in the context of national regulatory systems that continue to maintain their distinctive profiles. As they are phased in, these distinctions will be accentuated, introducing more complexity into the business situation as well as added adjustment requirements. This opens up the possibility that what business managers may celebrate ideologically, they may rue in practice. In distinguishing between their ideological orientations and interest calculations, Huelshof offers a way of cutting through the public relations fog surrounding the internal market, providing insights into the likelihood of medium-term industrial reorganization, even as industrial restructuring proceeds in the Eastern Länder.

As Andrei S. Markovits and Alexander Otto demonstrate in their highly original analysis in Chapter 2, the situation is similarly complex for organized labor. Any agreed position about the internal market would provide the German Trade Union Confederation (DGB) with significant leverage at EC level through the European Trade Union Confederation (ETUC) since the DGB is the largest and most active component of that regional body. But the fit between ideology and perceived risks to jobs and union membership implied by the internal market is different from union to union. German industrial relations law creates a regime that provides labor with a voice in industrial firms through works councils and representation on boards of directors. If the internal market means an increase in merger and acquisition activity within the Community, the question arises as to how organized labor's hard-won positions will be maintained. Other aspects of the German regulatory regime, such as levels of health and safety protection in the workplace, may also produce differing responses to the internal market, as may the palette of policy preferences with respect to work time, weekend work, cooperation with other EC union organizations, and other important issues.

In Chapter 3, Simon J. Bulmer shows that the prospect of German reunification brought to the fore the changing and somewhat contradictory fears and expectations of Germany's neighbors. Will Germany's attentions drift eastward? Will it dominate the other states in the Community? Following the central theme of this volume, Bulmer resists the temptation of interpreting the German-EC relationship in aggregate terms. Instead, his analysis proceeds from the individual policy networks that connect the two entities. Neither the EC nor the Federal Republic is a highly centralized policy-making structure. In Germany, policy-making is parceled out on both horizontal and vertical axes. Added to this is the fact that federal ministries jealously guard their spheres of responsibility, effectively fragmenting policy-making. In macro-economic policy-making, the government must contend with the independence of the Bundesbank. Moreover, Germany is a federal state in which significant powers of policy formulation and execution are assigned to the Länder. Bulmer evaluates these networks as constraints that can potentially mitigate any concerted action in the EC. The implication is that instead of *a* German-European policy, *many* German-European policies exist.

But what about the regional *effects* of the implementation of German policy preferences? Can it be that German *intentions* are beside the point? The fact of domination, the functioning of the EMS, can also be evaluated from the point of view of the other EC member states. This is what Paulette Kurzer and Christopher S. Allen do in Chapter 4 with respect to Belgium, Denmark, and the Netherlands. The effects of a large state's policy-making do not "stop at the water's edge." German policy-making institutions constitute the setting and establish the parameters within which economic policy is made for the small, open political economies on its borders. This reality has had adverse implications for this constellation of small "social democratic states." Kurzer and Allen's insightful contribution is defined by a curious situation. Despite the theoretical possibility for elaborating divergent economic and monetary policies, these countries have *chosen* to submit to German policies. That this occurs at all is attributed to the role of the central bank authorities in each of the countries in question. Variations in policy response are attributed to institutional differences among members of the group in the financial sector.

There is good reason to believe that it was precisely *because* of the size of these countries that the policy management problems in social-democratic Belgium, Denmark, and the Netherlands were not viewed as being particularly significant for the project of social democracy per se. But the struggle for redefinition of the social-democratic project was not only a matter for small states. If there had been any doubts about the acute need for such a change of perspective, it was put to rest by the defeat, at the hands of the foreign exchange traders, of the French socialist reflationary program that disrupted the EMS in 1983.

The contributions that have been introduced up until this point deal with Germany's connections to the EC within a national frame of reference, either from the point of view of Germany or its neighbors. Chapters 5 and 6 entertain the problem of decentering the policy-making subject from the national setting and refocusing this subject regionally. Two openings offered themselves in this regard, focusing on the social and environmental fallout of the internal market. Accordingly, the two chapters devoted to this subject analyze the reactions of the Social Democrats and the Greens to regional integration up through the Maastricht negotiation process.

Although the decline in effectiveness of nationally focused social democratic solutions had clearly revealed itself by the end of the 1970s, the regional stage for such an undertaking had been preempted by the EC internal market agenda. In this context the negotiation of the Single European Act and the internal market program, both with the blessing of the French Socialist government, confirmed less the triumph of neoliberalism than the impossibility of pursuing social democratic ends in a national framework and the dubiousness of a purely national strategy at whatever level. But what was the socialist alternative to be at the EC level? The French Socialists did, after all, control the national government and could try to affect regional affairs even after the policy defeat of 1983. Certainly, the meaning of the installation of French Minister of Economics and Finance Jacques Delors as EC Commission president in 1984 is to be found in this context.

In this changed atmosphere of the 1980s, Delors revived the moribund plans for Economic and Monetary Union of the 1970s. Then as before, the centerpiece of that objective had to be the "domesticization" of the Bundesbank. For that project, however, it was vital to mobilize allies in Germany. Who better than the German Social Democrats? Moreover, Delors could also enlist allies in the European Parliament for this project. Since the first direct elections to the European Parliament in 1979 (the same year EMS was launched), a group of members of the European Parliament had been working on a proposal to move the Community into the political realm with a European Union Treaty (Lodge 1986). But in playing this game, Commission President Delors, Socialist President Mitterrand, and the French Socialist Party were pressing the limits of the national action framework.

In the short term, however, the Socialists were unable to control the EC agenda, so that Delors's main accomplishment during his first presidency was to preside over the internal market reform embodied in the Single European Act (Burstein 1991). Significantly, Delors made the case for EMU on technocratic grounds, as a highly desirable extension of the internal market. It was on that basis that he was permitted, in December 1988, to assemble a high-level group drawn from the EC's central bank governors to look into the feasibility of EMU and draft the appropriate proposal. In light of steady progress in internal market matters and the prospect for EMU, the stage was set for the introduction of a "social dimension" at the Community level.

The social dimension provided a potential rallying point for European socialists. In Chapter 5 Robert Ladrech continues the social-democratic theme introduced by Kurzer and Allen in examining the incentives—and disincentives—for forging a reasonably cohesive, transnational collective identity endowed with a capacity to act effectively in dealing with the EC. Ladrech traces the development of the German Social Democratic statements on the EC through the debate that culminated in the new party program, adopted in 1989, and that party's attitude toward the Maastricht process. He records the rapid intensification of relationships between the German Social Democratic Party and the French Socialist Party and the parallel process of joint action with respect to expanding the competence of the European Parliament.

It is well to recall at this point that it was not so much the sudden electoral success of Europe's center-right parties, but fragmentation of the center-left, that accounts for Europe's conservative governments in the 1980s. The 1983 Bundestag election confirmed the defection of the Free Democratic Party to the Christian Democratic Union, but it was also the occasion for the electoral breakthrough of the German Greens at the national level. The same political development occurred, with a lag, in France. The first delegation of Greens to the European Parliament, elected in 1984, were dominated numerically by the Germans. The 1989 election to the European Parliament produced a French ecological contingent that was larger than the German.

Chapter 6, on the German social movement sector and the Greens, paints an apparently paradoxical picture. The most rhetorically international, indeed, even antinational of the German parties had adopted one of the most nationally oriented political strategies. Repelled by its growth ethos and technocratic remoteness, fearful of its drift toward military ambitions, and appalled by the process of market creation under the Single European Act, the Greens started the last decade in a posture of fundamental opposition to the EC. In the aftermath of the Maastricht negotiations, their skepticism about the Community is unabated, though there are forces at work that are making the Greens reconsider their strategic outlook vis-à-vis the EC.

Chapter 7, by James Sperling, places the discussion in a transatlantic context. Starting from U.S.-German and U.S.-European trade and investment patterns that make Germany less dependent on the United States than other European countries, Sperling infers a level of interest engagement that is not conducive to a high degree of commitment to resolve transatlantic problems. Three factors—economic cultures, conflicts of interest, and institutional weaknesses—combine to reduce still further the probability of reconciling macroeconomic policies. The central mechanisms for effecting such a reconciliation are the Bundesbank and the EMS. But very different constituencies compete to control these mechanisms. They must serve domestic policy, European economic convergence, and transatlantic cooperation simultaneously.

Demands associated with German unification and Maastricht-mandated economic and monetary union are obviously high priorities. Unfortunately, in light of the weak performance and high deficit levels of the American economy in recent years, German unification, undertaken on the basis of the politically mandated one-to-one West Mark/Ost Mark conversion, led to large gaps in real interest rates in the Atlantic area. A most dramatic expression of the difficulties of reconciling the demands placed on the EMS and the Bundesbank in all three arenas came in the week prior to the French referendum over Maastricht in September 1992. That opinion polls correctly foresaw only a bare majority of the population voting in favor of the treaty induced speculative attacks directed at the pound sterling, forcing it out of the ERM. The escudo, the peseta, the lire, and the punt all had ultimately to be devalued against the DM. Meanwhile, massive support operations successfully propped up the French franc. Moreover, as Sperling points out, the bases of transatlantic cooperation are shrinking as a consequence of the emerging architecture of the "European House." Fears of the costs of not contributing to the systematic economic revival of Eastern Europe and the Soviet successor states—instability, authoritarian solutions, mass migration—reinforces German preoccupation with Eastern Europe. Plans floated by the Commission for a European Economic Space indicate the understandable desire to press forward with schemes of regional cooperation whose ultimate effect would be to reinforce the Eurocentric trade patterns discussed previously.

The role of Germany has been the key to the evolution of the European state system since the Peace of Westphalia of 1648. In the nineteenth century, Germany's first try at territorial unification was undertaken as a conservative, authoritarian power, driven by a combination of industrial dynamism, heady nationalism, and aristocratic atavism.

Germany embraced military defeat and territorial truncation in the form of a republic, but the Weimar construct was never able to contain Germany's unresolved acute social conflicts. By emphasizing the national framework, resistance to the Treaty of Versailles, particularly the associated reparations provisions, advanced the consolidation of a new political formula that served to mobilize the German middle classes against the workers and "their" government, indeed, "their" constitution. It can be argued that the genius of

Weimar culture issued from these social tensions. But they also produced a pronounced political polarization that ultimately submerged modern and nascent postmodern political alternatives implied by the Weimar artistic firmament. The international economic turbulence ushered in by the New York stock market crash of 1929 programmed a stark political showdown whose main effect was the forcible reorganization of an already politically divided German working class under a right-wing dictatorship. As a class, German workers were neutralized not only by terror, but also by a new strategy of capital accumulation that restored employment, even as it cut wages. In this sense, the Nazi plan for transforming Germany's capitalist economic design for military production effectively married policy and politics and goes a long way toward explaining the lethality of the Nazis' uncompromising territorial revisionism as they went about subjugating and recomposing Europe.

Out of the ruins of the continent two separate German republics were permitted to emerge, but only after the Holocaust was acknowledged at the Nüremberg war crimes trials and only on the basis of the Yalta agreement. The advent of the Cold War brought de-nazification efforts to a premature end. For the West German state, there was national sublimation in industrial dynamism and later in the politics of the Atlantic Alliance. The myth of socialist construction encouraged a parallel sublimation of the past in the East German state. Semipermanent, large-scale allied military deployments as well as cultural exchange programs and the effect of returning German exiles created a thoroughly North Atlantic ambience in the Western state.

All of these were important conditions for the emergence of Germany's impressive social movement sector out of the first postwar generation, the '68ers. Economic growth created its own ills, but also the differentiated social structure and altered living arrangements that provided a social subject to challenge them. Nüremberg and occupation, in devaluing the parents' generation, emancipated the children to challenge their authority in all spheres. They were set free to criticize all sacred cows of the Cold War, particularly the Faustian deal between American strategic interests and Germans who wanted to expunge the dark past from memory. In this, they were helped both by the ideology and institutions of political consensus in postwar Germany and by ready access to the American realities of dissent and opposition. The former helped prevent a Weimar-type polarization of collective identities; both the former and the latter facilitated the emergence of the new identities and sensitivities that characterize the contemporary social movement sector.

In this liberal democratic institutional matrix and cultural landscape, it was not until the mid-1980s that the national motif once again surfaced, this time very much in a defensive posture, very possibly because of the successes of the postwar generation in transforming the terms of political discourse in Germany. How else to interpret the fact that when territorial unification came a third time, it came as a complete and not altogether welcome surprise? This was particularly true for the movement sector and the Green Party, the only West German political party to promote a two-Germany solution in the initial months after the breach of the Wall. The wave of violence against foreigners and anti-Semitic actions attributed to right-wing formations in 1991-1992 was equally a Western and an Eastern phenomenon associated with the seamy underside of *Modell Deutschland* as it struggled to absorb—for this is what unification amounts to—the former German Democratic Republic. Though there had been some troubling complicity of middle-class onlookers at some of the attacks, the fact that hundreds of thousands of German middle-class citizens went into the streets in peaceful solidarity with *Ausländer* demonstrates the marginality of the perpetrators.

The authors of this volume chart the diffusion and concentration of German power in the EC. Their contributions demonstrate that Germany's relationship to the European Communities is neither one-sided, nor unidimensional.

## REFERENCES


Burstein, Daniel (1991). *Euro-quake.* New York: Simon & Schuster.

Cox, Robert W. (1981). "Social Forces, States and World Orders: Beyond International Relations Theory," *Millenium. Journal of International Studies* 10, no. 2 (Autumn), pp. 126-155.

——— (1983). "Gramsci, Hegemony and International Relations: An Essay in Method," *Millenium. Journal of International Studies* 12, no. 2 (Spring), pp. 162-75.

Cutler, Tony, Colin Haslam, John Williams, and Karel Williams (1989). *1992—The Struggle for Europe. A Critical Evaluation of the European Community.* Oxford: Berg Publishers.

DePorte, Anton (1979). *Europe Between the Superpowers: The Enduring Balance.* New Haven, CT: Yale University Press.

Deubner, Christian (1979). "The Expansion of West German Capital and the Founding of Euratom," *International Organization* 33, no. 2, pp. 203-228.

Diebold, William Jr. (1959). *The Schuman Plan. A Study in Economic Cooperation.* New York: Praeger Publishers.

Hanrieder, Wolfram (1969). *The Stable Crisis.* New York: Norton.

——— (1989). *Germany, America, Europe. Forty Years of West German Foreign Policy*. New Haven, CT: Yale University Press.
Holland, Stuart (1976). *The Regional Problem*. New York: St. Martin's Press.
——— (1980). *The Uncommon Market*. New York: St. Martin's Press.
Katzenstein, Peter (1987). *Politics and Policy in West Germany: A Semi-sovereign State*. Philadelphia: Temple University Press.
Keohane, Robert, and Stanley Hoffmann, eds. (1991). *The New European Community. Decisionmaking and Institutional Change*. Boulder, CO: Westview Press.
Lankowski, Carl (1980). "Germany and the European Community. Anatomy of a Hegemonial Relation." PhD diss., Columbia University, New York.
——— (1982). "*Modell Deutschland* and the International Regionalization of the West German State," in Andrei Markovits, ed., *The Political Economy of West Germany: Modell Deutschland*. New York: Praeger.
Lodge, Juliet, ed. (1986). *European Union: The EC in Search of a Future*. London: Macmillan.
Ludlow, Peter (1982). *The Making of the European Monetary System*. London: Butterworths.
Maresca, John (1987). *To Helsinki. The Conference on Security and Cooperation in Europe, 1973-1975*. Durham, NC: Duke University Press.
Marjolin, Robert (1989). *Memoires 1911-1986*. London: Weidenfeld & Nicolson.
May, Bernhard (1982). *Kosten und Nutzen der deutschen EG-Mitgliedschaft*. Bonn: Europa Union Verlag.
Minc, Alain (1989). *La grande illusion*. Paris: Bernard Grasset.
Puchala, Donald (1990). "The European Common Market and the Resilience of the National State," *Il Difficile Cammino Dell'Europa Unita*. Pavia: Facolta die Scienza Politica, pp. 66-86.
Robertson, A. H. (1966). *European Institutions. Cooperation: Integration: Unification*. New York: Praeger Publishers, 2nd ed.
Schwartz, Thomas Alan (1991). *America's Germany. John J. McCloy and the Federal Republic of Germany*. Cambridge, MA: Harvard University Press.
Simonian, Henry (1985). *The Privileged Partnership: Franco-German Relations in the European Community 1969-1984*. Oxford: Oxford Univeristy Press.
Stirk, Peter M. R., ed. (1989). *European Unity in Context. The Interwar Period*. London: Pinter Publishers.

# PART I

# SECTORS

# 1

## German Business and the 1992 Project

Michael G. Huelshoff

This chapter explores the impact of the 1992 program upon business in the Federal Republic of Germany (FRG). Two groups of issues are explored. First, what motivates German business support for 1992, ideology or interest? This question is assessed first by examining the projected impact of the program on the various member states of the European Communities (EC) and second by examining the attitudes of German business elites toward the completion of the internal market. It is found that Germany is not projected to be among the biggest winners, and that German support for 1992 is based mostly on ideological grounds rather than on German interests. There is doubt among business elites about the relative and absolute gains of 1992 for Germany. Most businesses are adjusting through rationalization, improved marketing, and product innovation rather than expanding capacity, foreign investment, or exports. Business leaders anticipate that the most significant change after 1992 will be increased competition in existing markets.

The second set of issues concerns German winners and losers from 1992. Criteria are developed to distinguish between winning and losing sectors of the economy, and examples of each are explored. Industries likely to adjust successfully to 1992 enjoy economies of scale or scope that can be exploited in the new European markets and have not been protected. Industries likely to suffer after completion of the internal market are characterized by high levels of protection and few scale or scope economies. Finally, the chapter assesses the effect of German unification on business support for European integration. It is argued that German business will not be diverted from the EC by the newly opening markets in eastern Germany and the former Soviet Bloc for two reasons: These markets are projected to grow only slowly, and the German economy will remain heavily dependent upon export markets in Western Europe.

## MOTIVATIONS OF GERMAN SUPPORT FOR 1992: IDEOLOGY OR INTEREST?

The first issue raised here concerns what motivates business support for the Single European Act (SEA) and its associated initiatives: ideology or interest. Most German business elites supported the founding of the EC, although some expressed concerns that the EC might not fully develop along free market lines (Bulmer and Paterson 1987), and some were concerned that EC protectionism might damage German trade interests in non-EC countries (Hanrieder 1967). Expressions of ideological support for the EC among business elites has remained strong since then (Bulmer and Paterson 1987), although European business support for completion of the internal market did not originate in the FRG.[1]

Ideology aside, German interests in 1992 seem clear. The German economy is strongly export-oriented, the EC is by far Germany's biggest market, and the share of German exports going to the EC is growing. To more fully examine business motivations and the role of ideology and interest in German business's preparation for 1992, three questions are explored: Which countries are likely to benefit the most from 1992? How much does German business expect to gain? How are the Germans preparing for 1992?

### Who Benefits?

On the surface, the German economy ought to gain disproportionately from the completion of the internal market. Microeconomic conditions could hardly be better. The FRG's much-vaunted technical education system has created one of the most highly trained work forces in Europe. German business leaders enjoy in many cases large cash reserves and good relations with lending institutions. German management has often been criticized for cautiousness, but there are signs in key sectors that it is learning to be flexible (Herrigel 1989). Codetermination and shop-floor representation guarantee that wage and productivity increases are often linked and that strikes are rare in comparison to many of Germany's European competitors.

Conditions at the macroeconomic level are equally as favorable. The independence and fiscal conservatism of the Bundesbank led to high levels of price stability, although this has eroded somewhat since German-German monetary integration in July 1990. Bonn is notably unwilling to intervene in markets without careful guidelines and with limited funds. Unlike many of the FRG's competitors, German business is not dependent upon state subsidies to remain competitive. Even the jump in oil prices caused by political instability in the Gulf in 1990 did not slow Germany's fastest rate of GNP growth in the EC (*New York Times* 1990b). Despite the recent worldwide recession and the unexpected costs of unification, the Germany economy remains stable.

For evident political reasons, the official, EC-sponsored projection of the impact of 1992 upon European business, the Cecchini Report, does not assess the relative impact of 1992 for individual members (Cecchini et al. 1988). But the report's emphasis upon the lowering of factor costs, realization of economies of scale, and rationalization leads one to the opinion that the Germans would be in a strong position to take advantage of the completion of the internal market. The Cecchini Report's projections, however, are controversial. While it projects GNP increases of between 2 1/2 percent and 6 1/2 percent across the entire EC, some estimates put the expected increases at 11 to 35 percent (*The Economist* 1989c). Others fear that savings realized in one area will be offset by new costs. Open borders, for example, will require internal controls to oversee transportation of hazardous materials (*Die Zeit* 1989).

European business elites are skeptical of these optimistic forecasts. A European *Wall Street Journal* survey found that 61 percent of business elites expected that 1992 would encourage national growth only slightly, and 60 percent expected that "local cultural and taste barriers" could continue to limit trade after 1992 (*Wall Street Journal Europe* 1988b). German business is a little more positive. The same 1987 poll found that German business expected a 5 percent increase in turnover and a 1 1/2 percent drop in unit costs due to 1992. Yet a later poll of the top 500 German firms found general skepticism toward 1992, with over half of the respondents expecting no more than a slight increase in business (*Die Welt* 1989).

Which states will benefit the most from 1992? While the data are inconclusive, they suggest that, due to interindustry trade, little specialization, and a high degree of wage convergence among northern European states (despite protection in some industries), 1992 is unlikely to lead to much growth in the North (*The Economist* 1990). The real beneficiaries may be southern Europe, particularly Greece, Portugal, and to a lesser extent Spain, where low wage rates and falling trade barriers may stimulate growth. A survey of German business leaders found that 22.2 percent expected Spain to be the major beneficiary of 1992, followed by France (16.4 percent), the FRG (15.7 percent), and Portugal (13.8 percent) (*Die Welt* 1989). On the other hand, another survey found that 62 percent of French businesspersons expect the FRG to benefit the most from 1992 and only 22 percent expect France to benefit the most (*Wall Street Journal Europe* 1988a).

In conclusion, the absolute and relative gains expected from 1992 are unclear. For the German economy, 1992 may not generate large benefits. First, there is controversy over the existence and size of real increases in GNP to result from completion of the internal market. Additionally, European business opinion is divided over the question of which country will benefit the most from 1992, and scholarly analyses suggest that the largest beneficiaries are likely to be found in the south, not in the north, of Europe. If accurate, these data point to continued German support for opening markets in Europe to be based more on ideology than on interest.

## German Expectations and Adjustment Strategies

Assessing the motivations of German support for 1992 cannot be limited only to analysis of projections of macroeconomic effects. In addition to GNP growth, 1992 means the reorientation of European business toward the European market and the intensification of economic activity within Europe. The spate of highly publicized takeover bids, joint ventures, and cooperative arrangements over the past few years is indicative of the changes in business attitudes resulting from 1992. Whatever the likely impact of the program on GNP, 1992 has already wrought significant changes in the European business environment.

A 1988 survey found that 79 percent of French business managers were aware of and responding to 1992, in comparison to 18 percent in the FRG and 5 percent in the UK (*Wall Street Journal Europe* 1988a). Another survey conducted by Consensus Research in London found that 62 percent of surveyed firms in France had developed a plan to address the challenges of 1992, with a further 26 percent still in the planning stages (*Frankfurter Allgemeine Zeitung* 1988). Similar figures for the FRG were 36 and 39 percent, respectively, and 30 and 23 percent for the UK. In the fall of 1988, 60 percent of German companies felt inadequately informed about the impacts of 1992, and many expected that the FRG's past success in penetrat-

Table 1.1
**Impact of 1992 on the Competitiveness of German Business (in percent and by industry)**

| Sector | Positive | No Impact | Negative |
|---|---|---|---|
| Manufacturing Industry | 28 | 55 | 17 |
| Raw Materials & Prod. Goods | 25 | 58 | 17 |
| Capital Goods | 33 | 53 | 14 |
| Consumer Goods | 24 | 56 | 20 |
| Foodstuffs | 23 | 56 | 21 |
| Construction | 9 | 65 | 26 |
| Trade | 16 | 68 | 16 |
| Wholesale Trade | 19 | 65 | 16 |
| Retail Trade | 14 | 70 | 16 |
| Services | 18 | 54 | 28 |
| Transportation | 13 | 50 | 37 |
| Hotels and Restaurants | 32 | 61 | 7 |
| Business Overall | 25 | 58 | 17 |

Source: DIHT, 1990a.

ing European markets would guarantee their success after 1992 (*Wall Street Journal Europe* 1988c).

German attention to the 1992 program has been growing in the past few years. A federal Economics Ministry program to provide information to small and medium-size firms has proven quite successful, and the number of conferences, meetings, seminars, and public debates about the impacts of 1992 in specific sectors of the economy has grown exponentially.[2] A survey conducted in the FRG in the summer of 1989 found that knowledge about 1992 was spreading, and that while about 60 percent of the public and industry were positive about 1992, a number of problems were also expected. These included increased taxes, loss of political independence, and increased bureaucratization (*Handelsblatt* 1989a).

The Diet of German Industry and Commerce (Deutsche Industrie- und Handelstag, or DIHT) conducts regular surveys of German business opinions (Korn 1988). Table 2.1 presents data from the Winter 1990 poll. The most

Table 1.2
**German Industrial Adjustments Planned for 1992**

| Sector | Rational-ization | Product Innovation | Improved Marketing | Foreign Invest-ment | Other Adjust-ments |
|---|---|---|---|---|---|
| Manufacturing | 35 | 25 | 30 | 5 | 5 |
| Raw Mat. & Prod. Gds. | 38 | 23 | 29 | 5 | 5 |
| Capital Goods | 33 | 25 | 30 | 7 | 5 |
| Consumer Goods | 34 | 23 | 32 | 5 | 6 |
| Foodstuffs | 38 | 25 | 33 | 2 | 2 |
| Construction | 48 | 15 | 21 | 2 | 14 |
| Trade | 31 | 10 | 45 | 4 | 10 |
| Wholesale Trade | 31 | 13 | 42 | 4 | 10 |
| Retail Trade | 33 | 5 | 51 | 3 | 8 |
| Business Overall | 35 | 23 | 31 | 5 | 6 |

Source: DIHT, 1990a.

striking finding is that in all sectors included in the survey, at least half of the respondents expect no impact from 1992. The strongest negative impact is registered in the transportation, food, and construction industries. Additionally, in only two industries, capital goods and hotels and restaurants, do as many as a third of the respondents expect positive implications. In light of the earlier survey findings, these data suggest that negative expectations seem to be growing. This may be due to the growing proximity of 1992, the reactions of competitor firms, and the impact of increased information about the program (DIHT 1990a). Even firms otherwise positive about 1992 are beginning to express doubts. Concerns have been raised, in particular, about the likelihood of continued foreign subsidization of industry, high German taxes, environmental protection costs, and the inflexibility of German industrial relations. Business elites fear that these factors are making Germany an uncompetitive environment for investment.

Despite these concerns, relocation outside the FRG is not a common response of German business to 1992. (See Table 1.2.) The most favored strategies are rationalization and improved marketing, followed by product innovation. In industries expressing the most skepticism about 1992—for example, food and construction—rationalization is the preferred response. These data were collected before German unification was realized. It is unclear what the new markets and investment opportunities in the eastern states of the united Germany will mean for business's investment strategies. The fall 1990 DIHT poll focused upon unification questions, without reference to the interplay of unification and internal market questions (DIHT 1990b)

Finally, one must take into account the opinions of the major political arms of German business, the business associations. There are several important business associations concerned with 1992, including the Federation of German Industry (Bundesverband der Deutschen Industrie, or BDI), the Federation of German Wholesale and Foreign Traders (Bundesverband des Deutschen Groß- und Außenhandels, or BGA), the Confederation of German Employers' Associations (Bundesvereinigung der Deutschen Arbeitgeberverbände, or BDA), and the DIHT (Bulmer and Paterson 1987).[3] All advise their members on how best to prepare for the completion of the internal market.[4] All support the 1992 project and lobby for freer markets in Europe. For example, the BDI proposes deregulation of the telecommunications sector, elimination of agricultural price supports, and the opening of labor markets—opinions often more free market–oriented than those of the center-right coalition in Bonn (BDI 1987, 1988; *Chemische Industrie* 1988). The BDI also emphasizes the need to strictly control the use of subsidies and the growth of bureaucracy in Europe (*Nachrichten für Außenpolitik* 1988; *Süddeutsche Zeitung* 1988c). The BDI and the BGA want to ensure that the 1992 project does not lead to "Europrotectionism" (BDI 1989). The BDA, concerned mostly with social issues, resists efforts to establish Community-wide standards for social policy (BDA 1989; *Süddeutsche Zeitung* 1989). The DIHT has noted needs in connection with the 1992 program for deregulation, tax harmonization, freeing of services, elimination of agricultural and steel subsidies, and establishment of a politically independent monetary system on the lines of the Bundesbank. The DIHT also sees a need to decentralize regional policy so as to maintain national competence (*Handelsblatt* 1988a). The DIHT has warned German industry against "euphoric expectations" about 1992 (*Süddeutsche Zeitung* 1988a) and defended the German business community when Chancellor Helmut Kohl accused it of reacting slowly to the program (*Handelsblatt* 1988b; *Süddeutsche Zeitung* 1988b).

A majority of German business elites do not expect significant increases in profitability or market share as a result of 1992. Support for the completion of the internal market, therefore, is largely driven by ideology rather than interest. While German business elites expect that completion of the internal market will make their operations easier, they do not expect an increase in their ability to export (as they are already quite competitive in export markets). Of course, some firms will realize increases in profits and market share after 1992. Further, the BDI and DIHT see in 1992 the opportunity to eliminate many of the evils that they have reluctantly accepted in the German economy, including agricultural subsidies and regulated markets. These findings suggest that ideology takes precedence over interest in German business support for 1992, but one should not lose sight of the tangible benefits that completion of the internal market will bring to many German businesses.

## 1992 AND GERMAN INDUSTRIES: WHO WINS, AND WHO LOSES?

We now turn to a second major issue: assessing winners and losers from 1992 within Germany. This effort is difficult for several reasons. First, it is unclear how much of the program will be completed, and when it will be completed. A number of fundamental issues have not been resolved, including tax harmonization and government procurement. Equally significant is the issue of monetary union. Without, at the least, stable exchange rates among EC members, it will be difficult to make the Common Market work. The inflation potential of recent increases in oil prices and German unification do not bode well for maintaining exchange rate discipline.

Additionally, German business elites emphasize the importance of eliminating state subsidies for industry in addition to completion of the SEA.[5] Article 92 of the Treaty of Rome specifies that states may use state aids and subsidies in certain restricted situations, while Article 115 allows the use of trade-restrictive measures if faced with instability in markets due to growing import penetration (Casperi 1988). Using these and other rationales, state subsidies in Europe grew to about $40 to 50 billion per year in 1989 (*Die Zeit* 1988). While EC members are required under Article 92 to submit to the Commission all proposed subsidies over about $200,000, there are reasons to suspect that these subsidies will continue. Not only are states increasingly reluctant to inform the EC even after the subsidies have been issued, but the sheer number of subsidies granted each year would quickly overwhelm the Commission's staff if it were required to vet each one. Additionally, the EC's track record on enforcing the subsidy review is mixed. The EC successfully ordered subsidy cuts in the cases of Italy's Alfa Romeo, Spain's ENASA truck maker, and British Aerospace's takeover of the Rover Group (*The Economist* 1989a). The Commission, however, was unable to guarantee timely compliance in the EC-led restructuring of the European steel

Figure 1.1
**Industry Characteristics and Impacts of 1992**

| Protectionism? | Economies of Scale | Economies of Scope | Neither Scale nor Scope |
|---|---|---|---|
| Yes | Losers: Raw Foodstuffs | Losers: Processeds Foodstuff | Losers: Trucking: Energy |
| No | Winners: Steel, Chemicals | Winners: Autos, Capital Goods,Textiles | Mixed: Pharma-ceuticals |

industry. The Commission continues to fight subsidies to the French auto firm Renault and electronics conglomerate Bull, with mixed success. These cases are only the most visible among the mountain of subsidy programs the EC must begin to address if the internal market is to be realized. An increase in the number of cases vetted by the Commission during the mid-1980s led some members to begin to anticipate Commission views before granting new subsidies and to avoid reporting new programs (Casperi 1988, p. 49).

Unresolved conflicts over the internal market and problems with controlling subsidization confound efforts to assess German winners and losers. But light can be shed on this problem by examining industry characteristics. Figure 1.1 summarizes three important industry characteristics: economies of scale, economies of scope, and protectionism. Industries enjoying existing or easily obtainable scale economies might be expected to benefit from opening markets in Europe. The extent of these benefits is likely to be determined by prior levels of openness in the relevant markets. Economies of scope, in contrast, reflect the flexibility of firms to respond to changes in demand (Junne 1990). Continued national differences in consumer preferences and changes in such preferences have made apparent in recent years the importance of economies of scope in many industries trying to maintain international competitiveness. Overriding these concerns is protectionism. While most German markets have been unprotected for some time, pockets of protection exist. Opening these markets will result in a strong competitive shock for firms selling in them. They may be forced rapidly to exploit scale or scope economies, and/or face falling profits and market share. Firms in these industries also will face greater difficulties in adjusting to the growth in intraindustry trade expected after 1992 (ibid.) Scale, scope, and protection, then, help to distinguish winners from losers.

## Potential Winners

Examples of potential winner industries include autos, capital goods, and chemicals, as well as some formerly weak industries such as steel and textiles. Not all firms in these industries will benefit equally from 1992. Some firms might not benefit at all. Yet these industries should do well overall. In each case, though, there are special problems that may limit profit-making.

In autos, Volkswagen is a likely winner. Volkswagen is the largest producer in Europe, slightly ahead of Fiat. It has invested heavily in flexible production facilities, which will allow it to take advantage, via economies of scope, of market niches after 1992 (*The Economist* 1989b). While Volkswagen already exports heavily in the EC—the share of its production sold in Europe has grown from 48 percent in 1973 to 74 percent in 1987 (Volkswagen AG 1988)—it is likely that the firm's profits will strengthen with the opening of the market. The other German producers, Daimler-Benz and BMW, have firm footholds in the high end of the market and in trucks. While they have expressed concerns about growing Japanese penetration of EC markets, the recent agreement to limit Japanese access to the European market until 1999 will help protect these firms. As yet they have few European competitors in these markets.

Götz Birken-Bertsch (1988) identifies four factors that are key to the realization of a free market in autos. First, the EC must adopt fully common emissions standards for autos. While EC agreements have reduced differences in emissions standards, distortions continue. Additionally, lack of tax harmonization limits the Europeanization of the market. Tax differences mean that a BMW 318i costs DM 2,500 less in Belgium than in the FRG and DM 55,900 more in Greece (Oehler 1990). Third, transportation policy must be integrated, especially taxes on trucking. Last, Birken-Bertsch notes that the treatment of foreign producers, in particular the Japanese, needs to be harmonized. This has largely been accomplished in the recent EC-Japanese arrangement limiting imports until 1999.

The German capital goods industry should also do well in the transition to 1992 (*Frankfurter Rundschau* 1989; *Schreyer* 1990). In key markets, the industry entered the 1980s behind its U.S. and Japanese competitors. Yet the industry has caught up. Investment in both product and process has improved the competitive position of the industry, which already exports much of its production. The elimination of trade barriers in Europe is likely to enhance exports. The machine tool industry, for example, will be in a position to defend and better itself due to economies of scope. The reinvestment programs of the 1980s tended to emphasize flexible production, leaving the industry well prepared for 1992 (Herrigel 1989).

Three other German industries also restructured during the 1980s, readying them for 1992: steel, textiles, and chemicals. In each case, realization of the full benefits of the completion of the internal market will require not only the removal of trade barriers, but also the elimination of foreign subsidies.

The German steel industry restructured through the 1980s, cutting capacity by about a third. Thanks to the EC's Davignon Plan and the stinginess of the Bonn government, capacity reductions focused upon the least-efficient facilities, such as the Saar steel works. German steel began to rely more upon high-quality, high-profit products, brought crude steel-making capacity into line with finished product output, and rationalized and concentrated production. Additionally, in many products there are economies of scale that the German industry has or will realize with more open markets in Europe. But the picture is not completely positive. Despite the success of the Germans in meeting their goals, many other European steel industries continue to be subsidized. Particularly troublesome for the German industry are subsidies in Italy and Belgium. The inability of the EC to enforce the strictures of the Davignon Plan—which was to end steel subsidies by 1985—bodes ill for a free European steel market. Additionally, steel imports may grow, if proposals to ease restructuring in Eastern Europe by opening steel markets are approved. Nonetheless, the German steel industry is well positioned to protect its position in European markets and to grow after 1992.

The German textile industry has undergone a similar restructuring over the past two decades (Neubauer 1990a). The crisis of the 1970s led German producers to rationalize production and reinvest, so that by 1990 the Germans had one of the most automated textile industries in the world. The Cecchini Report projects only a small increase in business in the European textile industry after 1992, but the German textile industry is preparing to expand. The strength of the industry is the large number of small and medium-size firms that can adjust production flexibly to account for differences and changes in consumer taste—again realizing economies of scope. At the same time, some producers are working to concentrate production in order to compete against large European firms after 1992.

The expiration and renegotiation of the current Multi-fiber Arrangement (MFA) is likely to enhance the German competitive position in textiles. This treaty limits the exports of Third World producers to the EC. Renegotiation will likely lead to higher levels of access to European markets for the Third World and Eastern Europe. Yet the Germans will benefit from the new MFA, as their French and Italian competitors will not, because they have rationalized production facilities and reinvested to realize scope economies. German textile producers project that they will realize larger shares of their competitor's markets when completion of the internal market and the new MFA pressure other European producers. As with steel, textiles are targeted by Eastern European states transiting from command to market economies. The rosy picture for German textile producers is complicated by growing eastern European demands for better access to EC textile markets.

Finally, the German chemicals industry is well positioned to benefit from 1992 (Stübinger-v. Olshausen 1988). German producers such as Bayer, BASF, and Hoechst are among the largest chemicals firms in the world. In some product lines, economies of scale can be enhanced with a further opening of European markets. In others, such economies already have been realized through existing Europeanization of investment. The big German chemicals firms also enjoy ample resources to ready themselves for 1992. As with steel, gains from 1992 depend to some degree on the elimination of foreign subsidies. In other European states chemicals industries have long received government support.

The situation in the pharmaceuticals sector of the industry is unclear (Pelzer and Reimertz 1989). Scale and scope economies are limited in the industry. The EC has yet to develop European-wide product standards for the industry, and tax and pricing policies remain unresolved. German pharmaceuticals markets have been protected from foreign competition. The larger producers, such as Bayer, will probably do well because they have operated in international markets for some time. The future of the small and medium-size firms in the industry is more problematic.

One significant problem plagues the German chemicals industry: environmental standards. German environmental standards are among the most stringent in Europe, and there is some concern that the extra costs associated with these standards will make the FRG unattractive to industry (*Frankfurter Rundschau* 1989). Harmonization of environmental standards in the EC is slow. Some analysts argue that the Commission is less interested in raising European environmental standards than in realizing the internal market.[6] EC policies of allowing some states to maintain higher environmental standards than others is unlikely to assuage the concerns of the chemicals industry about environmental costs.

The industries most likely to benefit from 1992, then, are the traditional strengths of the German economy: autos, capital goods, and chemicals. They enjoy little protection, have strong export records, and can take advantage of scale and scope economies. Additionally, the restructuring that has occurred in the German economy over the past couple of decades will pay off. Formerly weak industries such as steel and textiles seem well positioned to take advantage of the new opportunities provided by 1992. Pressure to open these markets to Eastern European producers, however, threaten the prospects of German steel and textiles. It is likely, as well, that the move to complete the internal market will enhance existing trends in German industry toward the high end of most product lines (Adams and Rademacher 1989). Realization of many of these benefits is dependent upon the elimination of foreign subsidization and public support for national champions.

## Potential Losers

Most firms projected to lose from 1992 have enjoyed protection that will be reduced or eliminated with the completion of the internal market. It can be expected that they will lose market share and be forced to restructure. It is unlikely, however, that any of these industries will collapse. But they are the weak points of the German drive toward 1992. Examples of loser industries include transportation, the food industry, and energy.[7]

The transportation industry will be strongly affected by the 1992 program in several sectors, including trucking. The German trucking industry is the most highly protected in Europe (Wacker-Theodorakopoulos 1989). Long-distance trucking is protected through high taxes, including fuel taxes. Additionally, a tightly controlled permit system limits the number of shipments allowed per shipper per year. The intent is to minimize competition in the shipping industry between trucking and the Bundesbahn, the federally subsidized rail system. Few of these permits are set aside for non-German truckers. Many permits allow only one-way transportation. Thus, foreign and domestic truckers are occasionally forced to travel empty because they cannot get a permit to carry goods on a return trip.

High taxes and the permit system have led to inefficiencies in the industry. Protection also has created strong lobbies that push to maintain the protection and resist opening the market. The transportation business associations are among the most vociferous opponents of 1992 in Germany. They also influence the Federal Institute for Long-Haul Trucking (Bundesanstalt für den Güterfernverkehr), the federal agency responsible for regulating the industry (Neumann 1988). The trucking industry complains of high German taxes, safety requirements, and emissions standards that make firms uncompetitive against foreign shippers.

The EC and the Bonn government are, however, moving ahead to free the transportation market. Bonn has proposed lowering some taxes to the EC average (still 25 times higher than French taxes) and imposing a highway usage tax in exchange for dropping the permits. The EC has proposed a "territoriality" system, whereby members would maintain existing taxes, but computer-readable devices would be installed in all trucks to determine which states the truck had traveled through to assess taxes. It is hoped that high-tax states such as the FRG would be forced to lower their taxes through market pressures. This proposal reinforces EC attempts to eliminate border controls (*The Financial Times* 1989a). The opening of the transportation market in Europe will increase competitive pressures in the German trucking industry and lead to cutbacks and business failures.

The food industry also faces problems adjusting to 1992. Unlike many other German industries, the food industry exports only a small part of its production—13.7 percent in 1989 (Neubauer 1990b). Additionally, the industry is relatively unconcentrated in comparison to its European competitors. The largest producer, the Oetker Group, has a yearly turnover of about DM 1 billion, in comparison to such giants as Dutch Unilever, with a turnover of about DM 50 billion. The Germans also rank behind France, Belgium, and the Netherlands in the number and size of supermarkets (ibid.). As a result, average profits in the German food industry are the lowest in Europe. Additionally, EC differences in tax rates distort some portions of the food markets. European tax harmonization is likely to raise German taxes for beer, wine, and tobacco, while lowering coffee taxes.

The German foodstuffs industry is also concerned about the "Cassis de Dijon" ruling of the European Court of Justice, which established the principle of the free movement of goods for similar products. This ruling has been used by the EC to force open the German beer and sausage markets, which had excluded foreign goods that contained preservatives and artificial additives. In at least these two markets, the elimination of German protection has not led to any significant increase in imports, but the industry fears that high German purity standards will leave them uncompetitive after 1992. Hence, the German food industry lobbies for more activity at the European level to ensure consumer protection, raise quality standards for food, and address the environmental impacts of the industry (Weinz 1988).

Consumer preferences constrain realization of economies of scale in most areas except raw foodstuffs. National differences in consumer preference encourage flexible production facilities and economies of scope. Some German marketers are pursuing joint ventures and foreign investment. Aldi, for example, is expanding into the Netherlands and Great Britain. Nonetheless, it is likely that, if the over 200 trade barriers in the European food industry are dropped in the course of the completion of the internal market, the German food industry will be forced to undergo significant rationalization.

Finally, the energy industry is also a problem for the Germans. Energy production and distribution has often been considered a natural monopoly, because fixed costs are a large proportion of total costs in the industry. For political reasons, states also wish to minimize their dependence on foreign sources of energy. Environmental concerns further complicate the picture. Heating oils and nuclear power are discouraged in Germany. A free market would allow imports of cheap, nuclear-generated French electricity, aggravating the strong German antinuclear lobby (*The Financial Times* 1989b; see Chapter 6).

The Germans are particularly sensitive about maintaining jobs in the coal industry. Coal miners are a strong lobby in Bonn. They successfully negotiated the so-called "Jahrhundertvertrag" in 1980, which maintains jobs in the industry by subsidizing coal prices and requiring German electricity-generating plants to use set percentages of German coal. To pay for the program, energy consumers must pay a tax (the "Kohlepfennig"), which in 1989 amounted to 8.5 percent of electricity prices. As a result, German coal cost about DM 255 per ton in 1987, in comparison to DM 157 in the United Kingdom and about DM 90 on the world market (Matthies 1989). The energy industry also labors under high taxes on heating oils.

In the FRG, these factors have led to an inefficient and expensive energy industry. Electricity prices in Germany, for example, were 25 percent higher than in the UK in 1987, 35 percent higher than in France or Belgium, and about 48 percent higher than in the Netherlands and Italy (Rekittke and Schulten 1989, p. 184). Between 1985 and 1987, electricity prices dropped by as much as a quarter in these countries, while they rose 6.4 percent in the FRG (ibid., p. 183).

Elimination of the large number of trade restrictive mechanisms in energy is a key goal of the European Commission. The EC's energy program emphasizes four points: the elimination of material, technical, and fiscal barriers to trade in the industry, particularly taxes and contracting regulations; the elimination of both subsidies for coal and existing distribution monopolies; harmonization of prices, in particular electricity and gas prices; and the harmonization of environmental standards, in particular for oil refineries (Matthies 1989).

The German energy industry strongly resists this program. Professor Joachim Grawe, head of the Association of German Electricity Producers (Vereinigung Deutscher Elektrizitätswerke, or VDEW) has said that "these endeavors are neither economically nor managerially feasible, nor in the interests of energy independence" (Nowak 1990).[8] Others in the industry have complained that opening the market will hurt small and medium-size firms and individual households.

Additionally, Commission opposition to the Jahrhundertvertrag has incensed the coal industry. The EC has pressured Bonn for several years to eliminate coal subsidies. The Commission ordered in March 1989 that the subsidies must end by March 1991 (*Handelsblatt* 1990a). The FRG appealed the decision to the European Court of Justice (ECJ). While the federal government on one side and the companies and the union on the other have agreed that the subsidies must be cut, they have been unable to agree on how, by how much, and by when (*Handelsblatt* 1989b). Issues in contention have included precisely how much coal is to be mined, the size of the subsidies, and the requirement that electricity firms purchase German coal (*Handelsblatt* 1989c). A German expert commission was appointed to study the issue, but the EC has continued to keep the pressure on Bonn to end the Jahrhundertvertrag (*Frankfurter Rundschau* 1990; *Handelsblatt* 1990b; *Süddeutsche Zeitung* 1990). The conflict intensified when Bonn moved recently to cut subsidies to free money for eastern Germany.

German energy markets will be forced open after 1992. The coal industry will be hardest hit, as the subsidies in the industry are phased out and German electricity generators can purchase more cheap foreign coal. Competition from the French will also grow, forcing more efficiency in the market. Effects on the oil refining industry will depend upon taxation and environmental policy. If taxes are lowered, heating oil will be more attractive; and if environmental standards in Europe are raised to German standards, the latter's costs will be more in line with European costs. If taxes are not harmonized and if the Germans maintain higher than average environmental standards, the German oil refining industry is likely to continue its only recently slowed precipitous decline.

In sum, examples of industries likely to suffer after 1992 include the transportation, food, and energy industries. They are losers because they have enjoyed protection that is likely to be eliminated or reduced and because their structures are inefficient on European standards. Only in foodstuffs do economies of scale and scope exist of which German firms might take advantage. Here again, the potential opening of the EC's markets to Eastern European goods, though generally supported by Bonn, further threatens the industry.

Some industries in the German economy can be expected to benefit from the 1992 program and some to suffer. On the surface, these data seem inconsistent with the general lack of interest toward the 1992 program expressed by German business elites in opinion polls. Taken together, the data suggest that the gains of 1992 can be expected to be unevenly distributed among and within sectors of the German economy. Further, the winners are not expecting to win very much. The losers will lose the protection they have enjoyed, although there is no evidence that these firms and industries will necessarily fold under a tide of European competition.

## CONCLUSION: UNIFICATION, 1992, AND GERMAN BUSINESS

German business, for the most part, will benefit from 1992, but the benefits will not be great. German business elites are skeptical of the overall significance of 1992 for their profitability. They also stress that the opening of markets must be accompanied by the elimination of subsidization in other EC states. Yet German business supports the 1992 program. The data presented here suggest that German support is driven mostly by ideological, and not economic, concerns. The key sectors of the German economy—autos, capital goods, and chemicals—are already heavily committed to exporting within the EC, and the elimination of trade barriers will make trade only a little easier. Rationalization in otherwise weak industries including textiles and steel places German firms in good positions to realize economies of scope and scale after 1992. The sectors of German business that fear 1992 have enjoyed protection that is threatened by completion of the internal market, yet for the most part they are resigned to facing the heightened competition that will take place after 1992. They account for only a small share of German GNP and have not attracted much support from Bonn.

The rapid changes in Eastern Europe and German unification have raised questions about the German commitment to Europe. On the surface, 1992 has virtually dropped off the map of the German business community. Business newspapers such as *Handelsblatt* have until recently focused almost exclusively upon the former GDR. This is not surprising. Unification is clearly an emotional issue for Germans. Also, the costs of unification will be huge. The Bonn government has made it clear that it expects most of the money to come from the private sector and that it expects German business to act patriotically to help integrate the former GDR into the FRG (Waigel 1990).

There are a number of important questions raised by German unification, including the extent to which Germany will be distracted from European integration by unification and the likelihood of more aggressive and demanding German positions in EC bargaining. Fortunately, both these questions have so far been resolved in favor of continued German passivity. The more fundamental question concerns the behavior of German business in light of unification and the opening of markets in Eastern Europe. Will Germany begin to reorient itself economically toward the East? Germany has traditionally enjoyed strong economic ties with the nations of Eastern Europe. Germany exported about $13 billion to Eastern Europe in 1989, more than twice as much as the United States, the next largest exporter to the region (Deutsche Bank 1990). Unlike other EC states, the Germans also can take advantage of the relations established between the former GDR and the other former COMECON states. Complaints already have been expressed in France and Belgium about the loss of German business in border regions (*The New York Times* 1990a).

Yet German business's fixation on the former GDR is likely to decline. Investment in the five new Länder has been slow until recently, and most projections are that it will take many years before they catch up. The problems with rebuilding the Eastern European economies will constrain foreign investment and profit-making in them for some time. It may be that the deficit of interest in 1992 among German businesspersons results from their preparations for completion of the internal market. The winners need to adjust only a little anyway, and enjoy ample cash reserves and access to credit to do so. The losers have, for the most part, accepted the inevitability of 1992 and are resigned to making the necessary painful cut-backs and rationalizations. Markets in Western Europe will remain important for German business, as will interest in further opening EC markets. But, as we have seen, German companies do not expect much new business after 1992. Whether EC markets can continue to be engines of *growth* for the German economy is another, unresolved question.

## NOTES

1. One of the earliest expressions of business support for completion of the internal market can be found in Wisse Dekker, "Europe 1990," speech given at the Centre for European Policy Studies, Brussels, 11 January 1985. Dekker was president of Philips NV, and had his staff prepare an action program that reflects closely the Commission's original White Paper on the Completion of the Internal Market.
2. Author's interviews in Bonn, FRG, January and February 1990.
3. Industry-specific associations also comment upon EC politics.

4. Author's interviews in Köln, FRG, February 1990. The DIHT, for example, publishes regularly "Wegweiser zum Europäische Binnenmarkt," which summarizes for business the legal and political steps taken each year toward completion of the Single European Act and comments upon outstanding issues.
5. The issue is raised often by the BDI and the DIHT. See also *Wirtschaftswoche* (29 January 1988).
6. Author's interviews in Brussels, Belgium and Bonn, FRG, January and February 1990. See also Hey and Jahns-Böhm (1989); and Hey (1990).
7. I do not examine the construction industry, which was expected to do poorly after 1992. The demands of reconstruction in the former GDR may cushion the industry. About twice as many construction firms were positive about the business year 1991 than was the case two years earlier (that is, before unification), and the number expecting worsening conditions dropped from 25 to 10 percent. Investment in the industry is also up. Explanations given for this optimism and increased investment include opportunities in the new German states and increased public housing expenditures. There remain, though, large differences in opinion among firms in the industry. See DIHT (1990b).
8. Translation is the author's.

## REFERENCES


Adams, Heinz W. and Helmut Rademacher (1989). "Quality from Germany—Strategisches Qualitätsmanagement." In Heinz W. Adams, ed., *Europa 1992.* Frankfurt aM: Frankfurter Allgemeine Zeitung, pp. 359-376.

BDA (1989). "Stellungsaufnahme zur Sozialen Dimension des EG-Binnenmarktes." Euro-Info Nr. 4/1989.

BDI (1987). "Memorandum zur Europapolitik."

BDI (1988). *Informationen und Meinungen.* "EG-Binnenmarkt zügig vollenden."

BDI (1989). "Completion of the Single European Market—Consequences for the European Community's External Economic Relations." IV/4-71-25/0.

Birken-Bertsch, Götz (1988). "Die Vollendung des Binnenmarktes und die deutsche Automobilindustrie," in Werner Weidenfeld, ed., *Binnenmarkt '92: Perspektiven aus deutscher Sicht.* Gütersloh: Bertelsmann Stiftung, pp. 59-66.

Bulmer, Simon, and William Paterson (1987). *The Federal Republic of Germany and the European Community.* London: Allen and Unwin.

Casperi, Manfred (1988). "The Aid Rules of the EEC Treaty and Their Application," in Jürgen Schwarze, ed., *Discretionary Powers of the Member States in the Field of Economic Policies and Their Limits Under the EEC Treaty.* Baden-Baden: Nomos Verlag, 1988, pp. 37-52.

Cecchini, Paolo, et al. (1988). *The European Challenge 1992.* Aldershot: Wildwood House Ltd.

Chemische Industrie (January 1988). "BDI-Memorandum: Vordringliche Maßnahmen."

Dekker, Wisse (11 January 1985). "Europe 1990." Speech given at the Centre for European Policy Studies, Brussels.

Deutsche Bank (1990). "Perspectives for Trade with the East." Deutsche Bank Bulletin.

DIHT (1990a). "Wettbewerbsfähigkeit und Anpassungsstrategien Deutscher Unternehmen im EG-Binnenmarkt." Bonn.

DIHT (1990b). "Wirtschaftslage und Erwartungen." Bonn.

*The Economist* (10 June 1989a). "Battle of Brittan."

*The Economist* (23 September 1989b). "Ready, Steady . . ."

*The Economist* (18 November 1989c). "The Lure of 1992."

*The Economist* (21 April 1990). "Advantage, Greece."

*The Financial Times* (6 July 1989a). "Brussels Wants Red Tape Cut for Trucks at Borders."

*The Financial Times* (26 September 1989b). "France Awaits EC Ruling on Cheap N-Power Sales."

*Frankfurter Allgemeine Zeitung* (29 March 1988). "Geringes Interesse der Finanzinstitute am Gemeinsamen Binnenmarkt."

*Frankfurter Rundschau* (23 March 1989). "Nicht nur Gewinner beim EC-Binnenmarkt."

*Frankfurter Rundschau* (16 February 1990). "Verträge einhalten."

*Handelsblatt* (11 January 1988a). "Reform der Agrar- und Finanzpolitik ist Voraussetzung für gemeinsamen Markt."

*Handelsblatt* (16 March 1988b). "Zügige Deregulierung in der Gemeinschaft nützt den Unternehmen."

*Handelsblatt* (16 June 1989a). "Das Programm Europa '92 erhält von vielen Bundesbürgern Vorschußlorbeeren."

*Handelsblatt* (22-23 September 1989b). "Vor einer schwierigen Kompromißsuche."

*Handelsblatt* (29-30 September 1989c). "Die Bonner Gratwanderung geht weiter."

*Handelsblatt* (9-10 February 1990a). "Bonn will Nachbessern."

*Handelsblatt* (16-17 February 1990b). "Keine Ende im Kohlepoker."

Hanrieder, Wolfram (1967). *West German Foreign Policy 1949-1963.* Stanford, CA: Stanford University Press, 1967.

Herrigel, Gary B. (1989). "Industrial Order and the Politics of Industrial Change: Mechanical Engineering," in Peter J. Katzenstein, ed., *Industry and Politics in West Germany.* Ithaca, NY: Cornell University Press, pp. 185-220.

Hey, Christian (1990). "Umweltpolitik in der EG: Kooperation Oder Konkurrenz der Standards?" in Rudolf Welzmüller, ed., *Marktaufteilung und Standortpoker in Europa.* Köln: Bund-Verlag, pp. 191-224.

Hey, Christian and J. Jahns-Böhm (1989). *Ökologie und freier Binnenmarkt.* Freiburg: Schwartz auf Weiss.

Junne, Gerd (1990) "Managementstrategien und Standortwahl," in Rudolf Welzmüller, ed., *Marktaufteilung und Standortpoker in Europa.* Köln: Bund-Verlag, pp. 84-99.

Korn, Peter (1988). "Chancen und Risiken bei der Vollendung des EG-Binnenmarktes," in Werner Weidenfeld, ed., *Binnenmarkt '92: Perspektiven aus deutscher Sicht.* Gütersloh: Bertelsmann Stiftung, pp. 51-56.

Matthies, Klaus (1989). "Deregulierung des Energiemarktes?" in Otto G. Mayer, Hans-Eckart Scharrer, and Hans-Jürgen Schmahl, eds., *Der Europäische Binnenmarkt.* Hamburg: Verlag Weltarchiv GmbH, pp. 175-194.

*Nachrichten für Außenpolitik* (4 January 1988). "BDI zur Europapolitik: Vorrang für Marktwirtschaft."

Neubauer, Ralf (1990a). "Textil- und Bekleidungsindustrie: Den Binnenmarkt bereits bewältigt," in Uwe Vorkötter, ed., *Aufbruch nach Europa.* Stuttgart: C. E. Poeschel Verlag, pp. 104-109.

——— (1990b). "Nahrungsmittelindustrie und Handel: Deutsche Zwerge gegen Europäische Riesen," in Uwe Vorkötter, ed., *Aufbruch nach Europa.* Stuttgart: C. E. Poeschel Verlag, pp. 139-144.

Neumann, Walter (1988). "Binnenmarkt auf Europas Straßen," in Werner Weidenfeld, ed., *Binnenmarkt '92: Perspektiven aus deutscher Sicht.* Gütersloh: Bertelsmann Stiftung, pp. 129-131.

*The New York Times* (3 April 1990a). "French-German Nerves Are on the Edge."

*The New York Times* (13 August 1990b). "Oil Prices to Slow Europe's Growth."

Nowak, Inge (1990). "Elektrizitätswirtschaft: Lange Leitung nach Europa," in Uwe Vorkötter, ed., *Aufbruch nach Europa.* Stuttgart: C. E. Poeschel Verlag, pp. 131-135.

Oehler, Klaus Dieter (1990). "Automobilindustrie: Strategie-Spiele," in Uwe Vorkötter, ed., *Aufbruch nach Europa.* Stuttgart: C. E. Poeschel Verlag, pp. 99-103.

Pelzer, Frank, and Alois Reimertz (1989). "Europa 1992: Der Euro-Pharma-Betreib," in Heinz W. Adams, ed., *Europa 1992.* Frankfurt aM: Frankfurter Allgemeine Zeitung, pp. 157-172.

Rekittke, Karl, and Rudolf Schulten (1989). "Mehr Wettbewerb in der Energieversorgung?" in Heinz W. Adams, ed., *Europa 1992.* Frankfurt aM: Frankfurter Allgemeine Zeitung, pp. 173-188.

Schreyer, Ulrich (1990). "Machinenbau: Gut und Teuer," in Uwe Vorkötter, ed., *Aufbruch nach Europa.* Stuttgart: C. E. Poeschel Verlag, pp. 136-138.

Stübinger-v. Olshausen, Ilse (1988). "Europäischer Binnenmarkt 1992 aus der Sicht der BASF," in Werner Weidenfeld, ed., *Binnenmarkt '92: Perspektiven aus deutscher Sicht.* Gütersloh: Bertelsmann Stiftung, pp. 75-77.

*Süddeutsche Zeitung* (20 February 1988a). "Gegen euphorische Erwartungen an den EG-Binnenmarkt."

*Süddeutsche Zeitung* (16 March 1988b). "EG-Binnenmarkt auf dem Prüfstand."

*Süddeutsche Zeitung* (20 April 1988c). "Playdoyer für den gemeinsamen Binnenmarkt."

*Süddeutsche Zeitung* (31 August 1989). "Deutscher Sozialstandard für die EG abgelehnt."

*Süddeutsche Zeitung* (31 January 1990). "Die milliardenschwere Bürde des Kohlepfennigs."

Volkswagen AG (1988). "Europäischer Binnenmarkt 1992," in Werner Weidenfeld, ed., *Binnenmarkt '92: Perspektiven aus deutscher Sicht.* Gütersloh: Bertelsmann Stiftung, pp. 67-70.

Wacker-Theodorakopoulos, Cora (1989). "Die Liberalisierung des Verkehrssektors durch den EG-Binnenmarket," in Otto G. Mayer, Hans-Eckart Scharrer, and Hans-Jürgen Schmahl, eds., *Der Europäische Binnenmarkt.* Hamburg: Verlag Weltarchiv GmbH, pp. 127-150.

Waigel, Theo (1990). "German Unity: Fiscal Policy Will Keep Its Sound Course." German Information Center.

*The Wall Street Journal Europe* (24 February 1988a). "Despite Squabbling, EC Countries Progress Toward Open Market."

*The Wall Street Journal Europe* (22 April 1988b). "Survey Finds National Pride May Stall Unification Effort."

*The Wall Street Journal Europe* (11 October 1988c). "Many Firms in the Dark About 1992."

Weinz, Wolfgang (1988). "Europäische Verbraucherpolitik: Das Gemeinschaftliche Lebensmittelrecht," in Werner Weidenfeld, ed., *Binnenmarkt '92: Perspektiven aus deutscher Sicht.* Gütersloh: Bertelsmann Stiftung, pp. 78-83.

*Die Welt* (13 January 1989). "Europa Sprengt Schranken für den Wachstumsschub."

*Wirtschaftswoche* (29 January 1988). "Etwas Weniger Europaduselei, Bitte Schön!"

*Die Zeit* (22 January 1988). "Abscheid vom Staatlichen Schutz."

*Die Zeit* (11 August 1989). "Falsch Kalkuliert."

# 2

# West German Labor and Europe '92

Andrei S. Markovits and Alexander Otto

## Introduction

In the middle of the 1980s many Europeans—especially businesspeople—bemoaned their continent's poor economic performance. Pessimistic in outlook, they worried about the lasting effects of their economies' "Eurosclerosis" in comparison with the seemingly boundless dynamism of Japanese and Korean production and the innovative flexibility of the American "job machine."[1] Barely five years, one white paper, one report, and a few bureaucratic decisions later, this Eurosclerosis has suddenly metamorphosed in certain circles into what could aptly be termed Euroeuphoria. With the acceptance of the Single European Act of 1987, the European Community (EC) member states pledged themselves to the concept of a European internal market. They decided to eliminate border controls, differences in technical regulations, and restrictions on competition in public procurement; to liberalize European financial markets; and to reduce differences in value added tax rates among EC member states. The proposed changes gave rise to a lot of optimism in the European business community. Baited by the prospects of the world's largest internal market, with 320 million consumers, imaginations in many a European boardroom are running wild with the possibilities for unprecedented growth, mergers, and ultimately profits.

In notable contrast to capital's and most governments' Euroeuphoria, labor has been on the whole rather troubled and confused by these momentous developments. Labor's position on Europe's internal market remains thus far lukewarm at best, most typically, however, virtually inert and often helpless. Above all, labor continues to behave reactively. It has yet to assume the initiative in seizing the agenda, especially in devising a coherent cross-national strategy for collective action.

This comes as no surprise if one takes a look at labor's great diversity in the twelve countries that were to form the internal market in January 1, 1993. Whereas labor's postwar history in the Mediterranean countries has been shaped predominantly by Communist unions, labor on the continent's northern rim and in Britain witnessed the primacy of social democracy through much of this century. Whereas the labor movement has been organizationally split along confessional and/or ideological lines in Italy, France, Belgium, Holland, Spain, and Portugal, and along craft lines in Britain, industrial divisions primarily characterize West Germany's labor organization.[2] Vast cross-national differences in wage rates, labor productivity, collective bargaining arrangements, and labor legislation make the formulation of common goals-let alone the implementation of common policies—a gargantuan (if not a Sisyphian) task for European labor.

Despite the presence of substantial formal barriers to transnational labor cooperation, there has been a rising interest in international activities among the European unions. The increasing importance of international issues has also been recognized by the German Trade Union Federation (Deutscher Gewerkschaftsbund—DGB), which is by far the largest and most active participant of the European Trade Union Confederation (ETUC).

In view of 1992, the DGB's foremost concern is the implementation of a legally binding social charter aimed at the protection of workers' rights. The DGB feels that the internal market does not provide adequate safeguards for working conditions and workers' co-determination rights. Therefore it fears that the position of the workers will be undermined by the liberalization of Europe's economy. In addition, the DGB demands more active regional policies on a European level and stresses the importance of international cooperation among European trade unions. But, despite its criticism of the internal market's missing social dimension, the DGB generally regards 1992 as a positive and necessary development.[3]

As a consequence of its numerical strength, the DGB has considerable influence on the ETUC's policies. Positionally, too, the dominance of DGB unionists among the ETUC's leaders provides further evidence for the power of the West German unions within the European labor movement.[4] Few experts doubt that the DGB's influence within the ETUC will increase during the 1990s. Vested with this "vanguard" role, the German unions' positions vis-à-vis the internal market have already assumed a centrality well beyond the immediate confines of the Federal Republic. An explanation of these union positions forms the core of this chapter.

By necessity this study largely deals with union positions rather than strategies. When we refer to the position of a union, we mean the attitudes of its leaders and officials toward an issue. A position encompasses the analysis and evaluation of the issue and the development of a response to it. Unlike a strategy, a position does not imply the existence or implementation of a concrete plan of action. As yet, the German unions still have not developed any detailed strategies that concretely address the challenges posed by the internal market. Thus our research mainly focused on an evaluation of the unions' positions toward the internal market. It is based on a thorough review of the union press and other published documents, interviews with key union leaders, and a survey of union members in Hamburg.[5]

By looking at the positions of four DGB member unions, we intend to contribute to a better understanding of trade union behavior in an uncertain international economic environment. In our analysis we have focused on two important explanatory variables affecting the positions and strategies of the German unions: union ideology and perceived economic interest. A union ideology induces members to identify with an organization that claims to promote their principles and goals. It creates stronger interpersonal ties that come from feeling part of a clearly defined group. Consequently, a union ideology not only facilitates the mobilization of members but also offers the members what Peter Lange and George Ross call incentives of "identity" and "sociability."[6] As Allan Flanders points out, ideologies are an important source of organizational strength: "By furnishing the group with an accepted and shared normative code they preserve its solidarity while at the same time giving to each individual his sense of personal worth."[7] Given the significance of union ideology for creating ties among union members and between leaders and the membership, trade unions have a strong incentive to preserve their ideology. In order to maintain these ties, the ideology of a union also has to be, at least minimally, consistent with its behavior.

In this way, a change in the economic environment such as the completion of the internal market is unlikely to translate directly into a union response formed on the basis of perceived economic interest. Instead, the nature of the response also will depend to a large extent on the ideology of the union. However, we do not view ideology as an immutable constraint on the behavior of a union. As the postwar history of the German trade unions has demonstrated, an ideology also can be modified by the union leadership in response to changes in the socioeconomic and institutional environment.[8] However, a change in ideology can create divisions among the membership. It may also weaken the credibility of the union leadership. Therefore, such a change is unlikely to occur unless the union perceives the presence of a significant gap between its ideology and the economic interest of the membership.

The relative importance of perceived economic interest and union ideology in determining union behavior largely depends on three factors. First, it is contingent on the union's perception of the size and certainty of the change in the economic environment. As the completion of the internal market still has relatively uncertain economic effects, we expect that ideology will play an important role in defining union responses until the economic impact of 1992 can be estimated more accurately. Second, the influence of ideology on union behavior will depend on the union's commitment to its ideology. Unions that do not have an explicit ideological commitment tend to follow their perceived economic interest in their policy decisions unless the change in the economic environment is still highly uncertain or likely to be small. In contrast, unions that are explicitly committed to an ideology will have greater difficulties in adjusting their positions to changes in the economic environment. In this way, a Communist union, such as the French CGT, is unlikely to endorse the internal market, which lacks a well-defined social dimension, even though union members may very well benefit from this development. Third, the relative influence of ideology and perceived economic interest depends on the nature of the union's behavior. In general, ideology tends to have a more substantial influence on union positions than on actual strategies. In notable contrast to union positions, it may be very costly for a trade union to adopt strategies that are contrary to the economic interest of its members. In this way, the implementation of a detailed strategy is generally preceded by a careful evaluation of its likely economic costs and benefits.

In this chapter we argue that union ideology has been the most important explanatory variable affecting the initial responses of the West German unions to the completion of the internal market. Given that the precise economic effects of European integration are still largely unknown and given that detailed strategies have not yet been implemented, unions rely on their respective ideologies as a predictable guide to action in a period of uncertainty. First we briefly describe the ideological frameworks informing the world of the four German unions forming the core of this study. Then we examine the sectoral economic changes that each of these unions can expect from the completion of the internal market. Having thus discussed two of the most important variables affecting union positions and strategies—ideology and economic environment—we then present the substance of our empirical findings by comparing the overall evaluation of the internal market by each of the four unions. Subsequently we contrast activist and accommodationist positions on the internal market by highlighting their substantial differences regarding work time reduction and possible collaboration with other European unions in the framework of 1992.

## THE IDEOLOGIES OF THE GERMAN TRADE UNIONS

While one of the most important legitimizing and solidarity-producing tenets of the postwar German labor movement has rested in its ideological unity and moderation, a closer look will clearly convey substantial differences in the *Weltanschauung* informing the politics of the DGB's member unions. Especially during the 1970s and 1980s, there developed two distinct groups inside the DGB, which we termed activists and accommodationists.[9] The activist unions in the DGB are fundamentally critical of Germany's political economy. Although hostile to communism and firmly anchored in the organizational boundaries of social democracy, the activists regard themselves as major players for social reform. They perceive themselves as advocates of progressive causes well beyond the confines of immediate union concerns. Taking the antagonism between capital and labor as a given, the activists regard industrial conflict as inevitable in the struggle for social change. Unions adhering to this point of view believe in the intrinsic value of mobilization in the name of universalistic solidarities that reach far outside the actual purview of union interests. Two of the leading activist unions, IG Medien (the media union) and IG Metall (the metalworkers' union), represent this wing of the DGB in our study.

In notable contrast to activism, the DGB's accommodationist unions stress the common interests of labor and capital in a modern economy such as the Federal Republic's. Accommodationism holds that unions and employers can find mutually satisfying solutions to their common problems through a close and cooperative relationship best called social partnership. In contrast to the activists' negative assessment of the German political economy, the accommodationists see the Federal Republic's political and economic institutions in a positive light. Far from seeing their mandate as one of substantially altering the existing conditions of the German political economy—as do the activists—the accommodationists perceive their primary task to be enhancing the legitimacy and effectiveness of the system, which they propose to do best by maximizing the economic interests of their immediate members without much radical fanfare and universalistic concerns. If the activists became allied with social democracy's radical elements and the so-called new social movements in the course of the 1980s, the accommodationists remained solidly in social democracy's traditional growth-oriented and reformist camp. Two accommodationist unions, IG Chemie-Papier-Keramik (the chemical workers' union) and Gewerkschaft Nahrung-Genuß-Gaststätten (NGG; the food workers' union), represent this wing of German labor in our study.

Several criteria played an important role in the selection of these four unions. Foremost, we wanted to include the most pronounced representatives of activism and accommodationism, respectively. This led us to include IG Metall and IG Medien on the activist side and IG Chemie on the accommodationist side. We also thought it important to analyze the positions of key actors within the DGB, which again led us to IG Metall and IG Chemie. With our decision to make IG Medien part of the study by virtue of its explicit activism, we needed a comparably small union on the accommodationist side, which we found in NGG. Last, hypothesizing as to how these unions' immediate interests might be affected by the internal market confirmed the validity of our choice. Our sample thus includes prospective "winners," and "losers," as well as mixed cases.

## THE EXPECTED ECONOMIC EFFECTS OF THE INTERNAL MARKET'S COMPLETION ON THE FOUR UNIONS STUDIED

It is impossible to predict the precise economic and social consequences of the internal market, which will largely depend on future economic policies, business strategies, and legal changes. However, given the great importance of the internal market for Europe's future development, many studies have already tried to predict the most likely economic and political effects of 1992. Naturally, the German trade unions have followed this research with great interest. In this section we shall therefore analyze what the unions can "rationally" expect from 1992 on the basis of the studies available.[10]

It is important to note that we focus exclusively on the changes associated with the completion of the internal market and not on each sector's expected future prospects in general. Our analysis also remains largely confined to the likely economic effects of 1992, disregarding changes among parties and shifts in the climate of government, to mention but two crucial political factors. Since employment and wages in each industry are closely related to that industry's economic performance, we view this approach as justified. In addition, we take into consideration other factors that affect workers' lives, such as, for example, work safety issues and the relative importance of multinational companies in each industry. By weighing these factors, we believe to have arrived at a balanced conclusion as to the effects of 1992 on each of the four unions' organizational purviews. Here are our results.

## Positive Expectations: The German Printers

The completion of the internal market is likely to benefit firms and workers in the printing and paper-processing industries, in which most IG Medien members are organized. Exports make up only 7 percent of sales in the printing industry because of language barriers, disproportionately high transport costs, and the need for punctual delivery of newspapers. However, the export of catalogs, books, and advertisements has steadily increased during the past years, and by 1987 exports of these goods were more than 2.5 times larger than imports.[11] In the paper-processing industry the pattern was not very different since exports exceeded imports by more than 200 percent in 1987.[12]

As the growth in the difference between exports and imports attests, the competitive disadvantages created by high wage costs and the short work week (under 40 hours) seem outweighed by other productivity advantages of German printing enterprises. In particular, the great productivity of the German printing industry can be explained by the substantial investments made since the 1970s and the highly skilled work force. Thus, the completion of the Internal Market is likely to benefit firms and workers in the German printing industry. The initial benefits will not be overly high because of the low nontariff barriers in this industry, but the removal of administrative formalities at borders may stimulate increased trade.[13] In this way an increase in industrial growth rates and employment can be expected.

In addition, the printers' co-determination rights and IG Medien's bargaining power are unlikely to be adversely affected by a growth of multinational companies resulting from the integration of the internal market. Most of the large printing firms still have a relatively limited international presence. Even though some of the sizable printing companies, such as Axel Springer and Bertelsmann, are in the process of international expansion, it seems unlikely that this will substantially weaken IG Medien's bargaining power because high transportation costs and language barriers will make locational shifts of production sites more difficult. Thus, the completion of the internal market is unlikely to have any adverse effects on German printers.

## Mixed Expectations: The German Metalworkers

Like the printing industry, the German metal industry is likely to be a winner in the internal market. The export-oriented automobile industry, for example, which already has a market share of 42 percent in the European Community, will undoubtedly benefit from the removal of substantial nontariff barriers in 1992.[14] Given the impressive productivity of the German automobile industry, it seems hardly surprising that most firms expect significant sales increases as a result of European economic integration.[15] The market shares of other sectors not characterized by high nontariff barriers—such as machinery and electronics—are not likely to expand significantly as a result of the internal market. In these sectors, higher industrial growth rates will be induced primarily by higher growth rates in the domestic economy.

Given the favorable prospects for the main sectors of the German metal industry, positive employment and wage effects can be expected from the completion of the internal market. However, several small sectors—such as the boiler and railroad equipment industry—which previously have been protected by high nontariff barriers, are vulnerable to restructuring changes that could have harmful consequences for the work force.[16] European integration also may undermine the social rights of metalworkers and the bargaining power of IG Metall. In the metal industry, unlike in printing, multinational firms play an important role. Given the absence of binding EC directives on workers' participation and consultation rights within multinational companies, the internal market may weaken the bargaining position of German metalworkers. Thus, despite favorable growth prospects in the metal industry, European economic integration may have certain negative consequences for IG Metall and some of its members.

## Mixed Expectations: The German Chemical Workers

The export-oriented German chemical industry also is likely to benefit from the completion of the internal market. Although superior technology and large economies of scale have given rise to high productivity in the German chemical industry, the direct effect of the internal market is bound to be limited because most parts of this industry are not protected by high nontariff barriers.[17] For example, as most chemical firms do not manufacture finished products, the advantages of VAT harmonization will only concern them indirectly.[18] The indirect effects of the Common Market, however, may be quite substantial because the chemical industry is extremely dependent on the Federal Republic's macroeconomic performance, which is likely to improve as a consequence of 1992.[19] Therefore wages and employment will most likely be positively affected as well.

However, the economic effects on some parts of the chemical industry still remain uncertain. For example, substantial government intervention has occurred in the pharmaceutical industry. Given the wide variations in prices among member states, the integration of pharmaceutical markets in the Community will probably have far-reaching implications for European pharmaceutical companies.[20] In particular, small firms that have benefited from market protection in the past may be displaced by the restructuring of the industry, which could carry adverse consequences for workers.

The completion of the internal market also may prove detrimental to the West German chemical workers for other reasons. With the exception of Denmark, the Federal Republic's work safety requirements and health regulations are the most stringent in the EC.[21] Were the EC to adopt lower minimum safety standards in its integration program, a downward leveling of work safety could be expected in the Federal Republic. The internal market also may undermine the bargaining power of unions and works councils, because many multinational firms operate in the chemical industry, and their presence is likely to become increasingly significant. Without effective consultation and co-determination rights, workers will have very limited power over the allocation of investments and production sites.

## Negative Expectations: The German Food Workers

In an evaluation of the sectoral effects of the Common Market, IG Metall found that only seven German industries are potentially threatened by the completion of the internal market.[22] These industries are characterized by low intra-EC penetration rates, high nontariff barriers, and the comparatively high prices that they charge for their products. Five of these seven industries belong to the food industry, which thus far has been well protected by the Federal Republic's stringent and restrictive food legislation. These "endangered" industries include the production of candy, chocolate, cocoa, pasta, beer, champagne, wine, mineral water, and other nonalcoholic drinks. Thus, a large part of the German food industry seems to be threatened by the completion of the Common Market.

The Federal Republic's food imports currently exceed its exports by 17.5 percent.[23] The internal market may cause the trade balance for food items to deteriorate even further. At this point it seems that the German food industry has not prepared adequately for 1992. According to one reliable source, many German firms may already have missed their chance to adjust to the changes triggered by the completion of the internal market.[24] In this way, it seems possible that 1992 will trigger a wave of takeovers by foreign firms that want to gain access to German food markets. This, together with the negative prospects for the industry, is likely to have adverse social consequences for the

German food workers. Given the relatively low income elasticity for most food products, it seems unlikely that these adverse developments will be counterbalanced by the expected improvement in the general economic climate.

Apart from the anticipated difficulties for the food industry, the social rights of the German food workers and NGG's bargaining power may be undermined by the process of European integration. In particular, the probable strengthening of multinationals is cause for additional worries for NGG in its attempt to protect its members from the negative social consequences of the integration process. Even though the economic performance of the hotel and restaurant industry is unlikely to be strongly influenced by 1992, a major part of NGG's membership could be negatively affected by the completion of the internal market.

Having completed our discussion of the two main independent variables that could affect trade union positions toward the completion of the internal market, we are poised to test the relative importance of union ideology and economic expectations in determining these positions. Were ideology to be the decisive variable, activists would be likely to view the integration process more critically than accommodationist unions. Unlike accommodationism, the activist ideology is generally opposed to growth-oriented "mega" projects, especially if they lack a well-defined social dimension, as still is very much the case with the internal market. Since activism places more emphasis on redistribution than on economic growth, unions adhering to the activist philosophy are bound to be more critical of 1992 than their accommodationist counterparts.

However, were rational economic expectations to be the decisive determinant of union positions, the unions that are most likely to be favored by the integration process (such as IG Medien) would also be the main supporters of 1992. Conversely, a union such as NGG, whose members have a good chance of being disadvantaged by the internal market, should oppose its completion. In the next section we discuss the relative explanatory power of both variables.

## THE OVERALL EVALUATION OF 1992 ON THE PART OF FOUR GERMAN TRADE UNIONS

To start with a cautionary note, it is important to realize that the unions' views of the internal market do not at this time amount to an official policy or to a well-formulated coherent position. It was still too early for that. Since in their publications DGB unions almost never stress their positional differences, our interviews and survey proved crucial to demonstrate the existence of interunion divergences regarding their positions on 1992.

Our findings highlight the marked differences between the positions of activists and accommodationists, thereby providing evidence for the important role of ideology in the unions' positions vis-à-vis the internal market. In contrast, we were surprised how relatively insignificant sectoral economic expectations and potential changes, which very well might have concrete effects on the unions' world of collective bargaining, were in shaping the unions' positions.

## The Activist Unions

The activist unions in the DGB are much more critical of 1992 than their accommodationist counterparts. In particular, it seems surprising that IG Medien, whose members are likely to benefit from the completion of the internal market, has the most critical position toward 1992 among all DGB unions. This attitude corresponds to this union's activist opposition toward all projects that it believes solely reflect the interest of the European business community. The activists' position reflects a "new left" *Weltanschauung* disdaining large size, economic growth, and loss of autonomy on the one hand and extolling localized empowerment, democratic control, and universalistic citizenship on the other. The activists' objections to the internal market could best be grouped into three categories.

### The Federal Republic as a Hegemonic Behemoth

Repeatedly, activists objected to 1992 as yet another vehicle to strengthen further an already much too powerful German economy. Making matters worse, so the activists say, would be the fact that this strengthening of the Federal Republic would inevitably occur at the direct expense of others in the EC, European countries outside the Community, and members of the Third World. For example, IG Medien's district secretary in Hamburg, Rolf Schuhmacher, feels that "the German economy has the obligation to help Third World countries which it has previously exploited. . . . However, because of the strong influence of big business in politics, such a policy will be very difficult to enforce. At least, we need to prevent that the mighty powers within the EC abuse the weak countries as provinces."[25] In the same context the activists criticize the Federal Republic's export prowess, which—given its acceptance across virtually all segments of the German public—amounts to veritable iconoclasm. IG Metall's leader Franz Steinkuhler has on a number of occasions referred to the Federal Republic's position as "export world champion" in a derisive and critical manner.[26] This view seems especially surprising given that the economic position of the German metalworkers is largely dependent on export performance.

Nonetheless, the "remedies" that the activists propose against Germany's high trade surpluses are not necessarily contrary to their members' economic interest.[27] Using a Keynesian framework of analysis, the activists favor a reduction of the Federal Republic's export surplus by increasing domestic demand. However, such a policy could even lead to a growth in exports if increased domestic demand solely reduced the surplus by raising imports. This increase in imports could in turn induce a growth of foreign demand for German exports. In short, the monetary value of exports could increase even as the trade surplus declines.

### The Issue of "Social Dumping"

Many activists worry that the internal market will create a downward leveling of workers' rights, a sort of "Portuguezation" of German industrial relations. In this scenario, the hard-fought gains of the German labor movement such as co-determination in the company boardroom and the shop floor will dissipate once 1992 is fully operational. While the activists share this fear with their accommodationist colleagues, their respective responses are tellingly different. In order to introduce German labor conditions in Europe's peripheries, the activists welcome German investment in Portugal, Greece, and Ireland even if they occur to the immediate detriment of workers in the Federal Republic. Activists believe that Germans have an obligation to share their wealth with Europe's less fortunate for the purpose of creating a more equitable and just collective order. However, the activists fear that the completion of the internal market will increase even further the already existing regional imbalances within the EC. According to the works council chairman of Broschek Druck Gmbh, Sonny Holz (IG Medien), "it is likely that the German printing industry will benefit from 1992. Nonetheless, I am an opponent of the internal market. It will boost investments in the printing industry . . . but after 1992 foreign printing enterprises will collapse as a result of intensified price competition. In this way, the Internal Market will have especially negative consequences for workers in other European countries."[28] In particular, the activists feel that the completion of the internal market may undermine working conditions in many other EC countries because of the absence of strong labor movements. In order to protect all workers from the consequences of 1992 and to prevent the widening of the economic gap among EC countries, the activists are willing to assume a leadership role in the European labor movement in the defense of workers' rights and working conditions. The activists believe that foreigners also have a right to benefit from Germany's economic prosperity, and therefore they firmly oppose all xenophobic parties and movements that have recently gained prominence in German politics. Thus, for example, were the inflow of foreign workers into the Federal Republic to increase with the completion of the internal market, many activist leaders would welcome this as a positive development.[29] Indeed, IG Medien's biweekly newspaper even argues that the current unemployment rate in Germany would be higher in the absence of foreign workers.[30]

### The Fear of Heteronomy and Bureaucratization

Activist leaders voice the worry that the internal market will lead to a loss in autonomy and an increase in bureaucratic decision-making. Unlike the conservative fear (à la Thatcher) that 1992 will mean a loss in national sovereignty to unaccountable Eurocrats in Brussels, the activists worry about a loss of democratic control due to excessive size and an increase in technocratic decision-making made indispensable by this very size. Here, again, the activists' affinity to a "new left" ideology is striking.

In conclusion, it is quite clear that elites in activist unions voice very critical opinions about the internal market. Nonetheless, IG Metall leaders generally regard the completion of the Common Market as a necessary development. They feel that any other alternative would lead to national protectionism that would ultimately damage all European economies. Moreover, these leaders believe that 1992 also may eventually prove advantageous to the workers, provided adequate social safeguards are taken from the very beginning. In this respect, IG Metall elites tend to view the internal market more positively than their activist colleagues in IG Medien. Our survey of union members conveys a striking confluence of their opinions and views with those of union leadership, at least on the issues concerning the European Single Market and German labor's responses to it. (See Tables 2.1, 2.2, and Figure 2.1.)

## The Accommodationist Unions

The accommodationists' attitude toward the internal market is much more positive and conciliatory than that of the activists. Union leaders have generally been confident that 1992 will create powerful growth stimuli. Moreover, accommodationists feel that this growth—and the internal market—will be very beneficial to German workers, German society, and the Federal Republic as a

Table 2.1
**Membership Attitudes: The Main Disadvantage of 1992**
**(3 choices per respondent)**

| | IG Medien | IG Metall | IG Chemie | NGG |
|---|---|---|---|---|
| Social rights of the employees are endangered | 77% | 63% | 51% | 60% |
| Germany is exposed to greater competition from low-wage countries | 41% | 36% | 63% | 67% |
| The poorer European countries will suffer from the economic superiority of the large industrial nations | 71% | 67% | 26% | 27% |
| The internal market favors only the interests of the multinationals | 65% | 67% | 42% | 20% |
| Downward pressures on work safety standards and consumer protection are likely | 6% | 27% | 42% | 47% |
| Environmental protection is likely to be less rigorous | 12% | 15% | 23% | 27% |

whole. The emphasis of the accommodationist unions on their support for Europe's economic integration therefore differs sharply from the activist unions' position, which stresses mainly the dangers of 1992. Even in tone one can detect a marked difference in the choice of words and phrases. Thus, while IG Metall published articles about 1992 under headings such as "Internal Market Diminishes the Rights of Employees, " "Jobs Created by the Common Market?" or, even more explicitly, "A Murderous Pressure," accommodationists stress the "Challenge of the Internal Market," are determined to "Use the Opportunities of the Common Market Decisively," and exhort people simply to say "Yes to European Unity." As to the substance, the accommodationists' position is much more national in scope, particularistic in its concerns, and trusting in the ultimate abilities of the establishment, be they the market, the German state, or the new European entity. In this way, even NGG favors the completion of the internal

Table 2.2
**Membership Attitudes: How Should the German Unions Respond to the Completion of the Internal Market? (more than one response possible)**

| | IG Medien | IG Metall | IG Chemie | NGG |
|---|---|---|---|---|
| Strengthen the cooperation with other European unions | 90% | 100% | 91% | 87% |
| Intensify the dialogue with employers' federations | 5% | 21% | 46% | 53% |
| Attempt to retain investments in Germany with more flexible strategies | 5% | 12% | 40% | 17% |
| Strive decisively for the 35-hour work week, even if there is an outflow of investments | 58% | 70% | 23% | 33% |

market, despite the fact that a large part of its membership may very well be harmed by European integration. Indeed, on a number of occasions accommodationists displayed downright enthusiasm for 1992. Here, too, we would like to group the responses into three categories.

## The Role of the Federal Republic

In marked contrast to the activists, the accommodationists believe that the Federal Republic has little obligation to help the poorer countries in Europe —let alone the Third World. The Federal Republic's primary obligation is to its own citizens, particularly its workers, who—as many accommodationists believe—will face increasing competition as a result of the internal market. In this way, the accommodationist unions demand from the state more educational programs designed to raise the qualifications of German workers, thereby ensuring their advantages over the expected foreign competition while at the same time helping the competitiveness of Germany industry. Accommodationists are eager to increase the productivity of German workers at the cost of others in Europe, thus making the Federal

Figure 2.1
**Membership Rating of the Effects of 1992**
**(highly negative = 0, no impact = 5, highly positive = 10)**

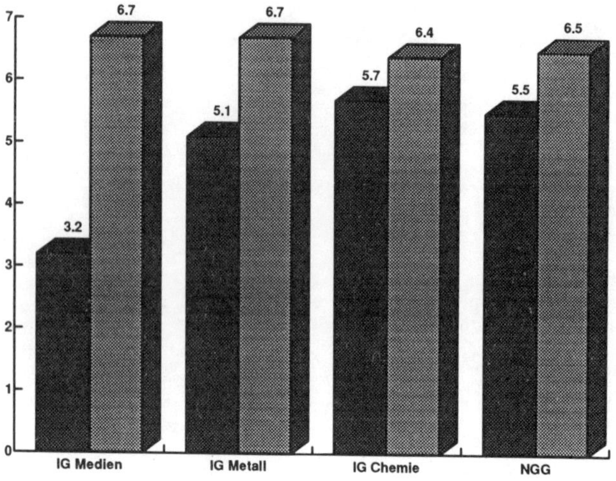


**Series 1: Expected Effect on the German Workers**
**Series 2: Expected Effect on the Economic Situation of the FRG**

Republic an even more attractive place for foreign investment. The accommodationist concern with Germany's international competitiveness also can be seen from the NGG's justification of higher wages in West Germany. According to the food workers' union, the failure of German wage increases to keep up with those in other EC countries would be damaging "because a further increase in the German trade surplus . . . could threaten the progress towards European unity [and] would soon lead to a revaluation of the mark anyway. Consequently, the external competitive advantage of the German economy would again be lost."[31] In contrast to the activist unions, the NGG does not fear that lower export surpluses may harm the poorer EC nations but rather that they may hinder the completion of the internal market. In this way, it becomes evident that the NGG is concerned primarily with Germany's competitiveness and the advantages the country can reap from the completion of the internal market.

Above all, accommodationists do not want to jeopardize one of their proudest contributions to what they believe remains perhaps the single greatest attraction of *Modell Deustchland*: social partnership. It has been this vaunted institution that accounts for the Federal Republic's great economic successes, and the accommodationists intend to keep it that way in an integrated Europe as well.

## The "Social Dumping" Issue

Just as the activist unions, the accommodationists, too, fear that the European economic integration process may undermine workers' co-determination rights. However, in contrast to the activists, the accommodationists mainly support the broadest possible harmonization of working conditions and worker participation in order to prevent a migration of investments and jobs to low-wage areas of southern Europe or Ireland. While the accommodationists—just like their activist counterparts—deplore the rise of xenophobia and racism in the Federal Republic, they are a good deal less enthusiastic than the activists about an increasing inflow of foreigners into Germany beginning January 1, 1993. For example, Hans-Peter Schröeder (IG Chemie), the works council vice chairman of the chemical firm Beiersdorf AG, feels that an increase of foreign immigrants is likely to lead to an increase of xenophobic tendencies in Germany.[32] According to Schröeder, this could disturb the social harmony between Germans and foreigners in the Federal Republic.

Conforming to their national concerns, accommodationist unions are worried not only about the protection of the rights and interests of German workers, but also of those of the German consumer. The NGG in particular accords this issue foremost priority in its evaluation of the Common Market. The completion of the internal market will lead to the harmonization of regulations concerning food products. The NGG fears that this process may endanger the health of the German consumer unless the highest safety and quality standards are guaranteed.[33] The NGG sees its demands on behalf of German consumers coincide with the economic interests of the workers in the German food industry.

Even though the accommodationist unions, just like their activist counterparts, worry about "social dumping," the nature of their respective concerns is profoundly different, thereby allowing the accommodationists to be a good deal more optimistic about the problem's solution. Having a more particularistic, that is, German-oriented, identity than the activist unions, the accommodationists' worries are more self-centered than those of the universalistic activists'. This, in turn, means that the accommodationists continue to have great faith in the regulative and protective powers of the German state and its ancillary institutions in helping German workers in an increasingly unsettled labor market. The accommodationists' trust in etatist policies extends from Bonn/Berlin to Brussels, thus making them less fearful of the impending changes. Above all, the accommodationists' confidence in economic growth outweighs their concerns in the potentially negative effects of social dumping.

### The Trust in the Powers that Be

In contrast to the activists, the accommodationists are not particularly enamored of expansionary fiscal policies. This bespeaks their profound trust in the "logic" of the market, especially when it is compared to the activists' skepticism regarding this arena. While the accommodationists' position may thus not necessitate close cooperation with foreign labor unions, it most certainly facilitates the dialogue with domestic employers. In addition to the accommodationists' basic trust in the market and the employers, it is their fundamental faith in the state that distinguishes them from the activists on this account. The state—especially when controlled by social democrats—will see to it that all adversities befalling German workers in the process of this worthwhile restructuring of European life will at least be bearable, if not completely avoided.

In conclusion, just as it is the case with the activists, here too ideologies and long-held general views about politics and economics define the accommodationists' overall position on 1992. As we tried to show, this assessment is overwhelmingly positive in tone and substance. While the accommodationists voice certain concerns regarding the internal market's possible adversities for the German workers, they also welcome 1992. Their concerns do not compare to the fundamental and wide-ranging criticisms voiced by the activists toward the internal market. This is all the more surprising since, pursuant to purely economic expectations, a number of accommodationist unions could legitimately voice major concerns about the internal market's potentially adverse effects on their members.

## FIRST STRATEGIES: WORK TIME, INTERNATIONAL LABOR SOLIDARITY, AND 1992

Perhaps no other issue has kept activists and accommodationists farther apart than their differing assessment of work time reduction as a strategy for labor and the national economy. It is interesting how these fundamental ideological differences, which divided German labor throughout all of the 1980s, have been reaffirmed on a European level for the 1990s. The divergence on this particular issue neatly highlights the different mindsets with which accommodationists and activists in the world of German labor approach the impending internal market.

Briefly, activists—spearheaded by IG Metall's 1978 to 1979 strike in Northrhine Westphalia's steel industry and the much larger work stoppage in the Federal Republic's metal and printing industries (involving IG Medien's predecessor, IG Druck und Papier, in addition to IG Metall) in the spring of 1984—have made the battle for the 35-hour work week the centerpiece of their overall strategy. More than any other strategy, the battle for the 35-hour work week encapsulates the essence of activism: First and foremost, the strategy is profoundly universalistic in that it aims to share available jobs with all workers, thereby uniting employed and unemployed in an act of solidarity. In addition, it is confrontational, challenging capital where it hurts by giving workers more fixed leisure time.

Accommodationists, led by IG Chemie, have opposed the 35-hour strategy with various degrees of vehemence. They see it as unnecessarily rigid, not very liked by workers (as opposed to radical union officials), and potentially disruptive of German production in an era of heightened global competition.

Both camps see the internal market strengthening their respective positions. To IG Metall and the activists, the 35-hour strategy seems ideally suited for 1992. Thus they coined the slogan "Europe Needs the 35." As Europe's most important and powerful union, IG Metall fully intends to transfer its vanguard role in the 35-hour controversy, which it assumed for a decade in the German context, onto the European plain. The union believes that the logic of the strategy fully applies to the Internal Market as well where strong unions pursuing universalistic class strategies will be sorely needed as a counterweight to the employers' overwhelming power. Thus, IG Metall sees its self-styled image of a "Gegenmacht" (countervailing power) in the Federal Republic replicable in the European context.

Of equal importance to the activists as the implementation of the 35-hour work week is their firm opposition to any weekend work. Ever since IG Metall succeeded throughout long and arduous battles in the 1950s and 1960s in attaining a free Saturday, the sanctity of a two-day weekend remained one of the most cherished achievements of the German labor movement. With the rapidly changing nature of production in the past few years, employers have demanded greater flexibility on the part of workers as to their working hours, which—so the employers hoped—might include weekends on occasions. Regardless of the employers' generosity in compensating workers for this necessary adjustment, IG Metall and IG Medien have refused to negotiate on this issue. Arguing that workers and their families have a right to enjoy their leisure collectively on weekends, the activists see the introduction of weekend work as an outright encroachment on their hard-won achievements and—worse still—as an undermining of private space that represents perhaps the last refuge and autonomous niche away from the inexorable logic of growth, capitalist accumulation, and bureaucratic dictates. Even if German workers lose in the short run because of their resilience on this issue—as has already happened when General Motors transferred work that it normally has done in its Bochum plant to its facilities in Zaragoza because the German workers refused to work on weekends—the activists intend to remain steadfast. Detlev Hensche, IG Medien's most outspoken activist, argues: "If we give in once, we will always be subject to blackmail. Therefore I can only advise to say no. Besides it is not necessarily bad if investments are spread more evenly, for example, also to Portugal and Sicily. At the moment we are only exporting unemployment with our trade surpluses."[34] Activists regard the resistance to weekend work and the struggle for the 35-hour work week as important contributions to social progress in Europe. They fully believe that these battles constitute a solid basis for the international solidarity of labor. Thus, the great importance accorded by the activists within the DGB to these issues is consistent with their strong beliefs in universalism and internationalism and with their challenges to the dictates of capitalism.

The accommodationists also consider work time issues crucial in labor's shaping its participation in 1992. Their approach, however, differs diametrically from that of the activists. Finding the resilience of the activists rigid, accommodationists are willing to negotiate openly with employers about weekend work and other work reduction schemes provided the resulting provisions will help tie—perhaps even attract—jobs to the Federal Republic. Accommodationists argue that the Federal Republic's competitiveness depends much more on flexible work hours than on low wages. They feel that the work time policies of the activists are out of step with new technological developments. They argue that employers should at least be guaranteed the optimal use of their expensive machinery if they are already saddled with high wage costs and the Federal Republic's extensive social net.[35] In the absence of considerable flexibility on work time issues, accommodationists fear that the Federal Republic will lose jobs to other European countries. To the reproach that the accommodationist position may be detrimental to the solidarity of the European labor movement, Horst Mettke, a key IG Chemie leader, replied that foreign labor unions also fail to contribute their fair share to this solidarity. Mettke stated: "I have had experiences with my European colleagues. We have massively tried to tell our European friends that we need to find a specific common basis. Then I was told: You know, if it helps our [i.e., non-German] competitiveness and if it prevents a rise in unemployment in our country [i.e., not Germany], then you have to understand that we take [the decision to work on weekends]. We do not have a problem with working on Saturday and Sunday."[36] Many accommodationists contend that the chance of preserving good working conditions in other European countries is very small given the weakness of the labor movement in most other EC nations. Thus, the German unions' primary task is to provide the best conditions for their own members by maintaining high levels of investments in the Federal Republic. This option, so the accommodationists believe, has thus far proven to be the most reliable for the welfare of the German working class.

Ideology also plays an important role in explaining union positions toward other European trade unions. The activists display their commitment to international labor solidarity by trying to augment their collaborative links not only with all unions belonging to the ETUC but also with those outside this largely social democratic federation, notably Communist-dominated organizations such as the French Confédération Générale du Travail (CGT) and the Spanish Comisiones Obreras (CCOO). At the company level, too, the activists seem very determined to pursue strong ties with the foreign equivalents of the Federal Republic's works councils. Thus, for example, an international consultation body has already arisen at Gillette, comprising union representatives from Spain, France, and Germany.[37] Called "Gisel" (Gillette Intersyndicale Européenne de Liaison), this organization intends to establish better communication and information links among the shop-floor representatives in the three countries. It also is designed to provide greater international solidarity in cases of industrial conflict. In Gisel IG Metall officials even work together with unions that do not belong to the ETUC, such as the Spanish CCOO.

In contrast to the activist unions, the accommodationists refuse to coordinate their activities with Communist unions from other European countries. IG Chemie even attempts to impose the principle of "social partnership" on the other member unions of the European Federation of Chemical Unions (EFCU). In this way, IG Chemie chairman Hermann Rappe warned his European colleagues that "we are for competition and the social market economy, and if you are against it, we have to fight it out."[38] Since many of the other EFCU unions refuse to adopt IG Chemie's accommodationism, genuine cooperation among the European chemical workers' unions will be very difficult to achieve. Thus, until now, the accommodationists' particularism has made them pursue a sauve-qui-peut policy that places little trust in the international solidarity of European trade unions. Instead, the accommodationists have sought closer cooperation with the German employers' federations in the preparation for the internal market. Unlike the activists, the accommodationists have formed study groups with the employers in order to discuss ways to respond to this major transformation that would prove optimal to both sides. Typically, the accommodationists first consulted the employers before they established contacts with foreign unionists. However, as Wolfgang Weinz, NGG's European secretary, notes: "NGG will have to discuss the consequences in case the employers fail to respond to the union's initiative. If we cannot work with the employers in the creation of international works councils, we will probably have to work without them."[39]

## CONCLUSION

The preceding analysis of the positions and first strategies of four German unions toward the completion of the European internal market underlines the primacy of ideology in determining union behavior. The study in no way denies the importance of economic interests in determining union positions and behavior. It merely shows that in matters of uncertainty and anticipation, unions—like many other decision makers—fall back on learned behavior and trusted terrain in formulating their views of the situation. They reduce the matter's complexity by fitting it into categories that they have learned to trust. Ideology then serves as a convenient method of minimizing uncertainty and reducing complexity. It is an important mechanism to attain the semblance of control in an otherwise uncontrollable situation. In short, it provides expected answers where only questions exist.

The more closely the West German unions can anticipate the exact economic effects of the internal market, the more we expect their positions to be defined by economic interest. Once the life of German workers will be concretely affected by the changes triggered by the completion of the internal market, union positions and strategies will have to reflect increasingly the interests of their members in order to prevent a loss of membership support. Ideology, of course, will never recede completely. Activists and accommodationists do in fact see the world around them in a different light. This has once again been made clear during the momentous events of 1989-90, which fundamentally transformed Europe and Germany. Whereas the accommodationist unions rushed to welcome the German Democratic Republic's demise and the Federal Republic's wholesale "takeover"of this moribund entity, the activists proceeded much more cautiously. To them, in notable contrast to the accommodationist view of the GDR, the East German experiment, though an obvious failure, in no way discredited the larger project of socialism. Moreover, congruent with a very popular position in the West German left, the activists accorded the GDR much legitimacy simply for being the first socialist—and explicitly antifascist—political construct on German soil.

Once union had become a fait accompli, the differences between accommodationists and activists persisted. Whereas the former were busily emphasizing the positive aspects of this unity, especially for the lives of East German workers who, for the first time, had the possibility to join free trade unions, the activists spent more time delineating the immense difficulties awaiting East German workers in a market-propelled capitalist society. Both wings of the West German labor movement have in the meantime proceeded to incorporate remnants of the old East German unions into the existing structures of the Federal Republic's DGB. Despite the enormity of this task, neither accommodationists nor activists have neglected their previous preoccupation with the European internal market. All German unions remain convinced that the events in Eastern Europe, as well as in Germany, do not in any way detract from the primacy of the project surrounding Europe 1992. If anything, German labor belongs to an ideological world in the Federal Republic that perhaps more than ever advocates Germany's integration into a strong European framework lest suspicions about Germany's "Sonderweg" and "Schaukelpolitik" once again become manifest. Despite all their ideological differences, it is quite clear that accommodationists as well as activists see the Western—European—ties of the Federal Republic as a sine qua non for the continuing economic prosperity and political democracy of Germany. Few within the unions question the legitimacy of this broad-based consensus. Moreover, as a modicum of certainty replaces much anxiety concerning this momentous reshaping of Europe's political economy, we predict that the German unions' actual strategies and day-to-day behavior will mainly reflect their trusted pragmatism, which has served them so well in the course of the Federal Republic's success story.

---

## NOTES

1. For an analysis of this relationship, see Manfred McDowell, "After Full Employment: European Social Democracy and the Politics of the American Model, " Ph.D. diss., Department of Political Science, Boston University, Boston, Massachusetts, 1990.
2. Besides the German Trade Union Federation, which is organized along industrial lines, there exist a small Christian labor federation and separate organizations for salaried employees and civil servants.

3. For a detailed review of the DGB's position toward the internal market, see Ernst Breit, ed., *Fuer ein soziales Europa* (Cologne: Bund-Verlag, 1989), and Gerd Siebert, ed., *Europa '92* (Frankfurt: Nachrichten, 1989).
4. At the time of this writing, Ernst Breit, the former head of the DGB, continues as chairman of the ETUC's executive committee. The European chemical and metalworker federations, both major actors within the ETUC, are also chaired by West German union leaders.
5. Much of the field research for this study centered on the city of Hamburg, the second largest German city after Berlin. It was a suitable location for the research, because all sectors studied are represented with large multinational firms. In particular, the Hamburg region is the center of the German printing and publishing industries. It is also the home of some of the largest firms in the food industry, metalworking, and chemical production. Moreover, Hamburg houses the headquarters of the food workers' union, Gewerkschaft Nahrung-Genuß-Gaststätten (NGG). In addition, Hamburg is a district center for all four unions comprising this study. Thus, the concentration of industry and union headquarters made it possible to conduct research effectively on the positions of the German trade unions toward the Internal Market.
6. Peter Lange, George Ross, and Maurizio Vannicelli, *Unions, Change and Crisis: French and Italian Union Strategy and the Political Economy, 1945-1980* (London: Allen & Unwin, 1982), p. 221.
7. Allan Flanders, "Trade Unions and the Force of Tradition" in *Management and Unions* (London: Faber & Faber, 1970), pp. 278-79. Flanders uses the term ideology in a pejorative sense. Therefore he employs the term tradition to describe the beliefs and values of trade unionists. We will not use this term for our own analysis because we believe it does not convey all dimensions of an ideology. In particular, the term tradition implies that the outlook of the unions could never be changed—a position with which we fundamentally disagree. However, Flanders's use of the concept of tradition corresponds very closely to our definition of ideology.
8. See Andrei Markovits, *The Politics of the West German Trade Unions* (Cambridge: Cambridge University Press, 1986).
9. Ibid.
10. From interviews with Gernot Müller from the DGB's research institute, Wirtschaftsund Sozialwissenschaftliches Institut des DGB (WSI), and with Harmut Bechtold from the DGB's major foundation, Hans-Böckler-Stiftung, as well as from the thorough study of union publications, we were able to get a good sense as to the sources on which the German unions have relied thus far in their assessment of the internal market's most likely effects on them.

11. "Überwiegend positive Aspekte für Drucker, " *Buchreport,* October 5, 1988; our own calculations.
12. IG Druck und Papier, *Arbeiten um zu Leben.* Heft 51: Schriftenreihe der IG Druck und Papier (Stuttgart: IG Druck und Papier, n.d.), p. 87.
13. Bundesverband Druck, "Ifo-Umfrage über erwartete Auswirkungen des EG-Binnenmarktes auf die Industrie," Mitteilung Nr. WP 37/88, July 13, 1988.
14. IG Metall, "EG '92 und die Standortdebatte" (Frankfurt: IG Metall, 1989).
15. Ifo-Institut, *Erwartete Auswirkungen des Europäischen Binnenmarketes auf die Industrie der Bundesrepublik Deutschland und der EG-Partnerländer* (Munich: Ifo-Institut, 1988), pp. 142-43.
16. Commission of the European Communities, *Social Europe—The Social Dimension of the Internal Market* (Luxembourg: Office for the Official Publications of the EC), p. 43.
17. Harmut Bechtold, "Chemiestandort Bundesrepublik Deutschland" (Düsseldorf: Hans-Böckler-Stiftung, Abteilung Mitbestimmungsförderung II, n.d.); European Trade Union Institute (ETUI), "Info 25: The Social Dimension of the Internal Market—First Part: Employment" (Brussels: ETUI, 1988).
18. Westdeutsche Landesbank, *Europa '92—Perspektiven für die deutsche Wirtschaft* (Düsseldorf: West LB, 1988), p. 38.
19. Bechtold, "Chemiestandort, " p. 7.
20. Commission of the European Communities, "The Economics of 1992," *European Economy,* no. 35 (1988), pp. 6971.
21. Reinhard Reibsch, "Bereits heute die Voraussetzungen schaffen," *Die Mitbestimmung* 35, no. 5/6 (May/June 1989), p. 324.
22. IG Metall, "EG '92, " pp. 37-40.
23. NGG, "Euro-Info, No. 1" (Hamburg: NGG, February 24, 1989).
24. Rainer Stinnes from the Munich consulting company Assocon, quoted in "Vorbereitung auf vollen Touren," *EW* (March 1989), p. 13.
25. Interview, 18 July 1989, in Hamburg.
26. For a detailed presentation of Franz Steinkühler's views on the European single market very much reflecting the overall caution and skepticism of the "activist" unions within the DGB, see Franz Steinkühler, "Chancen humaner Zukunftsgestaltung gegen Kapitalmacht und Sozialdumping: Gefahren und Perspektiven ausgewerkschaftlicher Sicht," in Franz Steinkühler, ed., *Europa '92: Industriestandort oder sozialer Lebensraum* (Hamburg: VSA Verlag, 1989), pp. 7-21.
27. See Margit Köppen, "Der Europäische Binnenmarkt 1993—Gefahren und Perspektiven aus gewerkschaftlicher Sicht," ms., IG Metall, Frankfurt, 1989.
28. Interview, 21 July 1989, in Hamburg.

29. This became especially clear in interviews with Rolf Schumacher (IG Medien; 18 July 1989, Hamburg) and Margit Köppen (IG Metall; 24 July 1989, Frankfurt).
30. "Ohne Ausländer wären viele Arbeitsplätze weg!" *Kontranunkt* 127, no. 11 (5 June 1989), p. 19.
31. NGG, "Euro-Info No. l" (Hamburg: NGG, 24 February 1989).
32. Interview, 25 July 1989 in Hamburg.
33. See, for example, NGG, "Die Position der Gewerkschaft NGG zur Vollendung des europäischen Binnenmarktes; Dasgemeinschaftliche Lebensmittelrecht" (Hamburg: NGG, April 28, 1987); and Wolfgang Weinz, "Europäische Verbraucherpolitik: Das gemeinschaftliche Lebensmittelrecht," in Forschungsgruppe Europaunter der Leitung von Werner Weidenfeld, eds., *Binnemarkt '92: Perspektiven aus deutscher Sicht* (Gütersloh: Verlag Bertelsmann Stiftung, 1988).
34. Detlef Hensche (IG Medien) in "Ihr löst einen Flächenbrand aus," Gespräch mit dem *Spiegel,* in Oskar Lafontaine, ed., *Das Lied vom Teilen* (Hamburg: Hoffmann und Campe, 1989), p. 273.
35. "Zeichen an der Wand," *Stuttgarter Nachrichten,* 11 February 1989.
36. Horst Mettke (IG Chemie) in "Ihr löst einen Flächenbrandaus," p. 273.
37. "Bei Gillette ein erster Europa-Betriebsrat," *Handelsblatt,* 10 February 1989.
38. Quoted in "Die Zeit der Freundlichkeiten ist endlich vorbei," *VDI-Nachrichten,* no. 23, 9 June 1989.
39. Interview, 18 August 1989, in Hamburg.

# PART II

# GERMAN HEGEMONY?

# 3

# Germany and European Integration: Toward Economic and Political Dominance?

Simon J. Bulmer

## INTRODUCTION: LOCATING THE "GERMAN QUESTION"[1]

Due to its very special history, Germany's role in postwar Europe has been the subject of considerable attention, both on the part of politicians and of analysts. Postwar concerns with Germany's role were shaped by the Cold War and the constraints it imposed. For the Western allies and domestic elites alike, the first concern was with preventing any accumulation of centralized German political authority. The West German state's emergence, with its dispersion of power downward, in the federal structure, and upward, through supranational integration, reflected the objective of deconcentrating political authority. By the 1970s, despite periodic French fears that the Ostpolitik might herald adrift to the East, perhaps a new "Rapallo," concern had shifted toward West Germany's economic power. Fears of an *economie dominante* had been one factor behind the preparedness of French President Georges Pompidou to enable British membership of the European Community (EC).

Paradoxically, it was also in the 1970s that countries began to be concerned about the lack of leadership from the West Germans. This first came to the fore with Chancellor Helmut Schmidt's reluctant acceptance in 1978 of employing the West German economy as a "locomotive" to haul the Western economies out of recession. In the 1980s it led to increasing concern that the Federal

Republic was failing to deliver political leadership within the EC of an order commensurate to its economic strength. This criticism was prominent in the period immediately preceding West Germany's presidency of the Council of Ministers in the first half of 1988. (See W. Wallace 1988.)

For the 1990s these concerns have been reformulated because of the issue of unification. To French elites unification has opened up the question of *wo liegt Deutschland?*—defining Germany's geopolitical location—and presents fears of a new Central European power to the East of the Rhine. The French response has been to propose, or support, increases in the tempo of economic and political integration as a means of binding the new Germany into the EC.

The British response, by contrast, has been more backward-looking. Constrained by its lukewarm attitude to supranational integration, Margaret Thatcher's government was unable to advance proposals along the lines of President François Mitterand's. Instead it suggested that the democratization of Central and Eastern Europe should lead to a reappraisal of the purposes of European integration and cooperation. It also advocated EC self-restraint in advancing grandiose schemes for further integration in case these should detract from the objective of completion of the internal market by the end of 1992. At the same time the government was concerned to assert its rights, as a victorious power, to participate in the negotiations on unification. Any belief that the British government was completely at ease with unification was undermined by the private, and subsequently retracted, comments of the former secretary of state for trade and industry, Nicholas Ridley, published in July 1990. His widely reported comments conjured up an image of the European Community becoming a "Fourth Reich," with annexation taking place through the dominance of the deutsche mark (DM). Thus European monetary policy was described as "a German racket designed to take over the whole of Europe. . . . This rushed take-over by the Germans on the worst possible basis, with the French behaving like poodles to the Germans, is absolutely intolerable."[2] While these sentiments did not represent official government policy, they reflected concern within Whitehall (and Westminster) about German power.

Developments in the autumn of 1990—the British government's entry in the Exchange Rate Mechanism and the replacement of Mrs. Thatcher as prime minister by John Major—did not signal an immediate reappraisal of attitudes. Fundamental British reservations remained on both Economic and Monetary Union (EMU) and political union as the two intergovernmental conferences opened in December 1990. Such a reappraisal remains inextricably linked with recognizing German power in the new Europe.

The concerns about increased German power are, once again, only part of the story. Voices from within the European Commission have been heard to suggest that unification will distract the Germans from completion of the internal market, Economic and Monetary Union, and other initiatives, to the extent that the already deficient German leadership in the EC will be further reinforced. Within the British government there was concern at the way in which German electoral concerns about farmers' interests were allowed to take precedence over the wider international trade issues to be discussed in the GATT ministerial negotiations in December 1990, shortly after the first all-German elections. Finally, some West German industrialists worry about their country's readiness to compete in the single European market.

The question of Germany's role in postwar Europe is clearly one of major importance. This chapter focuses on Germany's evolving role in European integration with a view to establishing whether it was/is/will be one of dependence, dominance, or leadership. As the subtitle of this volume indicates, hegemony and containment have been presented as different perspectives on (West) Germany's role in the EC (for instance, in Lankowski 1982 and Bulmer and Paterson 1987 respectively). It is clear that German economic and political influence will increase as a result of unification. However, it is argued here—employing a neoinstitutional approach—that Germany will remain a constrained and contained power in the short to medium term. Moreover, any deepening of the European integration process will have the tendency to extend these constraints.

## A DIVIDED GERMANY AND EUROPEAN INTEGRATION

In his study—covering the period from Bismarck to the late 1970s—Calleo (1978, p. 4) identified two dimensions of the German problem. The first relates to the recurrent conflict between Germany and its neighbors; the second to the problem of assuring internal democratic stability. The first is an external perspective that is reflected in the fear that a unified Germany presents a threat to its neighbors' independence because of its size and dynamism. The second, internal perspective is that Germany's domestic constitution—its political, economic, social, and cultural systems—has been responsible for this expansionism. There is, then, a clear link between the external and internal dimensions of the German problem. How these two dimensions of the German problem have been addressed in the postwar context is of crucial importance to understanding both West Germany's and a unified Germany's role in European integration.

## The External Dimension of West German Support for European Integration

The external dimension initially placed West Germany in a position of dependence. Foreign and defense policy areas were subject to allied control until 1954-55. Until it became redundant with the establishment in 1952 of the European Coal and Steel Community (ECSC), the International Ruhr Authority placed the West German economy under control. From this starting point emerged the chosen policy of Chancellor Konrad Adenauer, namely integration into the West. Adenauer's policy was one of seeking to establish the Bonn Republic's international credentials by freely entering into agreements that would place constraints on West German autonomy. In this way the new state could gain a status comparable to that of its peers and could gain acceptance internationally.

The means by which these goals were achieved, as is well known, was through a set of international and European bodies. Germany's acceptance of Marshall aid and the United States' international economic policy—termed by Maier "the politics of productivity"—bolstered domestic support for liberal, or "ordo-liberal," economic policy goals (Maier 1978). The external dimension to this policy should not be underestimated. Had the Federal Republic sought to pursue a more autarkical policy, it would have been exposing itself to potential disagreements with the United States not only over international economic policy but also, via issue linkage, in the security and defense arenas. In these, West Germany's dependence on the United States was explicit due to Cold War geopolitics and the U.S. nuclear guarantee. Clearly, then, it was not just international economic institutions that set the parameters for West Germany's foreign economic policy.

The creation of a liberal trade system was part and parcel of American sponsorship of the Euratlantic partnership, institutionalized in the North Atlantic Treaty Organization (NATO). Bringing West Germany into NATO could not be attempted at an early stage because of the popular fears in neighboring countries of German rearmament. Indeed, the first attempt at this was within the framework of the proposed European Defense Community. With the failure of this body, membership of NATO was achieved via Western European Union (WEU) and the Paris treaties. While this arrangement finally lifted the allies' control powers, West Germany's status was still different from other members because of the restrictions institutionalized via the WEU.

Beyond the Atlantic/Euratlantic context, European cooperation and integration formed the second set of institutional frameworks integrating West Germany into the new postwar circumstances. Supranational integration owed its origins to the postwar imperatives of the Cold War. It was, in its way, an attempt to tackle the German problem. By seeking to bind the Federal Republic into the European Coal and Steel Community, the Schuman Plan aimed to give the French government (and, eventually, those of the Benelux states and Italy) influence over West German heavy industry. The means were economic but the objectives were political: the gradual expansion of functional cooperation from two limited sectors to much more comprehensive coverage. Although the process of functional expansion has been characterized by fits, starts, and setbacks rather than the smooth progression suggested by some integration theorists, the same basic pattern of intensifying economic integration to secure political goals remains as before. Emphasizing the interconnectedness of the Euratlantic and European frameworks, the ECSC had the support of the U.S. administration, which saw it as an opportunity "to free West German industry from the strait-jacket of post-war controls and Allied restrictions and to use it as the engine for growth in Europe" (Berghahn 1986, p. 112).

From the West German perspective, support for integration offered many potential prizes: establishment of international reliability with the closest Western neighbors; regaining (incomplete) sovereignty over the coal and steel sectors; a potential "security community"; and a core market for industrial goods (Hrbek and Wessels 1984, pp. 45-54; Bulmer and Paterson 1987). Nor should it be overlooked that participation in European integration brought important, although less tangible, benefits for addressing the internal dimension to the "German problem" of recurrent political instability. Here the contribution was the community of values that European cooperation and integration assured in terms of support for basic human rights, democracy, social justice, and the rule of law (Hrbek and Wessels 1984, p. 48): the same values that currently attract East European interest in the EC. For West Germany, all these benefits stemmed from its initial position of dependence.

The external dimension to ensuring (West) German stability in the postwar period was thus achieved, both on the part of the allies and German elites alike, by actively embracing the conditions of interdependence, penetration, and integration. (See Saeter 1980, p. 8.) Interdependence is represented by the FRG's international economic openness, highlighted in particular by trade relations with other EC member states. Penetration refers to the way in which the action of foreign governments has a direct influence, via such institutional links as NATO and the EC, on West German domestic politics. As years have gone by, so increasingly has the reverse influence also become applicable. Integration is closely associated with this but extends beyond structures and institutions to the substance of policy. Thus many German policies are difficult to isolate from their European context; indeed, they are dependent on it. West

German foreign policy, for example, is extremely difficult to detach from its context in European Political Cooperation (EPC), the framework for the coordination of foreign policy between EC member states.

If interdependence, penetration, and integration were actively sought in the Atlantic and European frameworks of West German foreign policy, this was not at all the case until the 1970s with relations with the German Democratic Republic (GDR). Relations with the GDR, often considered by non-Germans as a foreign policy issue but by West Germans as an internal matter, in fact were at the interface of both. Without the achievement of a suitable superpower relationship, inter-German relations could not be developed. The reaction to the 1952 Soviet Note demonstrated this situation only too clearly. Once superpower circumstances permitted, however, West Germany's Ostpolitik was conducted by means of inducing functional cooperation, credit arrangements, and other aspects of interdependence.

## The Internal Dimension of West German Support for European Integration

Within the Federal Republic, acceptance of European integration was far from unanimous in the 1950s. It was rejected until the mid-1950s by the Social Democrats (SPD) and aroused opposition within the Free Democrats (FDP) until the mid-1960s. Even among Christian Democrats there were disagreements about whether integration should be about expanding economic markets or strengthening political union. The latter division was paralleled to some extent by divisions in industry, where the interventionist policy instruments with which the High Authority of the ECSC were endowed were opposed in some quarters. The creation of the Common Agricultural Policy led to serious concern on the part of the German Farmers' Union that West German agriculture was to be sacrificed on the altar of European integration, but, with time, this position moderated.

Within the governmental machinery, the situation was relatively straightforward under Konrad Adenauer's chancellorship because of the tight rein he kept on foreign and European policies. It was only really with the establishment of the Common Agricultural Policy (CAP) in the 1960s and the creation of the EC's own resources budget in the 1970s, that individual ministries (at this stage agriculture and finance) took on policy responsibilities with their own institutional logic. The Foreign Office's involvement in European integration had been as something of a latecomer. This was because of its late development due to allied controls over foreign policy until 1955; Adenauer's wish to take personal change of this policy area; and the economics ministry's responsibility for the details of policy relating to the coal and steel sectors and those relating to the Common Market.

The federal system, although it was developed as one of the foundations of the West German state, did not emerge as a difficulty of European integration during the 1950s. At the time of joining the ECSC only one state, North-Rhine Westphalia, was significantly affected by the limited overlap of competences with those of the Länder because of the geographical concentration of the coal and steel sectors. With the creation of the European Economic Community (EEC), there was much greater potential overlap of competences, but, because of its framework treaty status, the Treaty of Rome failed to give immediate cause for serious Länder concern. In any case, the provision under Article 24 of the Basic Law for the Transfer of Sovereignty to supranational organizations was a kind of institutional counterbalance to any loss of authority on the part of the Länder.

What these circumstance show is that the western part of a divided Germany had embraced friendship with the French, the process of supranational integration, the Atlantic Alliance, and the institutions of the capitalist economy as its fundamental terms of reference. By the end of the 1970s, the vast majority of the institutions of government and of other political actors were treating European policy matters as routine, to be dealt with by the appropriate technical committee or section; specific institutional arrangements for EC policy were very much the exception. Within the ministries the vast majority of EC business was dealt with at a technical level, with the ministerial level being more concerned with those policy areas where party political capital could be gained or with matters of greater urgency. (See Bulmer 1986.) These structural factors had the potential to influence the content of West Germany's European policy, in the way advanced in the interpretations of the new (or neo-) institutionalists, such as March and Olsen (1984) or Hall (1986).

More generally, the FRG's policy in the EC had, as Hanrieder commented about the German political economy, "purposes that are simultaneously political and economic, domestic and foreign, amenable as well as resistant to governmental direction" (Hanrieder 1982, p. 59).

## West Germany in the EC: Dominance or Dependence?

By the 1970s and 1980s the Federal Republic had become the leading economy of the EC and had built up a strong reputation for good behavior (as a Musterknabe). So, in a period where it had considerable potential influence, was its role in the EC characterized by dominance or dependence? This immediately necessitates consideration of all the dimensions of the West German political economy, as identified by Hanrieder.

### Resources

Politically, West Germany's strengths derived from several sources. The first of these was its central position in shaping the state of relations between the two halves of Europe via inter-German relations (including by economic means such as making loans to the German Democratic Republic [GDR]). As the 1980s progressed, the FRG increasingly occupied a pivotal position in the transformation of East-West economic, political, and military relations. In the earlier 1980s, however, the freedom of maneuver here was constrained by the state of superpower relations, especially given the GDR's pro-Soviet line at this time. Second, the FRG's strategic importance lay in Cold War geopolitics, which ensured that the defense of West Germany was of central importance to NATO. Moreover, the FRG represented (and represents) the main European contributor to NATO's conventional defenses. However, the constraints of NATO policy-making clearly counterbalanced theses factors. Similarly, the FRG's nonnuclear status could be seen as a further counterbalance when compared to Britain or France. (See Bulmer and Paterson 1989.)

Essentially, these are background factors to the specific issue of West German power in the EC, although they have a more immediate relevance to foreign policy cooperation via the EPC. Within the EC the FRG's main assets derived from economic strength. The West German economy has been the strongest in terms of gross domestic product (GDP) and represents approximately one-quarter of the EC's GDP (in 1986, 26 percent). In terms of trade performance, the FRG has been responsible for about a quarter of both the EC's external and internal trade. This position has been further underpinned by the large trade surpluses that the FRG has built up. The West Germans' deutsche mark (DM) is one of the three leading international currencies of the Western world, and the most important one within the EC. Finally, the West Germans have been the leading net contributor to the EC budget; in 1985 they contributed 28.2 percent of the EC budget's "own resources" and received only 17.0 percent of the payments made under EC expenditures (Shackleton 1989, p. 130).[3]

Have these characteristics of economic strength been translated into political influence within the EC? The evidence of an activist German

European policy is rather scant, particularly if one confines matters to governmental actions. An activist European policy would require some kind of central authority guiding policy along a clear direction. However, since the period when Adenauer was setting out the guidelines of West German foreign and European policy, there has been little evidence of this occurring. A number of reasons can be cited. These relate in large part to the domestic structure of EC policy-making.

## Constraints

First of all, the party political salience of EC policy had declined by the 1970s; the scope for making political capital from a policy for which there was a broad consensus was very limited. The emergence of the Greens failed to change this situation, since all the parties sought to take on an "environment-friendly" posture.

Second, the gradually increasing range of policy areas covered by the EC led to the supranational dimension permeating the vast majority of federal ministries; only the ministry of defense and ministry for inter-German affairs were excluded from this trend. This situation led to "competing European policies," as individual ministries extended their *Ressortpolitik* (house policy). A number of policy issues demonstrated this, but none more so than the question of reform of the Common Agricultural Policy (CAP). West German agricultural interests were defended vigorously during the 1970s and 1980s. This proved possible because the minster of agriculture was able to increase his ministerial autonomy in relation to the finance ministry, in the EC Council of Agriculture Ministers, where accountability to coalition policy was less easy to enforce.

Third, the organizational responses to European policy in the individual ministries was such as to ensure that policy remained in the hands of specialists and was, in consequence, not very amenable to centrally coordinated initiatives. Agricultural policy represented one of the few areas where intracoalition party politics played a role, which is often overestimated. Both agriculture ministers since 1969 (Ertl, FDP, 1969-1983; Kiechle, CSU, 1983-1993) have been from smaller political parties, anxious to give themselves a profile in Bonn.

Fourth, a number of areas of EC competence are not exclusively within the competence of the federal government. Exchange rate policy (as coordinated since 1979 within the European Monetary System) is a matter for the autonomous Federal Bank in Frankfurt. The Federal Bank is the most significant of a range of parapublic institutions—see Katzenstein (1987, pp. 58-80)—that are entrusted with the running, or regulation of, individual policy areas. Others relevant to EC policy include the Federal Cartel Office (EC competition policy) and the Federal Environmental Office. Technical standards, such as the ubiquitous DIN standards, are often the product of meso-corporatist negotiation or even "private interest government."[4] These arrangements represent a different institutional configuration of the same phenomenon as parapublic institutions, namely bridging "the gap between public and private'" (Katzenstein 1987, p. 58). In both cases the effect is to make EC policy areas or policy issues much less amenable to the federal government's influence.

Fifth, there is the impact of the federal system. Apart from foreign and foreign economic policy, few areas of EC competence are exclusively the concern of the federal government but are shared with, or even held exclusively by, the Länder governments. At one extreme of the spectrum there are policy areas such as secondary education and broadcasting regulation, both addressed by the EC in recent years; by, respectively, the LINGUA program on language teaching and the EC directive on cross-frontier broadcasting. In these cases the federal government's political authority to negotiate on behalf of the Länder in the EC Council of Ministers was limited. The constitutional position is more open to dispute because the federal government claims that its responsibility for foreign policy means that it alone can actively negotiate with foreign governments, such as in the EC Council of Ministers. However, the Länder governments would argue that, under the principle of subsidiarity, the Basic Law gives them exclusive domestic competence for the cultural and education policy areas, and that this legal principle should take precedence.[5] Then there are the many policy areas in which the Länder are primarily involved in the administration of policy. Nonetheless, they still may have valid points to feed into the federal government because it is they, the Länder, that will continue to administer policy, even if it emanates from Brussels rather than Bonn. In all these cases the Länder have political and/or constitutional claims to participate in West German EC policy-making.

Prior to the Single European Act (SEA), Länder consultation had been conducted largely on informal lines, following an agreement reached between Chancellor Schmidt and the Länder minister presidents in 1979 (Bulmer and Paterson 1987, chap. 8). This had provided the basis for consultation until the SEA but had been unsatisfactory to the Länder because of the federal government's narrow interpretation of the range of issues on which they had to be consulted. In consequence, the Länder governments took the opportunity presented by the SEA, with its strengthening of the EC's constitutional powers, most notably on environmental matters—largely the domestic responsibility of the Länder—to negotiate a more formalized position. Here again, therefore, there are important constraints upon any centrally steered strategy for West German European policy.

A final constraint, apart from the obvious one that it is the commission rather than individual member governments that are supposed to put forward policy initiatives, is the persistent preference for joint initiatives with other governments. Unlike the previous constraints, then, this an external one, albeit self-imposed. The Franco-German partnership has been the most usual framework for such initiatives, including the holding of regular summit meetings (the European Council), the creation of the European Monetary System (described by Ludlow 1982, p. 290 as "arguably the first major act of German leadership in the history of the European Community" but still presented in Franco-German clothing), and proposals for an intergovernmental treaty on foreign policy cooperation, tabled at the 1985 Milan session of the European Council. Another German initiative, originally launched by Foreign Minister Hans-Dietrich Genscher, and particularly concerned with EPC, became the Genscher-Colombo initiative, once Italian support had been canvassed.

## BALANCE SHEET

So what evidence is there of West German political leadership within the EC? During the 1970s and 1980s, German initiatives on EC policy were invariably presented in bilateral or multilateral form. There were occasions when the federal government acted as a drag on EC developments, for instance when it became concerned in 1973 that it was becoming the "paymaster" of the EC. This led to a reluctance to contemplate new EC policies with significant expenditure components. Agreement to the European Regional Development Fund, for example, was held up by this. More recently, the finance ministry's concern about the costs of EC policies has been less pronounced because the British government, with its concern about the financial costs of membership, has (unwittingly?) served as a proxy (H. Wallace 1988). In consequence, the federal government has been "saved" from taking up a non-communautaire stance in the Council of Ministers or the European Council.

A comparable situation obtained with German policy toward the Common Agricultural Policy. Due to its farm sector's comparatively high-cost operation, especially in southern Germany, the agriculture ministry also served as a drag upon CAP reform. However, this was achieved without encountering a great deal of adverse publicity. Among the explanations for the lack of criticism of the German government were: confusion over Bonn's policy, given the finance ministry's wish to restrain EC spending; and the role of the French government (responsible for a larger agricultural sector) as the agriculture ministry's proxy/supporter in the Council of Ministers. Ultimately, with the CAP reforms agreed on in 1988, the agriculture ministry may have suffered a setback, but it occurred during the West German presidency of the Council of Ministers. As a result the government was able to emerge credited with solving a budgetary crisis that was partly of its own making!

The presidency of the Council of Ministers more generally represents an opportunity for individual member states to place their imprint upon the EC's development. However, despite the success of the January-June 1988 West German presidency—in solving the budgetary crisis, in maintaining the momentum on the legislation for the single market, and in supporting the establishment of a committee to look into Economic and Monetary Union—it is difficult to attribute this positive balance sheet solely to the German government. Some of it can be put down to the good fortune of presiding at a time of increased momentum on integration. Given its much more limited diplomatic resources, the Irish presidency's success in the first half of 1990 was no less impressive and helped by factors beyond its control, namely the timing of changes in Eastern Europe.

On foreign policy matters the FRG has played a fairly "mainstream" role within the EPC. Its support for procedural innovation, such as through the Genscher-Colombo initiative, has been based on the perception that the EPC may serve as a useful proxy for a West German foreign policy and certainly as an "emancipation factor" (Rummel and Wessels 1983). So, although the FRG was a medium-size power with considerable strategic importance, its ability to influence world events could increase only insofar as it consulted with its partners via the EPC. Yet this very act of consultation also served to make German policies amenable to the influence of partners. Measured against the United Kingdom, with its potential to follow the Anglo-American "special relationship" (for example, in supporting President Ronald Reagan's bombing of Libya rather than the more moderate "European" view) or to be pulled into unilateral policy steps by postcolonial or ideological considerations (for example, the unilateral lifting of sanctions against South Africa following the release of Nelson Mandela in 1990), the evidence of West German unilateral leadership is relatively limited.

Turning to economic influence, there is perhaps more evidence of a dominant West German role, but there are two qualifications. First, economic strength and influence have largely been achieved through export-led growth. This, in itself, exposed the West German economy. It is often overlooked that the FRG is consequently dependent on the well-being of its EC partners' economies, since they represent its core market. Second, although German economic strength is perceived to have influenced its partners in the EC, this cannot be seen as the result of a deliberate, coordinated policy on the part of the federal government.

Regarding export-led growth, the Federal Republic has developed into the state most dependent on foreign trade of the Group of Seven. According to figures for 1986, exports of goods by West Germany accounted for 27.2 percent of its gross domestic product; the United Kingdom was next with 19.5 percent (OECD 1988). So, although the FRG became the world's largest exporter of goods and services in 1986, the economy's continued success is dependent on remaining sensitive to trends within the international economy. Moves toward liberalizing trade in services, both via GATT and completion of the single EC market, represent challenges to an economy that has tended to have a closely regulated service sector. In addition, the more that large trade surpluses are accumulated, the more that other countries—in the EC or internationally—expect West German sacrifices for the collective economic good. The so-called locomotive experience of 1978 was the product of such pressure but has been interpreted in the FRG as a major contributory factor to the increase in public debt in the early 1980s and to the current account deficits of 1979-1981 (Kreile 1989, pp. 15-17).

Has West German economic strength been deliberately deployed for unilateral advantage? The classic example cited is that the EMS exchange rate mechanism (ERM) has a deflationary effect on other members due to the predominance of the DM. This criticism has been made by the French (for example, after the Socialist government's U-turn on economic policy in 1983) and by the Italians. The basic argument is that the EMS is unbalanced because of the DM's dominant role. As a result, other states are required to adopt German economic policy priorities. "In other words, weak-currency countries must bear the burden of adjustment by disinflationary (and therefore low growth) strategies, while there is no leverage on trade surplus countries such as Germany to revalue" (Flockton 1990, p. 68). Of course, attitudes toward the DM's power in the EMS are influenced by the individual observer's attitude toward West German economic policy. For those member states that favor tight control over inflation and have close trade links with the FRG, the grounds for criticism are not so great. For the larger member states, the decline in policy autonomy is more striking politically. Even so, some British economists advocated joining the ERM specifically because of the failure of domestic policy to tackle inflation; the discipline of the DM was actively courted!

It would appear, therefore, that the EMS affords clear sectoral evidence of German hegemony in the EC. However, using economic methodology based on interest rate movements within the EMS, Smeets (1990) argues that the evidence is not so clear-cut. Germany has tended to lead the short-term interest rate behavior of other countries in the ERM; but, with the exception of the Netherlands, Smeets finds no evidence of influence regarding long-term rates. Moreover, he cautions against taking the short-term interest rate experience as evidence of German hegemony. He points out that prioritizing counterinflationary policy has been widespread among OECD countries; it is not solely the result of EMS membership. Given this priority on the part of other EMS currencies, Smeets argues that any deflationary effect can be explained just as much by the currency markets demanding higher interest rates in those countries with a worse historical record on countering inflation than the FRG, as a kind of risk premium. His conclusion is that German dominance of the EMS is not proven.

Leaving aside this contested economic dimension, there is also the political aspect: Has the alleged deflationary effect of the DM on other ERM currencies been the result of a deliberately orchestrated West German European policy? Given its constitutional autonomy, the Federal Bank is clearly not executing governmental policy. In this sense it is difficult to see a coordinated West German attempt to stamp its ideas on other member states. This would be contrary to the principles of the *liberale Ordnungspolitik,* whereby the federal government and other agencies merely provide the framework, while the economic process is responsible for the rest. Indeed, if there is a threat of German dominance, it seems to derive less from governmental policy than from the strong position of individual companies. Relatively secure from hostile takeovers from foreign competitors (by virtue of complex ownership structure) and helped in some cases by the strategic thinking of a "house" bank, West German companies are well placed to pursue expansionist plans for the single market. The acquisitive strategy of the insurance company Allianz or the (domestic) merger between Daimler-Benz and Messerschmidt-Bölkow-Blohm create very strong firms on the EC stage. Ultimately, however, developments such as these run up against the competition legislation of the EC, which involves the vetting of mergers above a certain monetary value.

In this assessment of the FRG's position prior to unification, it has been argued that the situation is not characterized by dominance. Nor is it characterized by leadership, which has seldom been exercised, and then indirectly or negatively. Equally, it is not characterized by dependence. The truth lies somewhere in between. The Federal Republic has doubtless been the EC's workshop, banker, and foremost exporter, but this has not been without a variety of external and internal institutional checks. The situation is arguably best described as "asymmetrical interdependence." However, with German unification, the picture has changed. What are the prospects for Germany's European role in the post–Cold War period?

## A UNIFIED GERMANY AND EUROPEAN INTEGRATION: TOWARD ECONOMIC AND POLITICAL DOMINANCE?

Offering a potential scenario for a unified Germany's European role is a very hazardous undertaking and is perhaps best left to the fairground fortune-teller, who makes no claims to be a political scientist. Nonetheless, by identifying the particular dimensions of the reformulated German question, it maybe possible to identify the variables.

### Context

First of all, it is important to note that the broader international context has changed. Any threat to the stability of Europe is as much the result of changes in the overall terms of reference, or "architecture," of the international politics of Europe as it is of the situation in a single state; the concern about German preponderance in Europe cannot be isolated to developments in the two Germanys. Germany retains its central position in the European continent, but the ending of the Cold War has facilitated a reunified Germany of almost 80 million inhabitants. In different ways, and in different states of morale, the two superpowers are signaling a withdrawal from their respective Cold War roles in Europe.

In the case of the United States, it has been argued that the Bush and Clinton administrations' reluctance to participate directly in running the economic aid program for the new democracies is indicative of a wish to see the (West) Europeans take responsibility for problems that most immediately affect them (W. Wallace 1990, p. 17). Similarly, the United States was initially rather reluctant to give economic aid to the ailing Soviet economy—for instance, at the Houston Western economic summit in July 1990—although it finally agreed to assist in December 1990. It is striking how, in recognition of the new European order, President George Bush had, first, made U.S.-German relations the cornerstone of his European diplomacy, and second, offered encouragement to further political integration in the EC.

For its part, the Soviet Union's efforts swiftly to reap the peace dividend from the ending of the Cold War were hampered by the slow progress of economic reform (*perestroika*), by the internal ethnic/nationalities problems, and by divisions within, and defections from, the Communist Party, all of which threatened the country's continued unity. Indeed, this was confirmed by the Soviet Union's disintegration following the abortive coup against President Mikhail Gorbachev in August 1991. The specter of internal turmoil in the former Soviet Union remains a potential influence on the broader context of Germany's role in Europe, and it is revealing that the German government had been the keenest to aid Gorbachev's Soviet Union prior to its collapse.

## Resources

It seems clear that Germany will play a bigger role in Europe than before. William Wallace recalls the comments John Maynard Keynes made about the European economy before World War I: "Round Germany as a central support the rest of the European economic system grouped itself, and on the prosperity and enterprise of Germany the prosperity of the rest of the Continent mainly depended" (W. Wallace 1990, p. 15). Wallace points out, moreover, that West Germany is the main trading partner of nine EC states, four in the European Free Trade Association (EFTA), together with Turkey and Yugoslavia; and is the second most important partner after Russia for most East European states (which, moreover, are seeking to distance themselves from dependence on Moscow).[6] German Economic and Monetary Union (GEMU), implemented at the start of July 1990, has been seen as the potential source of an economic miracle in the former GDR. Furthermore, if the united Germany were able to maintain the GDR's trade links with other East and Central European countries, the German economy would be a very potent force. In the medium and long term, therefore, the German economy does indeed look capable of forming the central support for the entire European economy. A report by the EC commission predicted that unification could add 0.5 percent to EC growth rates over the medium term (quoted in the *Independent,* 16 January 1990). The DM's potential growth as a reserve currency—other things being equal—for Eastern and Central Europe looks clear.

This economic power offers much potential political leverage too. Germany's position in European politics is no less pivotal than in the 1980s. The superpower constraints on German foreign policy have been reduced significantly. German exceptionalism—in terms of its nonnuclear status and the restrictions under the Western European Union treaty—represents a less significant general constraint in a climate of nuclear disarmament and reduced military tension.[7] Furthermore, within the institutional structure of the EC, the unified Germany could justifiably make a case for extra members of the European parliament and an increase in the weighting of its vote in the Council of Ministers.

## European Uncertainties

Does this all amount to Germany as a shackled Gulliver being transformed into a liberated man-mountain, to use the terms of Swift's *Gulliver's Travels*? Or does it amount to the nightmare of a "Fourth Reich"? The answer to these questions would be a clear yes if West Germany had pursued autonomous foreign and foreign economic policies over the post-war period. It has not. Rather, its record on remaining true to the Euratlantic system and to European integration suggests that these scenarios can best be averted by a continued emphasis on interdependence, penetration, and integration. Indications thus far are that Chancellor Kohl and Foreign Minister Genscher's successor, Klaus Kinkel, are actively seeking a continuation of these external links. The political elite is still conscious of the concerns of neighbors about increased German power. The initial failure of the Kohl government to recognize Poland's sensitivity to the setting of the eastern boundaries of a unified Germany arguably represents its only misreading of international opinion.

At present it remains unclear which international organization will form the overarching framework for pan-European relations. The Conference on Security and Cooperation in Europe (CSCE) appears to be the only existing framework for allowing Europe to develop a new security arrangement. However, fundamental reorganization will be necessary if this body is to take on new functions, including the one of giving security assurances to Germany's neighbors to the north, south, east, and west. German membership in NATO will offer some international security guarantee as long as NATO's membership remains appropriate to the security needs of the 1990s.

The European integration process offers continuity in addressing the German question, since this was intrinsic to the establishment of the ECSC.

The revival of the integration process in the late 1980s, although the result of unrelated international pressures, has at least given the EC much greater dynamism and importance. Without the advances offered by the SEA, the EC might have been marginalized still further by the events of 1989. As things stand, there are still a number of potential conflicts between the unification process and the economic integration already in train from the SEA onward (Kirchner 1990).

First, how far is the "Europe" of the EC an appropriate geographical, political, and economic entity? Its membership ranges from the Mediterranean to Scandinavia; from (with unification) Central Europe to the Balkans; and yet it does not include all states from any of these four subregions. This situation has been modified by the October 1991 agreement on the establishment of a European Economic Area (EEA) between EC and EFTA countries. However, a further arrangement would be necessary for the states of Eastern Europe; otherwise the EEA would risk institutionalizing outmoded European divisions. Applications for EC membership from Turkey, Austria, Sweden, Norway, Finland, Malta, and Cyprus are a further complicating factor. All these questions open the perennial dilemma of integration: wider or deeper? The British government has indicated some wish to open this debate even though it potentially detracts from the issue of accommodating a unified Germany in the EC. A looser community—such as surely would ensue—could afford Germany more power rather than reduce its influence by sheer weight of membership numbers.

The EC Commission has certainly identified ways of increasing its profile and broadening the scope of Community activity. Its willingness to run the economic aid program to the Eastern European democracies (on behalf of the Western industrialized states) has brought it into a new role of potential foreign policy authority; witness its response in suspending aid to Romania when the newly elected government drafted miners to clamp down on antigovernment protests.

Second, there is the question of how far German unification is compatible with European integration. Certainly, an array of detailed potential conflicts can be envisaged, of which the following are only a sample.

## State Aids and Competition

Phasing out state aids to East German industry is proving to be both a painful and a necessary process. The shock of massive restructuring in East German industry, where labor productivity was estimated at 40 percent of West German levels, will be necessary if the unified state is to avoid accusations of breaking EC state aids rules.[8] The sectors undergoing particularly painful adjustment are textiles, steel, consumer goods, and shipbuilding. Competition policy issues have been raised. Allianz's purchase of a 51 percent stake in the former GDR state insurance monopoly; Lufthansa's proposed stake in the GDR's state airline, Interflug; the purchase by Ruhrgas of 35 percent of the GDR's gas network. These and similar moves suggested anticompetitive consequences at a time when the single-market program is designed to increase competition. It appeared that such moves would escape regulatory control in the period between GEMU and full unification. Thus the GDR was not in the EC—and subject to its laws—until unification took place; the Federal Cartel Office's terms of reference related only to market position in West Germany; and the East German Competition Protection Office was only belatedly given regulatory powers after GEMU ("West Germany raid on the East raises monopolies fear," *The European*, 20-22 July 1990).

## Economic and Monetary Union

The initial assumption had been that GEMU might destabilize the DM and thus jeopardize its stability in the EMS. This, in turn, it was feared, would obstruct progress toward Economic and Monetary Union along the lines proposed in the Delors report, which foresaw irrevocable fixing of exchange-rates in the last of its three-stage plan. However, an alternative viewpoint is that GEMU has led to the Federal Bank abandoning some of its institutional conservatism. The achievement of GEMU within eight months' of the breaching of the Berlin Wall indicated an adaptability in policy that had previously been thought missing. In particular, the ability of the Kohl government to force through GEMU, despite the Federal Bank's reservations, indicated that political objectives could overrule the more technical monetary policy concerns of Frankfurt.

How, then, do these apparently contradictory indications square with the negotiations commencing in the intergovernmental conference on EMU? The outcome is a strong commitment from Bonn to the principle of EMU but on the Federal Bank's terms of there being an independent European central bank. This located the German negotiating position in a familiar role—that of pro-European rhetoric linked to technical reservations. The convergence conditions agreed in Maastricht in December 1991 will necessarily require other member states to adopt the deflationary policies normally pursued by Germany, if EMU is to be achieved at the end of the decade. German diplomatic skill will be required within the EC in order to avoid accusations of hegemony and imposing the German model on other member states.

While this debate was conducted in the intergovernmental conference on EMU, the debate on the DM's dominant role in the EMS has taken on a new turn. The costs of German unification has resulted in a big rise in public borrowing; from less than 1 percent of gross domestic product to about 4.5 percent in under a year. (See "Germany's Damaging Deficit," *The Independent,* 3 January 1991, p. 22.) Chancellor Kohl's domestic policy decision—as part of the federal election campaign—that no tax increases would be required to pay for unification—a decision later reversed—resulted in an upward pressure on German interest rates. This pressure is then transmitted to other countries within the EMS Exchange Rate Mechanism, exporting, or sustaining, high interest rates by virtue of the German currency's prominent position. For the United Kingdom, confronted at the end of 1990 with the onset of an economic recession and desirous of a cut in the domestic interest rate, the interdependencies between members of the Exchange Rate Mechanism were all too clear. An interest rate cut was incompatible with staying within the EMS at the existing alignment. German unification seemed set to have a deflationary effect on weaker EMS currencies, adding to the broader debate about the DM's deflationary effect within the EMS.

### EC Distributional Politics

Although it seems to be in the distant past, only a little over six years have elapsed since the Iberian enlargement of the EC. This still not fully digested incorporation compounded existing concerns that completion of the single market would result in the emergence of a more pronounced core-periphery relationship within the EC. The February 1988 European Council agreement to make a significant increase to the resources of the structural funds sought to rectify this. However, the membership, via unification, of the structurally backward GDR has raised this issue again. In fact, EC aid to the former GDR did not divert EC budgetary resources away from the existing poorer member states. However, unification might in the medium term divert inward investment (including by German capitalists) away from Spain and Portugal, for example, toward East Germany and Eastern Europe. Although these developments can only be speculated on, German unification could easily upset the distributional issues of the EC's budgetary politics. As the largest net contributor to the EC budget, Germany's exposure to funding both unification and increased side payments to poorer

EC states would be clear and perhaps a focus for domestic political forces critical of the EC. Negotiations over a new EC budgetary horizon are putting Germany's position to the test.

### Other Concerns

Beyond these potential problems lie a range of detailed concerns: the eligibility of East Germany's large agricultural sector for support from the CAP; ensuring that any transitional arrangements—be they state aids, environmental standards, or others—are adequately policed so as not to undermine the moves toward fairer competition that are intrinsic to the single market; and so on. These issues were addressed by the EC Commission's Task Force on German unification during 1990. (See Commission of the EC 1990.)

## Continuing and New Constraints?

Against this background of issues, what estimation can be made of Germany's future role? Successful avoidance of German preponderance will be dependent on voluntary acceptance of external constraints and a continuation of the domestic political structures that limited West Germany's role in the EC.

The German economy, from unification, has been subject to the EC Treaties (with special transitional arrangements). Given the strengthening of supranational powers currently under way, this should act as a brake on German economic owners. This will be the case particularly as the momentum toward Economic and Monetary Union is maintained. The dissatisfaction with Germany's dominant position in the EMS had already led to some changes in 1987 (the Nyborg agreement). The French government has clearly seen EMU as a way of strengthening the institutional penetration of German politics and counteracting potential hegemony; this was clear from President Mitterrand's shaping of the informal summit and the Strasbourg European Council session in December 1989. There is further support in Italy for advancing toward EMU as a way to avoid the DM's being a hegemonic currency (Ciampi 1990).[9] The deepening of integration thus offers one potential route to maintaining the components of interdependence, penetration, and integration that have formed the bedrock of West Germany's European role.

The alternative scenario, implicit in the British government's approach, appears less appropriate. The opening up of the EC to the newly democratized states—restated at the Maastricht European Council—is attractive in bolstering newfound political freedoms. But is it economically feasible in anything other than the medium or long term? The British fear of losing sovereignty appears to be more a reflection of a "British problem" than an attempt to solve a German one. To continue advocating a Europe of sovereign states, as Mrs. Thatcher did in her Bruges speech in 1988, seems to ignore the lessons of history regarding German power. An opening up of the EC to East European states may have the effect of reducing Germany's strength through increasing numbers. However, premature entry could create serious economic dislocation, jeopardize the single market, and cause the kind of Central European instability that history suggests should be avoided.

German power within the EC will also be dependent on domestic politics. Looking back at the domestic constraints of the 1970s and 1980s, it is pertinent to ask whether unification will lead to their disappearance. Given that unification increasingly appears to be absorption of the GDR by the Federal Republic, this looks unlikely. No suggestions have been made that government will become more centralized around the chancellor; that Prussian bureaucratic traditions of *Sachlichkeit* will be cast off; that the Federal Bank's autonomy will be conceded and other parapublic institutions brought under governmental control; or that the federal system will be dismantled. On the contrary, these constraints look likely to persist or even be strengthened. The federal system in particular appears to be a possible source of additional constraints as the already assertive federal states are joined by the new Länder of the former GDR, with their particular demands regarding EC policy. As already noted, the German government's policy on the GATT Round suggests that sensitivity to the farm lobby is unlikely to decrease. Finally, the institutional constraint of the coalition government has been reinforced by the improved performance of the Free Democrats, who continue to hold important European policy portfolios.

The external and internal constraints on Germany's European power look set to continue for some time. And in the short to medium term they will be reinforced by the full public policy agenda that unification provides. The anticipated East German economic miracle remains for the future as the painful process of economic and political reconstruction takes place and budgetary deficits mount. Major problems exist regarding the infrastructure of the former GDR and indeed regarding the infrastructural integration of unified Germany. In addition, the westward migration continues within the new state. Some of the assumptions about the new Germany's centrality in the European economy have been shown to be erroneous. For instance, the ability to capitalize on the former GDR's trade links with the East would occur only if, first, those partners had sufficient hard currency and, second, other non-German "hard currency" suppliers cannot offer better quality than concerns in the former GDR. These preconditions will be difficult to meet.

## CONCLUSION

The future role of Germany will be of central importance to Europe. Economically, there seems little doubt that Germany has the potential to be a hegemonic power. However, this potential can be limited by a further "upgrading of the common interest" of the type envisaged by neo-functionalist integration theorists in such conditions of dynamic disequilibrium. To the extent that integration stagnates or even recedes, the risk of German economic hegemony increases. Even if integration were to stagnate, it would be important to remember the economic and particular employment dependence of Germany on the EC market. Interdependence—even asymmetrical interdependence—has two sides; it is not hegemony.

Politically, the scope for German dominance is less clear-cut. It presumes a more centralized pattern of government than has existed hitherto, perhaps brought about by single-party government. However, the argument advanced in this chapter has been to emphasize the continuing domestic, and developing external, constraints upon German power in Europe. Interdependence, penetration, and integration—the terms given by Saeter (1980) to encapsulate (West) Germany's European and global relations—do not conform to the old realist notions of power. Rather—like the features of the German domestic political system—they conform to a pattern of power-sharing. So, if institutional arrangements have tamed German "power," we should not be surprised if Germany remains Europe's "gentle giant" or, in German, *der stille Hegemon*!

## NOTES

This is a revised version of paper originally delivered at the 1990 annual meeting of the American Political Science Association, San Francisco, 31 August, as part of the "Germany After the Cold War" panel, convened by Carl Lankowski. I am grateful to the British Academy for the financial support that enabled me to attend. I am also grateful for comments received, including from Peter Katzenstein, the discussant. Subsequent versions of the paper were given at a conference at St. Antony's College, Oxford, and as part of a "Germany Between East and West" seminar series at the University of Manchester, where further useful comments were received. I take full responsibility for the final product.

1. I use the term *German question* to refer to the postwar situation.
2. Quoted in *The Independent,* 13 July 1990. Ridley resigned from the Thatcher government on 14 July 1990 because of the intemperate language used in the interview. Following Michael Heseltine (former secretary of state for defense—resigned), Sir Geoffrey Howe (former foreign minister—demoted), and Nigel Lawson (former chancellor of the exchequer—resigned), Ridley became the fourth ministerial casualty of European policy in as many years. By the end of 1990 the resignation of Sir Geoffrey Howe as leader of the House of Commons and deputy prime minister and, most spectacularly, of Mrs. Thatcher herself increased the casualty list still further.
3. Figures from the Annual Report of the EC Court of Auditors. As Shackleton notes, the Germans were "generally prepared to accept the situation in light of [their] high level of prosperity."
4. DIN is the abbreviation for the Deutsches Institut für Normen (German Standards Institute). On meso-corporatism, see Cawson 1985; also see Bulmer (1989) on its importance in Germany.
5. Articles 30, 70, and 83 implicitly embody the principle of subsidiarity, namely that policy should be formulated and administered at the lowest level of government possible. In 1989 the Bavarian government challenged the federal government before the Federal Constitutional Court on the grounds that Bonn had taken insufficient account of the Länder governments when negotiating the EC's broadcasting directive. The Bavarian government's attempted temporary injunction was dismissed—see 2BVG (Federal Constitutional Court Reporter) 1/89—but the broader question of contested competences remains.
6. The relevant EC and EFTA countries are the United Kingdom, France, the Netherlands, Belgium, Denmark, Italy, Portugal, Spain, Greece, Sweden, Norway, Switzerland, and Austria.
7. The "Gulf Crisis," however, tended to underline continued German exceptionalism because of the internal constitutional constraints on deploying forces outside the NATO area. The federal government's decision in January 1991 to deploy aircraft to bolster Turkey's defenses was condemned internally by the opposition parties. On the other hand, given the military commitments made by the United States, Britain, or France, this deployment could be criticized externally as having no real value in the context of removing Saddam Hussein from Kuwait.

8. See the working document (EP 141.753) entitled "The Structure of the GDR Industry and Problems of Transition and Integration in the Common Market," prepared for members of the European Parliament's temporary committee on the impact of German unification on the European Community. Also see Bulmer (1992).
9. Ciampi is governor of the Banca d'Italia. See also the reply from Karl Otto Pöhl, his German counterpart, in the same issue.

## REFERENCES


Berghahn, V. (1986). *The Americanisation of West German Industry*. Leamington Spa: Berg Publishers.

Bulmer, S. (1986). *The Domestic Structure of European Community Policy-Making in West Germany*. New York: Garland, Inc.

——— (1989). "Unity, Diversity and Stability: The 'Efficient Secrets' behind West German Public Policy?" in S. Bulmer, ed., *The Changing Agenda of West German Public Policy*. Brookfield, VT: Dartmouth Publishing/Gower, pp. 13-39.

——— (1992). "Completing the European Community's Internal Market: The Regulatory Implications for the Federal Republic of Germany," in K. Dyson, ed., *The Politics of Regulatory Change in Germany*. Brookfield, VT: Dartmouth Publishing/Gower.

Bulmer, S., and W. Paterson (1987). *The Federal Republic of Germany and the European Community*. London: Allen & Unwin.

——— (1989). "West Germany's Role in Europe: 'Man-Mountain' or 'Semi-Gulliver,' *Journal of Common Market Studies* 28, no. 2, pp. 95-117.

Calleo, D. (1978). *The German Problem Reconsidered. Germany and the World Order, 1870 to the Present.* Cambridge, MA: Cambridge University Press.

Cawson, A. (1985). "Introduction. Varieties of Corporatism: The Importance of the Meso-Level of Interest Intermediation," in A. Cawson, ed., *Organized Interests and the State: Studies in Meso-corporatism*. London: Sage Publications, pp. 1-21.

Ciampi, C. (1990). "Fur einen Vertrag zur europaischen Währungsunion: Hegemonialwährung Keine Lösung," *Integration* 13, no. 1, pp. 3-8.

Commission (1990). "The European Community and German Unification." *Bulletin of the European Community,* April supplement. Brussels.

Flockton, C. (1990). "The German Economy and the Single European Market," *Politics and Society in Germany, Austria and Switzerland* 2, no. 3, pp. 54-70.

Hall, P. (1986). *Governing the Economy: The Politics of State Intervention in Britain and France*. Oxford: Polity Press.

Hanrieder, W. (1982). "Germany as Number Two? The Foreign and Economic Policy of the Federal Republic," *International Studies Quarterly* 26, no. 1, pp. 57-86.

Hrbek, R., and W. Wessels (1984). "Nationale Interessen der Bundesrepublik Deutschland und der Integrationsprozess," in R. Hrbek and W. Wessels, eds., *EG-Mitgliedschaft: ein vitales Interesse der Bundesrepublik Deutschland?* Bonn: Europa Union Verlag, pp. 29-69.

Katzenstein, P. (1987). *Policy and Politics in West Germany: The Growth of a Semi-Sovereign State.* Philadelphia: Temple University Press, pp. 58-80.

Kirchner, E. (1990). "West German Policy and DeepeningIntegration in the European Community." Paper presented at the International Studies Association, Washington, D.C., 10-14 April 1990.

Kreile, M. (1978). "West Germany: The Dynamics of Expansion," in P. Katzenstein, *Between Power and Plenty: Foreign Economic Policies of the Advanced Industrial States.* Madison: University of Wisconsin Press, pp. 191-224.

——— (1989). "West Germany in the International Political Economy: Model, Villain or Scapegoat?" *Quaderni Papers,* no. 13. Rome: Istituto Per Gli Studi Di Politica Internazionale, March.

Lankowski, C. (1982). "*Modell Deutschland* and the International Regionalization of the West German State in the 1970s," in A. Markovits, ed., *The Political Economy of West Germany.* New York: Praeger, pp. 90-115.

Ludlow, P. (1982). *The Making of the European Monetary System.* London: Butterworths.

Maier, C. (1978). "The Politics of Productivity: Foundations of American International Economic Policy after World War II," in P. Katzenstein, ed., *Between Power and Plenty: Foreign Economic Policies of the Advanced Industrial States.* Madison, WI: University of Wisconsin Press, pp. 23-49.

March, J., and J. Olsen (1984). "The New Institutionalism: Organizational Factors in Political Life," *American Political Science Review* 79, no. 3, pp. 734-749.

OECD (1988). *OECD Economic Surveys: Germany 1987/1988.* Paris: OECD.

Rummel, R., and W. Wessels (1983). "Federal Republic of Germany: New Responsibilities, Old Constraints," in C. Hill, ed., *National Foreign Policies and European Political Cooperation.* London: Allen & Unwin, pp. 34-55.

Saeter, M. (1980). *The Federal Republic, Europe and the World.* Oslo: Universtetsforlaget.

Shackleton, M. (1989). "The Budget of European Community," in J. Lodge, ed., *The European Community and the Challenge of the Future.* London: Frances Pinter, pp. 129-147.

Smeets, H.-D. (1990). "Does Germany Dominate the EMS?" *Journal of Common Market Studies* 29, no. 1, pp. 37-52.

Wallace, H. (1988). "The Federal Republic of Germany and Changing Coalition Habits: The Paradox of Leadership," in W. Wessels and E. Regelsberger, eds., *The Federal Republic of Germany and the European Community: The Presidency and Beyond.* Bonn: Europa Union Verlag, pp. 297-304.

Wallace, W. (1988). "Germany's Unavoidable Central Role: Beyond Myths and Traumas," in W. Wessels and E. Regelsberger, eds., *The Federal Republic of Germany and the European Community: The Presidency and Beyond.* Bonn: Europa Union Verlag, pp. 276-85.

——— (1990). "Deutschlands zentrale Rolle: Ein Versuch, die europaische Frage neu zu definieren," *Integration* 13, no. 1.

# 4

## United Europe and Social Democracy: The EC, West Germany, and Its Three Small Neighbors

Paulette Kurzer and Christopher S. Allen

### INTRODUCTION

The integration of the European Community (EC) into the single market and the increasing desire of Eastern European countries to participate in some form have made clear that convergence of economic, monetary, and fiscal policies is in the offing. Since this has been largely a movement led by elites (Sandholtz and Zysman 1989), trade unions and the left have been very slow to pose any challenge to the terms of this transformation. Moreover, the unification of Germany and its greater weight within the Community—and all of Europe—would seem to imply to the smaller Western European nations the idea that this convergence would take place at their expense. In other words, conventional wisdom would suggest that the Germans would dominate this process of convergence.

This chapter examines the relationship between the West German political economy and that of its smaller neighbors—Belgium, Denmark, and the Netherlands. Our thesis is that the combination of membership in the European Community and the EMS (European Monetary System) seriously constrains the economic policy options of the social democratic parties in the three countries. Germany's leadership in the EMS forced them to adopt deflationary policies creating higher than average levels of European unemployment (Economist Intelligence Unit 1989). Many studies stress the "disciplinary" character of the EMS, but what is meant by that? And who "disciplines" whom? The second part of the question is easily answered: Germany disciplines the others. The first part is more complicated because different versions of this theme exist (Ungerer et al. 1986). In the late 1970s, German governments preferred slow growth to inflation or full employment. With the tacit consent of the participating EMS countries, they purposefully deflated the domestic economy. German business and labor, however, had the means to withstand an explicit deflationary climate. Countries with a weaker industrial structure and less resilient export sector required extra stimuli to restore business confidence and labor market equilibrium. The most constraining element of the EMS is that a "go-alone" strategy is no longer viable (de Grauwe 1987). If economies grow faster than that of Germany, the current account starts to record deficits. These external deficits would then put pressure on the exchange rate, require central bank intervention, and provoke speculative currency transactions. If the exchange rate intervention were to fail to stabilize the currency within the bilateral margins, which is likely, the participating central banks and finance ministries must convene several meetings to decide on an exchange rate realignment.

The EMS entered into a more stable period after the relative uncertainties of the inflationary period of 1979 to 1983 because economic policies did indeed increasingly converge and because the requirement to seek prior consultations was tightened (Artis and Taylor 1988; McDonald and Zis 1989). To be sure, the convergences in prices and interest rates did not correspond to a convergence of real variables such as investments, growth, and employment (Ungerer 1989). Again, the kind of deflationary regime that Germany can sustain might be fatal to the economic health of weaker economies.

Changes in exchange rates affect the export competitiveness of the country's trading partners. An EMS member must demonstrate that other remedies have been exhausted and that the devaluation will not be used as a makeshift measure but will be accompanied by appropriate economic changes. Economic reforms include budget cuts, mandatory pay freezes, and the abolition of cost-of-living indexation. Requests for the change are collective decisions, and a central bank cannot sell or buy the currency of another country without the permission of the issuing central bank. Germany, the center country, runs monetary policy for the whole system because it holds the key currency and must be consulted prior to an exchange rate realignment (Giavazzi and Giovannini 1989).

In their defense, the Germans have argued that international competitiveness for all of Europe must be a primary criterion of any economic policy, and deflationary policies are a primary means to that end. In one sense, this is a straightforward story of a larger country influencing a smaller one (Bulmer and Paterson 1987), yet this issue has deeper significance as European—and German—unity continues at breakneck speed. The questions we are asking are: (1) Why have the small countries so readily accepted these circumstances? and (2) How have the Germans escaped strong criticism from these countries—as well as others—for their strong role in shaping the economies of its small neighbors? This latter question will likely continue to resonate among many European countries.

We are suggesting, however, that these events should not be seen in a "zero-sum" perspective. While the Germans clearly dominate—and will continue to dominate—the European economic and political environment, the post-1992 world is unlikely to produce a *Deutschland über alles.* European integration would not be proceeding at such a pace if Germany's neighbors perceived such a tendency. At the same time, Germans remain powerfully aware of twentieth-century history and are unlikely to take action that would increase the suspicion of their less economically advantaged neighbors. These events suggest that the dominant economic policy model for the post-1992 European Community will not be a stark, binary choice between German hegemony and a resistant group of small countries. Rather, we are arguing that a nuanced combination of domestic and European trends will likely be the direction toward which Germany and its small neighbors will proceed.

The first section of the chapter outlines the main domestic and international features of the German institutional model as it shapes the framework for European economic policy without imposing its will on its neighbors. The second section analyzes the outcome of economic liberalization and deregulation for organized labor and social democratic fiscal and labor market intervention in the three smaller democracies, given their dependence on West Germany. The third section attempts to explain the linkages and replication of these patterns of neoliberalism.

## *RAHMENBEDINGUNGEN*: THE GERMAN DOMESTIC INSTITUTIONAL FRAMEWORK

The institutional adaptation of the Federal Republic has been based on a fundamentally different view of regulation and is crucial for understanding Germans' view of the structure of their economy, as well as their view of others'. For Germans, regulation is not a rule-based static one but one based on a dynamic "structure" in which there is close coordination between market and state actors to create a stable outer regulatory framework (*Rahmen*) within which flexible and adaptive market response can take place. The terms market and state (and by extension, deregulation and regulation) are not mutually exclusive poles but are overlapping concepts that need to mutually reinforce each other for either to function. In other words, the German system of private-public interaction has not been a binary choice of "more" or "less" government, but a strategic relationship that has underpinned the economy since the end of World War II.

When a market economy was reestablished after World War II, the so-called Freiburg School economists who were so influential in the economic foundation of the Federal Republic wanted to ensure that an effective and "organized framework" policy would protect its operation from undue public interference and all inflationary tendencies. They thus put a premium on policy that was designed to foster a stable set of expectations in the private sector. Public policy was to be aimed at four major goals:

1. Upholding the primacy of monetary policy, on the grounds that a stable money supply would make anti-cyclical policy unnecessary. Hence, a strong central bank (Bundesbank) was to be the guardian against any misuse of power by the political authorities.
2. Seeking an open international economic system, in reaction to that Nazi policy of autarchy. Hence, these economists supported greater economic contacts with the United States and Western Europe, and they saw exports as the key to German growth.
3. Increasing market competition, but within the context of an "orderly market framework." Such a framework could be provided by banks and industry associations in conjunction with limited action by the state. In a sense, Freiburg economists such as Walter Eucken saw the whole nation as a unit within a setting of international competition. Hence, some cooperation among firms was quite acceptable in that it would lead to a positive sum outcome for the German economy.
4. Seeking a limited measure of state intervention. The role of the state was to provide a stable legal and social order, including an important measure of social security, as well as infrastructural measures to aid in the establishment of a higher market equilibrium. One of the "Social Market" economists, Wilhelm Röpke, gives one of the most telling descriptions of the importance of "Framework" regulations:

> [our program] consists of measures and institutions which impart to competition the framework, rules, and machinery of impartial supervision which a competitive system needs as much as any

> game or match if it is not to degenerate into a vulgar brawl. A genuine, equitable, and smoothly functioning competitive system can not in fact survive without a judicious moral and legal framework and without regular supervision of the conditions under which competition can take place pursuant to real efficiency principles. This presupposes mature economic discernment on the part of all responsible bodies and individuals and a strong impartial state. (Röpke 1982, p. 188)

This system of framework regulations gives a different twist to the usual market versus state dichotomy, so prevalent in discussions of Britain and the United States on the one hand and of France and Japan on the other. While the German institutional structure is clearly a market-based one, it does not exhibit the laissez-faire rhetoric of the Thatcher and Reagan/Bush governments. And while the German state is very much present in economic and political life, it does not exhibit the dirigisme of the French or Japanese public sector. Rather, it acts as a "semi-sovereign" state (Katzenstein 1987), that is, a state that is present in shaping the environment in which the economy functions, but not one that directs the minute details of economic life.

This "framework" system has allowed the Germans to set the outer boundaries of their financial relationship to their smaller neighbors without directly imposing solutions on them. This pattern suits the German style in another way as well. Namely, their position as the increasingly dominant power in Europe has given Germans much greater visibility than during the so-called Economic Giant/Political Dwarf period from the 1950s through the 1970s. However, the Germans have also preferred to let their position in the EC give them cover from being seen as the dominant player in Europe. In other words, Katzenstein (1982) has argued that the Germans do not want to be seen as the Japan of Europe, aggressively challenging their neighbors for superiority. Put simply, the Germans have argued that they favor not a "German Europe, but a European Germany," and their policies on EMS issues at least overtly reflect this philosophy.

## THE INTERNATIONAL NATURE OF GERMAN CONSTRAINTS

The institutional structure—and the ideational legacy (that is, fear of inflation) that reinforced it—were certainly important reasons for the Germans' ability to constrain the economic policy options for their three small EMS neighbors. However, Ton Notermans (1990) suggests that an international dimension needs to be given greater weight, namely, the role of the DM as a "second" reserve currency. He argues that the relative decline of the dollar after the collapse of the Bretton Woods fixed exchange system in 1971 slowly pulled the DM into much greater prominence during the 1970s and 1980s. He suggests that the Bundesbank's need to maintain the DM's strong position was a greater brake on German—and the small countries'—macroeconomic policies than purely domestic institutional factors. While Notermans wants to use his internationally oriented argument as a counter-weight to domestic-oriented explanations, John Goodman (1990, pp. 21-27) sees the role of monetary policy in the EC as more of an interdependent phenomenon than a stark, binary choice. He states that other large states (France and Italy)—together with Germany—play the dominant roles in the EMS, in response to which the smaller countries accede. As we suggest later, the small countries' accession to more restrictive monetary policies may be due either to lack of power in challenging Germany—and other large states' hegemony—or to a realization that their fate is inextricably tied to that of Europe as a whole. We address the relative merits to the two sides of this argument in the next section. In fact, Goodman argues that the internationalization of monetary policy toward a more European dimension may potentially diminish the Bundesbank's role in maintaining the kind of restrictive monetary policy that has been pursued since the late 1970s and is the foundation of the EMS. Bulmer and Paterson (1987, pp. 14-22) take a position similar to Goodman, in that they argue that Germany's domestic position is far more important in this equation than Notermans would suggest. Certainly the increasing role of the DM is an important factor, but this international dimension should also be seen as part of the German desire to act at the international level in order to solidify the policy-makers' domestic position.

Whether the primary cause was international or domestic, the specific effects of German leadership on European integration for Belgium, Denmark, and the Netherlands has been to reduce the scope for Social Democratic policies and to reinforce the influence and power of anti-Keynesian agents (Camiller 1989; see also Kurzer 1992). First, the dominant effect of the Bundesbank on the EMS vis-à-vis the national governments in these three countries has been to enhance the voice of the respective central banks (Symonds 1985). The Bundesbank has played this role since the creation of the EMS and has thereby enhanced the importance of monetary policies (and exchange rate policies) at the expense of budgetary intervention and fiscal innovation in other EMS countries. The central bank is a natural spokesman for fiscal prudence and sound money, but its voice does not always automatically carry a lot of weight. However, with the EMS and the priority on stabilizing exchange rates and low inflation, central banks became more important actors and became fully incorporated in the economic policy process during the 1980s. In essence, they took anti-Keynesian and anti-social democratic positions on market intervention and credit allocation. The second European integration during the late 1980s has allowed domestic business to seek alliances and build coalitions with other business, thereby circumventing labor and putting the labor movement at a disadvantage. During the 1970s, domestic firms might have needed the cooperation of the domestic labor movement. Now they can find allies in the EC Commission and other firms and leave labor to fend for itself without the opportunity to foster similar coalitions with non-domestic forces. Again, this undermines social democratic power and its ability to steer business into a certain direction (Scharpf 1987). Finally, the result of integration has been a much greater internationalization of the domestic economy, not only in terms of export ratios and foreign direct investments, but also in terms of financial deregulation on capital flows. This too inhibits a return of social democratic governments with social democratic agendas. While they can return to power, they often do so without the same agenda as before (Pontusson 1984).[1]

Clearly, European integration is hard to understand without looking at the Bundesbank's role in the economic process and the EMS. But this is essentially a carry-over from its domestic patterns and emphasis. For the German state, the Bundesbank has clearly circumscribed the possibilities for expansionary activities even during the center-left years of the Schmidt governments. As Jeremiah Riemer has argued, there was only a three- or four-year "Keynesian Interlude" in the late 1960s and early 1970s and then the Bundesbank's more restrictive policies curtailed this brief period of Keynesianism (Riemer 1982). However, the significant issue of this chapter is that these restrictive policies did not substantially damage the German left and unions. Since the German economy has been based on an export-led strategy of high-quality goods, these policies did not produce the kind of heavy unemployment that took place in Belgium, Denmark, and the Netherlands. In essence, the Germans have simply externalized their costs on their little neighbors.

What Germany can survive is likely to be extremely harmful for smaller neighbors. While understanding German hegemony is a key piece of the puzzle, there is still a gap in explaining why there has not been greater solidarity between the German unions and the SPD and the socialist parties in the smaller countries. At each level, West Germany has acted as a powerful brake on attempts by social democratic governments in the smaller EC countries to escape from these restrictions. At the institutional level, the Bundesbank has clearly circumscribed the possibilities for expansionary activities. At the market level, West German domestic forces have never pursued great stimulatory policies. This did not hurt the German political left and the trade unions, as they were advantaged by the strength of the West German economy. International "costs" are a moot point for the Germans as they simply externalize them. However, what Germany can cope with proves extremely harmful for its smaller neighbors. All of the small countries are usually dependent and exposed, but the compensating mechanisms differ because another dimension of dependence relates to institutional linkages. This linkage is provided by membership in the EC. Especially for the smaller countries, the EC shrinks the little space that was left to protect themselves from overexposure to economic dependence.

## THE SMALL MEMBERS OF THE EMS: BELGIUM, DENMARK, AND THE NETHERLANDS

Here we argue that the consolidation of German-type institutional frameworks through the EMS displaced earlier, more pro-labor arrangements in the smaller democracies. But why did the countries tolerate the subordination of their welfare program for the sake of economic harmonization and European federalism? We are not suggesting a German conspiracy to rule the economic affairs of its smaller neighbors. Rather, a convergence of interests has arisen between the central bank personnel in the high public spending countries and the German leadership. Monetary authorities in Belgium, Denmark, and the Netherlands sought to redesign the policy process in favor of balanced budgets, low interest rates, and price stability. The objective of the German authorities is to secure a zone of monetary stability to further foreign trade. Central banks in the other countries realized that EMS membership would augment their policy impact if they switched their authority to an intergovernmental agency that would quell any possible opposition to monetary restrictiveness. Monetary integration became a convenient pretext for rolling back the advances of the welfare state and for placing a moratorium on public sector growth and social spending. Table 4.1 highlights the notably inferior economic performance of the small EMS member-states.

The figures are self-explanatory. The smaller members inside the EMS did worse than both the Community at large and the small European countries

Table 4.1
**Economic Performance of Small European States and EMS Member-States[a] and Nonmembers[b] 1980-1985**

| | Real Growth | Unemployment | GFCF[c] |
|---|---|---|---|
| EC | 1.4 | 9 | -0.6 |
| Small EMS | 1.0 | 10.8 | -0.9 |
| Small non-EMS | 2.5 | 2.5 | 2.0 |

Source: OECD, Economic Outlook Historical Statistics 1960-1985
[a] Belgium, Denmark, Ireland, Netherlands
[b] Austria, Finland, Norway, Sweden, Switzerland
[c] Gross Fixed Capital Formation

outside the EC. The question is therefore why would governments in Belgium, Denmark, and the Netherlands tolerate economic hardships that appear to be directly linked to participation in the EMS? We must first establish why the hardship of a fixed parity with the German mark coupled with membership in the EC has led to such a startling economic deterioration. One possibility is that unlike the larger EMS members, the foreign trade of the smaller members is more oriented toward the EC. Whereas the larger countries benefited from the fiscal expansion initiated by U.S. President Ronald Reagan, due to a narrow export distribution the smaller members derived only indirect benefits from the stimulation of the U.S. economy (Vona and Bini Smaghi 1988). Only a marginal fraction of the export flows of the Low Countries and Denmark is destined for non-European markets. Second, their economies coped with public finance, labor market, and industrial imbalances. A deflationary regime seemed to have aggravated some of these problems, at least in the short-term.

We can therefore speculate that the smaller countries could have asked for special treatment in light of their structural problems and weak labor market performance. Denmark could have argued that since a significant portion of its trade was with Britain and the Nordic countries, a weighted basket of currencies that included those of its other trading partners might be a better alternative. Instead, however, the three small countries—Belgium, Denmark, and the Netherlands—were the only ones *not* to ask for any special antidote to lessen the pain of reduced policy autonomy. As a matter of fact, it is very likely that not implementing the rules of the EMS would have been advantageous for the small countries because their actions do not affect the outcome of the overall arrangements. Such a line of action ought to have endowed them with the freedom to do what needed to be done without having to fear retaliation or pressure from other countries. They did not do so, however, because central bankers in charge of monetary policy and the value of the currency argued strongly in favor of membership and compliance to the rules.

## THE EMS, CENTRAL BANKS, AND FISCAL CONSTRAINTS

A large body of literature richly documents the effects of short-term pressures on discretionary macroeconomic policy-making. Yet public spending and inflationary biases of economic policy-making exhibit substantial national variations. Political scientists claim that differences in social spending and inflation must be seen against the background of a united left and strong labor movement. Disciplined trade union federations are more likely to enforce wage restraints and thereby temper inflation pressures. Labor-led government coalitions are more likely to spend public monies on welfare programs and are more likely to intervene in market forces. Both high levels of public spending and low levels of inflation are traced to the political resources of the left and organized labor. Economists, however, have documented another reason for the variability in inflation rates and different tradeoffs between price stability and employment (Burdekin and Willett 1992; Burdekin and Laney 1988; Schor 1985). Central banks with well-defined constitutional obligations to preserve price stability are often in a position to lead the discussion on different economic policy options without having to take into consideration employment or general welfare issues. Appointment rules and the terms of the board of governors also add to or distract from the institutional autonomy of the central bank. Intrusive surveillance by elected officials seriously constrains the ability of central banks to set monetary policy independently from government. Similarly, the obligation to finance budget deficits resulting from parliamentary action undermines the authority of the central banks to curb government spending to combat inflationary tendencies. Institutional and appointment rules define the scope of autonomy of central bank behavior.

Central banks of Belgium, Denmark, and the Netherlands have witnessed a substantial loss of institutional autonomy since the 1960s. External factors were the growth of international capital markets and increased exchange rate volatility. Both complicated the task of central banks to safeguard the national currency and defend it against monetary debasement. Internal developments were the growing budget deficits and large government commitments on future social programs. Central banks had to stand by and watch the gradual growth of public deficits and national debt. Though these central banks once might have had the appropriate institutional leverage to deal with governments' deficit spending, that was now overtaken by a more liquid world and open financial markets. None of the three central banks was by law obliged to finance government deficits, but the governments of Belgium and Denmark borrowed abroad to finance their social programs and industrial bail-out measures. However, monetary policy in the three countries tended to be restrictive, and inflation rates, often an indication of central bank power, were either at or below the European average.

Institutionally, the central banks of Belgium, Denmark, and the Netherlands fall somewhere between integrated and independent central banks. An example of the latter is the Bundesbank, which is independent both in policy decisions and in appointments. Integrated central banks are under formal control by the political authorities and must pay attention to a host of economic objectives. None of the three central banks is tightly controlled nor can any totally ignore the summonses of elected officials. Of the three, the Danish Nationalbank is the weakest.

## DENMARK: TOTAL FINANCIAL LIBERALIZATION

In 1936 the Central Bank Act of Denmark established formal parliamentary supervision over money and credit. However, the act was a product of a tortuous compromise in which the social democratic bloc granted the greatest concessions. While the bank supervisors are recruited from parliament, various government ministries, and from the professional interest groups of labor and business, the actual leadership is in the hands of the board of management. Members of the board are elected by the bank supervisors or appointed by the crown (government). Directors of the board of management cannot be dismissed by the government or another institution, and their tenure lasts until retirement at age seventy. In the end, the juridical position of the Danish central bank is autonomous and parliamentary control is weak (Uutitalo 1984). The unfavorable position of the Danish economy in the international system limited the authority and activities of the Danish Nationalbank. Whenever the Danish central bank lowered the discount rate to boost, say, housing construction, the economy quickly registered sizable current account deficits. Increased consumption led to increased demand for imported goods. The monetary policies of the central bank were therefore routinely shaped by the need to defend the country's international reserves. Social democratic–led cabinets were also defeated by the vulnerable position of the Danish economy as an expansionary fiscal program threatened to widen current account deficits beyond sustainable levels. The Nationalbank therefore possessed the institutional autonomy to set monetary policy separate from government. But its independence was largely nominal since the structural weakness of the economy did not leave many options open (Johansen 1987; Pekkarinen 1989).

The economic recession hit Denmark harder than most other countries. Unemployment rose in one decade by a factor of eleven, from 1 percent in 1973 to 11 percent in 1983. Deficits on the balance of payments increased fivefold (in current terms) between 1975 and 1980. Public sector debt skyrocketed. To reduce the number of unemployed, government agencies increased their share in the total labor force to 31 percent in 1982, from 10 percent in 1960 (OECD 1988, p. 37). More public sector employment and greater social expenditures produced a gross debt of 74 percent of gross domestic product (GDP) in 1984. Interest rate payments accounted for 2 percent of public expenditures in 1973 and rose to 13 percent in 1983. Net interest payment increased from zero to 5 percent of GDP from 1970 to 1985 (OECD 1988, p. 40). Tensions in the industrial relations system and the wage solidarity program of the trade union confederation hierarchy sparked wage competition and led to extra generous pay settlements (Einhorn and Logue 1989, p. 246; Esping-Andersen 1985, p. 211). During the incumbency of the social democratic–led coalition in the 1970s, contrary to the trends in other countries, banking regulations and controls over external capital flows were tightened in an unsuccessful effort to keep domestic interest rates below those of its major trading partners. This was part of a "sheltering" strategy aimed at expanding the public sector to absorb the unemployed and at avoiding a depletion of foreign exchange reserves. The Nationalbank and professional economists in the major research institutes suggested an entirely different approach that consisted of financial liberalization and deregulation. The president of the Nationalbank repeatedly pointed out that capital controls were ineffective. However, in the absence of a credible commitment to a fixed exchange rate, the Nationalbank retained the various controls with the purpose of divorcing domestic from international interest rate fluctuations. The removal of exchange and capital controls, therefore, could be administered only after the government had broken with its traditional dependence on small devaluations (Damgaard 1989).

In the summer of 1982, the crisis package of the socialists failed to win parliamentary approval, and they resigned. A liberal-conservative coalition replaced them and presented its own budget that fall. The thrust of the new government program was to promote competitiveness of private business through a reduction in interest rates, inflation, and wage scales. It froze wages for five months, suspended the wage indexation for two years, increased taxes, and raised employee contributions to education and social security (ETLA, IFF, IUI, IOI 1987, p. 67). The Danes themselves noted the inherent danger of liberalizing the financial system and removing capital controls. The Nationalbank, though it had never been very successful, would now have no prospects of regulating the supply and price of credit (ETLA, IFF, IUI, IOI 1987, p. 68). However, the cost appeared minor. Net central government debt amounted to 40 percent of GDP in 1983, and its consolidation started right after the installment of the new cabinet. Membership in the EMS has helped to arrest public sector growth as the liberalization of capital movements influenced interest rates and brought them in line with the international level. By adhering to a firm exchange rate policy, the authorities sent a clear signal that they were willing to use instruments other than devaluation to restore the economic balance. This, in turn, allowed for lower interest rates as confidence in the Danish krone is stable (OECD 1988, pp. 57-58).

Danish authorities, for a while at least, thought that they could get away from the rules of collective exchange rate management. In 1979, when the socialist-led coalition was still struggling to design a crisis package, the Danish crown was devalued by 5 percent to improve competitiveness. It was part of a package that also included permanent modification of indexation mechanisms. Danish officials proceeded very informally, and called the Council of Ministers to report their decision, and acted unilaterally. In February 1982, the socialist-led cabinet wanted to devalue again to improve competitiveness and approached the members of the monetary committee with the request for 7 percent devaluation. The Council of Ministers and central bank officials rejected this request and approved a smaller realignment of 3 percent (Thygesen 1984). A few months later, the socialist cabinet had resigned. Membership in the EMS has eliminated the option of competitive (though small) devaluations and has increased the economic exposure of Denmark. Since international (European) trends had a distinctive deflationary and restrictive bias, the Danes had no choice and soon fell into line. In the meantime, the Nationalbank has been able to accomplish what it had tried to achieve the past decade: a stable exchange rate and relatively low interest rates. However, this has been at the expense of social goals associated with social democracy, such as universalistic social entitlement rights and income redistribution.

In 1982-1983, the big step was taken to liberalize capital markets and do away with prohibitions or restrictions on capital flows. The effect has been to enlarge Denmark's sensitivity to trends in Germany's short-term interest rates. For all practical purposes, it has no longer an independent monetary policy and is more than ever obliged to follow the gyrations of Germany's exchange rate regime (Smeets 1990; Steinherr and Schrevel 1988).

## THE NETHERLANDS: VOLUNTARY SURRENDER TO THE DM

In contrast to Denmark, in the Netherlands large current account surpluses (not recurrent deficits) constantly threatened to undermine the targets set by the bank for domestic liquidity growth. In the absence of rigid exchange or capital controls, capital inflows were substantial so that monetary restrictiveness and credit ceilings were usually ineffective. The bank's response was to encourage the export of capital by nurturing the reputation of the guilder as a stable reserve currency. It also tried to keep interest rates low so as to discourage an inflow of capital. While Danish real long-term interest rates were on average 5.2 percent from 1973 to 1979, Dutch real long-term interest rate were 1.1 percent.

The healthy financial position of the economy heightened the prestige and reputation of the bank. Dutch parliament and government exercise relatively modest influence on the money and credit policies of the Netherlands Bank. According to the Dutch Banking Act of 1948, the ministry of finance reserves the right to give instructions to the central bank. This provision has never been invoked. The treasury is allowed to take up a low ceiling of interest-free advances. However, these advances may be used only to cover temporary requirements. The bank, in turn, is not obliged to provide funds to the government. In general, the minister of finance and the central bank governor collaborate amicably (Kurzer 1988).

For the Netherlands Bank, the management of the country's exchange rate and money liquidity is eased by a comfortable surplus on current transactions (usually around 1 percent of GDP). By comparison, the Danish Nationalbank saw the external deficit grow from an annual average of 2.1 percent from 1968 to 1974 to 3.5 percent from 1974 to 1979. It is no surprise that the Netherlands Bank has consistently pursued the twin goals of low inflation and a balance-of-payments equilibrium with considerable success until the turmoil of the mid-1970s and that it actively promotes the guilder as an international reserve currency and a substitute for the German mark (Schotsman 1987). It also follows that the healthy external position of the

Netherlands adds to the reputation of its central bank. With a great variety of instruments at its disposal, the Netherlands Bank is an influential voice in policy-making.

In the 1970s, the bank suddenly faced two ominous developments that were more or less beyond its control. Wage negotiations in the Netherlands were based on consensual and centralized negotiations in bilateral or tripartite committees. One of the important preconditions for the smooth implementation of annual wage agreements was the authority of the top leadership to enforce the stipulations of the central accords. In the 1970s, industrial militancy and the disappearance of cultural/religious animosity led to a transfer of power from the confederation to the constituent unions, and the system of postwar wage restraints gave way to a more fluid and combative era of unenforceable central agreements and large wage drift. The socialist cabinet intervened after 1974 with mandatory wage agreements, but coercive incomes policies usually were aimed at narrowing wage differentials of different groups, and the cabinet continued to protect the value of real incomes of workers (Braun 1987; Fobben 1989; Wolinetz 1989). In short, wage and pay ceilings were set to guarantee the purchasing power of wage-earners and salaried employees and did not arrest the growing danger of cost-price inflation.

The second development that interfered with the operations of the bank was the unanticipated effects of natural gas wealth on the domestic economy. Since the price of natural gas is linked to the spot price of crude oil, government revenues received an enormous windfall after 1974. Natural gas receipts of the central government tripled from 1979 to 1982 and accounted for 7.2 percent of total government revenues in 1982 (OECD 1984, p. 35). With these royalties, the government could finance or maintain the social expenditures and transfer payments despite an economic turndown. Generally, public debt interest payments were not large by international standards, but the rapid growth in public outlays and the sudden collapse of energy prices after 1982 led to a rapid increase in public indebtedness to 55 percent of GDP in 1985.

For a long time, the bank believed that centralized wage negotiations could cope with the twin burdens of rising public expenditures and economic stagnation. However, divisions within the trade union federations, competition between public sector workers and blue-collar workers, and class polarization made a return to an era of wage restraints and labor unity impossible.

Subsequently, the Netherlands Bank asked for extensive deindexation of wages and salaries and the removal of a coupling mechanism that tied public sector salaries and social benefits to private sector wages. So long as the Social Democrats were in power, the likelihood of a direct attack on the welfare state was small. In 1977, after winning the national elections, the social democratic party searched desperately for coalition allies among the Christian democratic bloc. Disagreements inside the Christian democratic party ruled out a continuation of a center-left coalition government. Instead, the Christian Democrats formed a coalition with the Liberal Party, but they refused to deviate from the postwar pattern of union consultation and social spending.

Party leaders agreed that something had to be done to arrest the growth in government spending and to induce higher investments. But the political will was not there to push through controversial or unpopular measures. In 1982 the atmosphere in the European Community had changed, and the external obligation to stay within the bilateral grid and move along with the Federal Republic in the grid of EMS currencies supplied the extra determination that had been absent previously. In rapid succession, the government suspended the automatic indexation of public sector wages and social benefits and secured a wage freeze. Public sector salaries were reduced by 3.5 percent, welfare payments were reduced, and eligibility criteria were tightened. Sickness benefits dropped from 80 percent of previous wage to 70 percent in 1986. Disability payments were scaled down to 70 percent of minimum wage. As in Denmark, unions were not consulted and the program was implemented without their full consent.

Instead, politicians led by the monetary authorities voluntarily surrendered any remaining monetary policy autonomy for the sake of low inflation and a strong guilder. The Netherlands more than any other EMS country is now fully incorporated in a DM zone. Both its short-term and long-term interest rates, which are more important determinants for investors and consumers, are set by the Bundesbank (Smeets 1990). It should be stressed that this was a voluntary decision, a decision that corresponded to the traditional preference for a stable exchange rate and maintaining confidence in the guilder as an international reserve currency.

## BELGIUM: THE FIGHT FOR THE FRANC

The ability of the Belgian National Bank to go against the desires of the government is severely curbed by its divided structure (Welch 1981). Though its governing board is filled with appointments from government and established interest groups, separate state agencies are in charge of auditing the credit system and setting liquidity ratios for the banking industry. The three major political cartels—liberal, socialist, or Christian democratic—have freely taken advantage of the gaps in central bank regulation to run up an enormous national debt while the commercial banks and financial groups have gotten away with minimal requirements for public reporting and with virtually no barriers on financial transactions (Kurzer 1988). The ministry of finance has the power to review all of the bank's operations through a commissioner who can veto any action that conflicts with the interest of the state. Despite these institutional limitations and lack of autonomy, the National Bank and its related agencies wield considerable influence in narrow areas. Belgian coalition governments suffered through a prolonged period of intense conflict in the 1970s and elevated the National Bank to being the sole manager of the country's monetary policy. Furthermore, financial holding companies are extremely powerful, and they monopolize many critical appointments in the political system. Ample studies show that the private sector has representatives in every public office and state agency (Craeybeckx and Witte 1983; Mommen 1987).

In the 1970s, the worsening economic climate and the uneven impact on Belgium's two regions (Wallonia and Flanders) and Brussels fueled a resurgence of communal clashes and polarized Belgian politics (Frognier, Quevit, and Stenbock 1982). Government coalitions, which had always been indecisive and weak, became even more fragile. Weak governments produced haphazard and contradictory policy measures that were often aimed at appeasing both linguistic groups and resulted in a remarkable growth in public expenditures. Quite obviously, local authorities and the central government could not finance the increased expenditures during an economic recession when tax revenues had begun to fall as well. Borrowing was the best alternative, and the gross public debt reached first 90 percent of GDP in 1982 and then an astonishing 120 percent in 1988. Interest payments on public debt were 6.6 percent of central government expenditures in 1983 (OECD 1989, p. 54). The chaotic public finances and the chronic trade deficit eroded the confidence in the Belgian franc. From 1979 until 1982, the Belgian National Bank made desperate attempts to defend the franc in the foreign exchange markets and spent in the process 430 billion francs ($10 billion [1982]) of its reserves.

The National Bank agreed that the only realistic solution was a steep devaluation. But as in Denmark, it refused to consider a devaluation until certain features of the postwar settlement had been dismantled. To help unstable governments with the formulation of a crisis package, the National Bank presented an elaborate economic plan in 1981 whose major themes were the abolition of the indexation clause and widespread pay freezes

(Craeybeckx and Witte 1983, pp. 444-447; McClan and Anderson 1985, p. 253; de Ridder 1986, pp. 45-73). As in Denmark, an exchange rate adjustment had to be accompanied by a phasing out of centralized voluntary wage negotiations and a reduction in social transfer payments to be obtained by tightening eligibility criteria and lowering payments. During the EC summit meeting in Maastricht in March 1981 Prime Minister Wilfried Martens had been openly criticized by the other heads of governments for the drain of the indexation system on the budget, but his coalition partners at that time, the Socialist parties, objected to the abolition of the wage indexation and the savings plan for the public sector (Deweerdt and Smits 1982).

One year later, Martens and top officials of his cabinet traveled to Washington, D.C., to attend the annual meeting of the International Monetary Fund (IMF). The following day, news reports announced that a devaluation was imminent. Quite clearly, the IMF meeting was used to discuss with the relevant counterparts in other countries the possibilities of a devaluation of the franc. But the issue had to be settled in the Monetary Committee in Brussels and Frankfurt first. Belgian delegates approached the EC with a request for a 12 percent devaluation and defended themselves by pointing to the many severe financial and economic imbalances; the Germans and French countered that such a sizable realignment would have an unforeseeable ripple effect on the parity grid. After intense around-the-clock negotiations, the compromise offer was 8.5 percent devaluation (Smits 1983).

The Monetary Committee of the EC approved a realignment after the Belgian government had outlined how it intended to safeguard the advantages of a cheaper currency by removing the comprehensive indexation system. But it got less than what it had requested. The result of the halfway settlement was that interest payments of the combined public sector are still around 11 percent of GDP. The bank has not been able to lower the debt/GDP ratio. With the fixed exchange rate, interest rates are determined by international factors and reflect movements of the Belgian franc in the exchange rate grid of the EMS.

Since late 1988, the decision-making powers of the Belgian National Bank have been strengthened in recognition of the new responsibilities of central banks in the economic developments of the Community. As a result of the banks's capacity to ignore the wishes of politicians, quarrels between advocates of welfare spending and monetary authorities will not likely arise soon.

What have been the consequences of EMS participation on the economic policy process of the three countries? In each instance, monetary questions were put at the top of the list of objectives to be accomplished, and they thereby displaced other goals relating to economic justice, income transfers, government spending, and union-business cooperation on wage policy.

## CONCLUSION

The process of European integration will certainly continue in the current direction. But, while the precise shape may not yet be determined, it is clear that a united Germany will be the leading force in this process. Moreover, as the preceding account has shown, German institutions—in both their domestic and international dimensions—have a powerful capacity to shape the framework for economic policy in the 1990s. However, precisely because the Germans have the power to call many of the shots, smaller countries—and less-favored regions of larger countries—may bear disproportionately greater burdens in the process. This latter caveat to the "Euro-euphoria" of the early 1990s may afford greater opportunity to social democratic parties. Historically, the success of social democratic and trade union movements has turned on their ability to project themselves as representatives of the powerless majority. To the extent that wage bargaining in mass production economies, Keynesian macroeconomic policies, and distributive welfare state benefits were able to "deliver the goods" to their constituency during the postwar years, then these policies were successful (Scharpf 1987). Yet the fragmentation brought on at the national level by the strengthening of the policy capacity central banks has dramatically undercut the effectiveness of these left-wing macro strategies. And simple defense of old macro strategies is no longer enough. More important, however, this restrictive package of policies had deprived the left of a crucial tool—a universal way to respond, and thus, a basis of solidarity.

Any successful social democratic response must go beyond mere defensive responses. We are arguing that a successful social democratic economic policy in West Germany—and then in the small countries—must combine both an aggressive left Keynesianism with an active left industrial policy approach that can resist the more restrictive tendencies of the Bundesbank-dominated EMS (Allen 1990). In essence, however, the possibility for stimulative economic policies in the small countries remain hostage to their dependence on the actions of their large neighbor. Either a "Red-Green" coalition or a Europeanwide pattern of economic stimulation seems the only chance for the small countries—and their labor movements and social democratic parties—to overcome their restrictive economic policies and high unemployment. In other words, while the primary short-term direction of Europe will take a conservative, investment-led pattern of growth, the quality of life in Europe remains dependent of the ability of social democracy to create alternatives that build on—yet go beyond—the center-right, German-led institutional pattern.

## NOTES

1. For example, in the case of Sweden, Pontusson has shown that even the most advanced form of Social Democracy—and one not burdened by membership in a German-dominated EMS—was hard-pressed to repeat, during the 1980s, its successes during the earlier period of its political dominance.

## REFERENCES

Allen, Christopher S. (1990). "Trade Unions, Workers Participation and Flexibility: Linking the Micro to the Macro," *Comparative Politics* (April), pp. 253-272.

Artis, M. J., and M. P. Taylor (1988). "Exchange Rates, Interest Rates, Capital Controls and the EMS: Assessing the Track Record," in F. Giavazzi, S. Micossi, and M. Miller, eds., *The European Monetary System.* New York: Cambridge University Press.

Braun, D. (1987). "Political Immobilism and Labour Market Performance: The Dutch Road to Mass Unemployment," *Journal of Public Policy* 7, pp. 310-329.

Bulmer, Simon, and William Paterson (1987). *The Federal Republic of Germany and European Community.* London: Allen & Unwin.

Burdekin, R. C. K., and L. O. Laney (1988). "Fiscal Policymaking and the Central Bank Institutional Constraint," *Kyklos* 41, pp. 647-62.

Burdekin, R. C. K., and T. D. Willett (1992). *Central Bank Reform: The Federal Reserve in International Perspective.* R. D. Auerbach. Public Budgeting and Financial Management.

Camiller, Patrick (1989). "Beyond 1992: The Left in Europe," *New Left Review* 175 (May-June), pp. 5-17.

Craeybeckx, J., and E. Witte (1983). *De Politieke Geschiedenis van Belgie.* Antwerpen: Standaard Uitgeverij.

Damgaard, E. (1989). "Crisis Politics in Denmark 1974-1987," in E. Damgaard, P. Gerlich, and J. J. Richardson, eds., *The Politics of Economic Crisis.* Avesbury: Aldershot.

de Grauwe, P. (1987). "International Trade and Economic Growth in the EMS," *European Economic Review* 31, pp. 388-398.

de Ridder, H. (1986). *Geen Winnaars in deWetstraat.* Leuven: Davidsfonds.

Deweerdt, M., and J. Smits (1982). "Belgian Politics in 1981: Continuity and Change in the Crisis," *Res Publica* 24, pp. 261-272.

Economist Intelligence Unit (1989). "Why Does European Unemployment Stay So High?" in EIU, ed., *European Community: Economic Structure and Analysis.* London: EIU.

Einhorn, Eric S., and John Logue (1989). *Modern Welfare States: Politics and Policies in Social Democratic Scandinavia.* New York: Praeger.

Esping-Andersen, Gösta (1985). *Politics Against Markets: The Social Democratic Road to Power.* Princeton, NJ: Princeton University Press.

ETLA, IFF, IUI, and IOI (1987). *Growth Policies in Nordic Perspective.* Helsinki: ETLA, IFF, IUI, IOI.

Fobben, J. W. (1989)."The Netherlands and the Crisis as a Policy Challenge: Integration or Ideological Maneuvers?" in E. Damgaard, P. Gerlich, and J. J. Richardson, eds., *The Politics of Economic Crisis.* Avesbury: Aldershot.

Frognier, A. P., M. Quevit, and M. Stenbock (1982). "Regional Imbalances and Center-Periphery Relationships in Belgium," in Stein Rokkan and Derek W. Unwin, eds., *The Politics of Territorial Identity: Studies in European Regionalism.* Beverly Hills, CA: Sage Publications.

Giavazzi, F., and A. Giovannini (1989). *Limiting Exchange Rate Flexibility: The European Monetary System.* Cambridge, MA: MIT Press.

Goodman, John B. (1990). "Do All Roads Lead to Brussels? Economic Policymaking in the European Community," Paper presented at the conference on the United States and Europe in the 1990s, American Enterprise Institute, 5-8 March.

Johansen, Hans Ch. (1987). *The Danish Economy in the Twentieth Century.* London: Croom Helm.

Katzenstein, Peter J. (1982). "West Germany as Number 2," in Andrei S. Markovits, ed., *The Political Economy of West Germany.* New York: Praeger, pp. 199-215.

——— (1987). *Politics and Policy in West Germany: The Growth of a Semi-Sovereign State.* Philadelphia: Temple University Press.

Kurzer, Paulette (1988). "The Politics of Central Banking: Austerity and Unemployment in Europe," *Journal of Public Policy* 8, pp. 21-48.

——— (1992). "The European Community and the Postwar Settlement: The Effect of Monetary Integration on Corporatist Arrangements," in Dale L. Smith and James Lee Ray, eds., *The 1992 Project and the Future of Integration in Europe.* New York: M. E. Sharpe.

McClan, W. D. and P. S. Anderson (1985). "Adjustment Performance of Small, Open Economies," in V. E. Argy and J. W. Neville, eds., *Inflation and Unemployment: Theory, Experience and Policy Making.* Boston: George Allen and Unwin.

McDonald, R., and G. Zis (1989). "The European Monetary System: Towards 1991 and Beyond," *Journal of Common Market Studies* 27, pp. 183-202.

Mommen, A. (1987). *Een Tunnel zonder Einde.* Amsterdam: Kluwer.

Moran, Michael (1986). "Theories of Regulation and Changes in Regulation: The Case of Financial Markets," *Political Studies* XXXIV, pp. 185-201.

Notermans, Ton (1990). "Domestic Preferences and External Constraints: The Bundesbank Between Internal and External Pressures," Ms., 4 May.

OECD (1984). *Economic Survey of the Netherlands, 1983/84.* Paris: OECD.

——— (1988). *Economic Survey of Denmark, 1987/88.* Paris: OECD.

——— (1989). *Economic Survey of Belgium, 1988/89.* Paris: OECD.

Padoa-Schioppa, T. (1984). *Money, Economic Policy, and Europe.* Brussels: Commission of European Communities.

Pekkarinen, Jukka (1989). "Keynesianism and the Scandinavian Models of Economic Policy," in Peter A. Hall, ed., *The Political Power of Economic Ideas: Keynesianism Across Nations.* Princeton, NJ: Princeton University Press.

Pontusson, Jonas (1984). "Behind and Beyond Social Democracy in Sweden," *New Left Review* 143 (January-February), pp. 69-96.

Riemer, Jeremiah (1982). "Alterations in the Design of Model Germany," in Andrei S. Markovits, ed., *The Political Economy of West Germany.* New York: Praeger, pp. 53-89.

Röller, Wolfgang (1989). "Stragegien der Banken: Europa 1992," lecture given at the Hotel Intercontinental Frankfurt, sponsored by the Institut für Kapitalmarktforschung, 15 February.

Röpke, Wilhelm (1982). "The Guiding Principles of the Liberal Programme," in Horst Friedrich Wünche, ed., *Standard Texts on the Social Market Economy.* Stuttgart: Gustav Fischer Verlag.

Sandholtz, Wayne, and John Zysman (1989). "1992: Recasting the European Bargain," *World Politics* 42 (October), pp. 95-128.

Scharpf, Fritz W. (1987). *Sozial-demokratische Krisenpolitik in Europa.* Frankfurt: Campus.

Schor, Juliet B. (1985). "Wage Flexibility, Social Expenditures, and Monetary Restrictiveness," in M. Jarsulic, ed., *Money and Macropolicy.* Boston: Kluwer-Nijhoff.

Schotsman, J. (1987). *De Parlementaire Behandeling van het Monetaire Beleid in Nederland sinds 1863.* The Hague: Staatsuitgeverij.

Smeets, H-D. (1990). "Does Germany Dominate the EMS?" *Journal of Common Market Studies* 29, pp. 37-52.

Smits, J. (1983). "Less Democracy for a Better Economy," *Res Publica* 25, pp. 130-51.

Steinherr, A., and de G. Schrevel (1988). "Liberalization of Financial Transactions in the Community with Particular Reference to Belgium, Denmark, and the Netherlands," *European Economy* 12, pp. 117-49.

Symonds, Matthew (1985). "The Very Model of a Central Bank," *Deutsche Bundesbank: Auszüge aus Presseartikeln* 58 (September 13), pp. 5-6.

Thygesen, N. (1984). "Exchange Rate Policy and Monetary Targets in the EMS," in R. S. Masera and R. Triffin, eds., *Europe's Money: Problems of European Monetary Coordination and Integration.* New York: Oxford University Press.

Ungerer, H. (1989). "The EMS and the International Monetary System," *Journal of Common Market Studies* 27, pp. 231-48.

Ungerer, H., O. Evans, T. Mayer, and P. Young (1986). *The EMS: Recent Developments.* Washington, D.C.:IMF.

Uutitalo, P. (1984). "Monetarism, Keynesianism and the Institutional Status of Central Banks," *Acta Sociologica* 27, pp. 31-50.

Vona, S., and L. Bini Smaghi (1988). "Economic Growth and Exchange Rates in the EMS: Their Trade Effects in a Changing External Environment," in F. Giavazzi, S. Micossi, and M. Miller, eds., *The European Monetary System.* New York: Cambridge University Press.

Welch, J. (1981). *The Regulation of Banks in the Member-States of the EEC.* London: M. Nijhoff Publishers.

Wolinetz, Steven B. (1989). "Socio-Economic Bargaining in the Netherlands: Redefining the Postwar Policy Coalition," *West European Politics* 12, pp. 79-99.

Wood, G. (1988). "European Monetary Arrangement: Their Functioning and Future," in D. E. Fair and C. de Boissieu, eds., *The European Dimension: International Monetary and Financial Integration.* Boston: Kluwer.

# PART III

# NETWORKS

# 5

## The European Left and Political Integration: A New Stage in Social Democracy?

Robert Ladrech

### INTRODUCTION

The actual seriousness of purpose toward European political integration has been rather perfunctory, despite the internationalist rhetoric of West European socialist and social democratic parties dating to the pre–World War I era and the commitment to a democratic and united European Community since the late 1950s. To be sure, over the past couple of decades some parties, for instance, the Belgian Socialists and the German Social-Democratic Party (SPD), have stood out from the rest in their support for European union. At the same time, while not explicitly rejecting the notion of a more politically integrated EC, the British Labour Party and French Socialist Party have been most reluctant to support political union. Yet, even with the SPD, "proposals for Europe while the party was in power were relatively infrequent and statements on Europe had a ritual obligatory quality" (Bulmer and Paterson, 1987, p. 140).

In light of the intensified pace of EC integration since the signing of the Single European Act (SEA) in 1985, has there been any discernible response or reaction on the part of the major social democratic parties of the EC, particularly in their European policy? This chapter addresses the attitude and strategy of the SPD, one of the most important of these parties, toward the resumption of economic and political integration. The acceleration of an EC policy-making dimension and the growing dilemma of nationally based social democratic orientations, especially in macroeconomic matters, has engendered a renewed attentiveness to the emerging modalities of the new architecture of Europe. One manifestation of this concern is the promotion of social democratic transnational party collaboration and cohesiveness at the European level. The faster-paced evolution of the EC has generated concern among Social Democrats to the extent that former objections to EC integration are now eroding in varying degrees depending on the party. For the SPD in particular, programmatic change emphasizing European political union and support for supranational organizational development is evidence of wider social democratic reaction to Europe 1992.

This chapter documents the growth of socialist transnational party cooperation and the internal developments of the SPD in this regard. The first section briefly discusses the general nature of socialist transnational cooperation and party activity at the European level before 1989. Next, the dilemma of an increased EC policy influence conflicting with national social democratic parties orientations is addressed. This provides the background for a discussion of SPD developments and, finally, wider EC socialist transnational activities.

## HISTORICAL BACKGROUND

When speaking of social democratic parties and European integration, the historical record is, at best, mixed. Featherstone (1988) has succinctly rendered individual histories of social democratic parties in all 12 member states in regard to their stance on European integration. His findings, taken up to 1986, demonstrated a variation in support. The spectrum extended from the pro-EC German SPD and Belgian Socialists to the reluctant French Socialists in the 1970s and the hostile British Labour Party through the early 1980s. Featherstone offers three main categories of reasons explaining the diversity of attitudes, although it is safe to state that the national situation in all 12 strongly affects policy toward the EC. The first area is pressure from internal party influences. This ranges from the role of ideology, internal elites and trade unions, to public opinion and government and opposition roles. Second, there are influences from the wider domestic political system, such as the impact of other political parties, perceptions of economic interest, and the historical context. Finally, there is the external dimension where particular events and influences may serve to affect policy in one or more parties, depending on the domestic situation.

In this external realm, cooperation between social democratic parties occurs in the form of the Confederation of the Socialist Parties of the EC (CSPEC), formed in 1974. Even so, in the mid-1980s "the socialist parties in the EC continue to find the establishment of common policies difficult" (Featherstone 1988, p. 332). Despite an official manifesto drawn up for the 1989 European elections, each party campaigned on its own nationally derived issues. One of the prime organizational factors precluding a stronger CSPEC is the requirement for national party representatives to reach a decision by consensus. This, in fact, is not the case in the Christian Democratic transnational party federation, the European People's Party, which considers itself a European party and employs majority voting.

Three sets of actors are involved in European-level party politics aimed at the European Parliament (EP). They are the transnational party federations, the political groups in the EP, and the national party organizations. By far the weakest are the transnational party federations, CSPEC in the case of the Socialists. Nugent notes that the principal weakness is that they "are not involved in day-to-day political activity in an institutional setting . . . [and] therefore have no very clear focus and cannot develop attachments and loyalties" (Nugent 1989, p. 124).

Political groups in the EP form the next set of actors. Since the 1989 European elections, the socialist group is the largest, though short of an absolute majority. These groups have a unique problem: They have no anchor in grass-roots politics. Rather, they are creatures of EP political activity. Although the groups have formed on the basis of ideological identification, national variations have prevented party group discipline from evolving as much as their national counterparts (Attina 1990).

Finally, this brings us to the role of national parties at the EC level. National parties are involved in three ways. First, national parties select candidates at European elections. Second, as is often noted, European elections have been run as national elections, essentially as referenda on the governing party, and, therefore, with primarily domestic implications. Finally, national party delegations in the EP groups sometime cause great strains. Problems do not arise "so much from the national groups having to act on specific domestic instructions . . . [but simply because] each national party group inevitably tends to have its own priorities and loyalties" (Nugent 1989, p. 131).

Obviously, a lack of coordination among national parties, including the social democratic, has prevented any significant presence at the EC level. Differences over integration and its pace and, indeed, the apparent irrelevance of the EC up to 1986 in the calculations of social democratic parties, accounts for this state of underdevelopment. The lack of popular election to the EP before 1979 also meant that campaign mobilization, a defining behavior of political parties, was absent. This fact simply furthered the inconsequential nature of EC institutions in the eyes of party leaders and activists alike. Reif and Niedermayer (1987) add that parties have "failed to fulfill what is their essential role in any democratic system . . . because there is no incentive for them to invest the necessary energy. The European Parliament neither determines legislation nor controls what little there is of a government, i.e., the Commission" (p. 165). Added to the lack of party consensus over European integration is the absence of a suitable forum to decisively affect EC policy-making. It is clear, then, that up to the adoption of the SEA and its implementation beginning in 1987, transnational party activity—the necessary means to present a significant political party presence at the supranational level—"has been bound up by the institutional limitations and weaknesses of the E.C. itself" (Pridham and Pridham 1981, p. 277).

## REGIONALIZATION AND THE SOCIAL DEMOCRATIC DILEMMA

> Until now most left-wing parties—whether Socialists or Social Democrats—have mainly used or proposed to use purely national instruments: separate systems of rules, national fiscal policy, industrial policy relating to their own country, etc. The Single Market . . . will automatically reduce the margin of autonomy of these national instruments. It will force the Left, whether in opposition or in power, to consider its actions in genuinely European terms. It is a challenge. (Fabius 1989, p. 45)

Judging from the variety of national social democratic responses to the worldwide economic crises of the 1970s and 1980s, some analysts have concluded that "ideologically social democracy is in a period of disarray" (Paterson and Thomas 1986, p. 16). For many governing parties in the 1980s, programmatic change was necessary. While in office, they pursued policies that appeared to blur the distinction between left and right. Economic policy, in particular, seemed aimed at revitalizing capital accumulation, and retrenchment characterized social welfare. As a consequence, "the responses of social democratic governments to the conditions of the early 1980's, when private-sector employment could be maintained only if business profits increased substantially, lacked a theoretical foundation" (Scharpf 1991, p. 270). For the parties themselves, activists and leaders alike not only had to integrate a pro-market stance into their programmatic statements but, at the same time, fend off challenges from new left parties stressing nontraditional issues such as ecology and decentralization. In many cases, as in France with the Parti Socialiste (PS) or, in Spain, with the Spanish Socialist Workers Party (PSOE), a clear party orientation in general policy matters was absent. In effect, socialist governments responded to recessionary conditions or crises in balance of payments with austerity and industrial programs that in many cases hurt their primary constituents, blue-collar workers.

For the parties that spent most of the 1980s in the opposition—for instance, the German Social-Democratic Party (SPD) or the British Labour Party—party leaderships were either renewed, as in the case of the Labour Party, or else forced by electoral rejection to review basic economic premises. In most cases, remaining references to nationalizations quietly departed, and more positive sounding references promoting economic growth and competition crept in. By the end of the 1980s, most major social democratic parties, in government or in the opposition, had begun to stress the need for the left to develop a plan for regenerating national economic capacities in a competitive international environment. The dilemma, as many have pointed out, is to discover some additional organizing concept that justifies the neoliberal economic policies, while distinguishing these parties from the liberal right. Attention to feminism, ecology, and so on—all issues having their place in modern left-of-center parties—still do not address the political and ideological problem of equality and fairness in the economic realm. This is the ideological dimension of the social democratic dilemma.

A more practical dilemma, one that has developed especially during the latter half of the 1980s, is the relative shrinking of national policy maneuverability in an increasingly interdependent and integrated European Community. In other words, national policy choices, primarily industrial and fiscal, and increasingly in such policy areas as the environment and health matters, have become more restricted. This has resulted as certain commitments to EC-denoted guidelines and arrangements, such as currency fluctuation within the European Monetary System (EMS) or directives intended to implement the Single European Act, influence ever broader areas of economic and social life. The efficacy of purely national economic recovery schemes has thus been brought directly into question. That national markets will, more than ever before, be dominated by transnational capital brings home to the left the fact that most of their theoretical and operational underpinnings are quickly becoming anachronisms. This recognition itself can produce party disorientations. For instance, in France, Socialist activists were only beginning to realize that the space within which they can act has narrowed as a result of "the internationalization of domestic economies and the political choice of the 1992 project. Many Socialists were bewildered... by Rocard's unwillingness to take stronger measures to combat inequality because they believed that the country had finally entered a period of "après-crise" when *rigueur* could be relaxed. But they were thinking of an earlier economic era. . . . The liberal, deregulatory logic of . . . 1992 . . . is impeccable" (Howell 1991, pp. 36-37).

Increasingly, citizens are confronted by policies developed at the supranational level by actors unaccountable to national electorates. To the extent that this is true, future analysis of the EC Council of Ministers and Commission may require a concept of national party *irrelevance*. Indeed, irrelevance or lack of authoritative party input may be a contributing factor to eventual party failure. This phenomenon is similar to what Cerny (1990) has called the increasing constraints on the capacity of parties to process key issues. He writes that "in the circumstances of the 1990s, as transnational interpenetration of structures and the refocusing of the state along lines of international economic competition come to channel and even drive the dynamics of political agency along new lines, the opportunities for political officeholders at the nation-state level to fulfill the expectations which voters, in particular, are supposed to have of them are likely to shrink further" (p. 144).

The current predicament is that the EC is not addressing in any substantive manner social democratic party goals that derive from their specific programmatic identity, for example, workers' rights, equality, and social regulation of the market. Moreover, it is generally agreed that the Social Charter advanced by Jacques Delors is neither the bulwark against exploitation nor the protector of workers' rights that social democratic parties or unions would have hoped for (Lodge 1989). How then have social democratic parties met the challenge of redefining their contribution in the political and economic realms? The movement toward acceptance of the single market, however grudgingly given, has been the first step in coming to terms with the recent dynamics of EC integration. The social democratic strategy is to speed up the political content of integration as a means of reexerting influence on the processes and consequences of the single market from a supranational position, thus complementing national-based tactics that operate more precisely at the intergovernmental level.

## PROGRAMMATIC DEVELOPMENT AND EC POLITICAL INTEGRATION IN THE SPD

The SPD has been a supporter of European Community integration since the late 1950s, especially after the party's first postwar leader, Kurt Schumacher, died. It was Schumacher who opposed Western European integration while the chance for German unification still appeared to be in reach. Once the party had accepted West German participation in the European Economic Community, the "demand for increased rights for the European Parliament was mentioned in the 1961 election campaign and then more strongly in a European Manifesto produced for the 1965 election" (Bulmer and Paterson 1987, p. 136). Even so, the next two decades witnessed other sources of party elite attention, for instance, Brandt's Ostpolitik of the late 1960s and early 1970s. Helmut Schmidt focused on economic matters rather than political institutional dynamics. With the party's return to the opposition in 1982, the overriding concern seemed to be with domestic issues such as the peace movement and the North Atlantic Treaty Organization (NATO) double-track decision, relations with the labor movement, and, of course, determining how to win the next set of legislative elections.

Another factor diverting attention away from matters of EC integration was the general consensus among the major parties—CDU, FDP (Free Democrats) and SPD—that European integration was indeed in West Germany's interest. Bulmer (1989) refers to this as the Europeanization of German politics. This process was completed by the end of the 1960s, and "difference on European policy were matters of nuance, or derived from differences over the substance of domestic politics. This broad consensus has shown continuity up to the present" (216). However favorable SPD references have been toward EC integration for 30 years, this feature of party policy was kept in the domain of the party Euro-experts. In other words, European integration was not an issue of broad interest within the party. What has begun to stimulate greater attention for this issue within the SPD in recent years is the current acceleration of EC integration and the impact of domestic concerns in the 1980s.

After an interval of relative stability in the party system, the SPD found the 1980s a complex period with new actors and issues complicating the programmatic orientation of the party. In that decade, the domestic political "balance of forces" changed for the SPD. Returned to the opposition in 1982 by the defection of its coalition partner, the Free Democrats, and confronted with the Greens, a new competitor on its left after the 1983 legislative elections, questions of electoral strategy preoccupied party leadership throughout the decade. The 1987 election, in which the Greens nearly displaced the FDP as the third largest party in West Germany, together with the SPD's worst showing in over 20 years, resulted not only in leadership criticism but in a reevaluation of the very program of the party. As the party's basic program, the Bad Godesberg document adopted in 1959 was still the repository of principles. In facing the challenge from the Greens, while trying not to alienate centrist blue-collar support, the SPD began in 1985 a review of its basic tenets (Braunthal 1989).

Although a strong supporter of greater integration through the 1980s, the SPD began to view EC matters as more than an external policy and increasingly as a means for solving German economic problems. The intentions surrounding the programmatic renewal, though, were caught up in intrafactional dynamics. According to Padgett (1989), elections to the party executive at the 1986 conference "revealed that in the party at large and in the middle levels of its hierarchy, the New Left was gaining ground" (131). Old and New Left representatives were in place on the leadership, with Hans-Jochen Vogel becoming party chairman (Old Left) and Oskar Lafontaine vice-chair (New Left). The question of European unity, interestingly enough, did not become a contentious issue between the two camps, as some might have expected. This expectation was based on the behavior of the New Left Greens. Bulmer (1989) has suggested that a "decline in popular support for integration [may have] a generational element . . . symbolized by the questioning of values undertaken by the Greens. Their attachment to integration remains ambiguous because of their criticism of individual policies" (226).

The SPD strategy of incorporating certain issues such as ecology might have diluted support for the EC. Yet, even after Lafontaine became chair of the program committee, the Old Left commitment remained. Recently, in regard to the potential benefits or negative implications for social democracy from the single market, Vogel has written that

> which of these two variants becomes reality largely depends on whether we leave things to develop by themselves or whether we can influence the direction and impose social and ecological criteria—i.e., whether the forces which want to and can influence this development are strong enough [and this] applies to the Social Democratic and Socialist parties in the Community, whose hitherto rather loose association must be built up into a political decision-making centre. That implies an increase in the Confederation's staffing and the transition to majority decisions. (1989, p. 89)

In December of 1989, the SPD finally adopted a new basic program replacing the 1959 Bad Godesberg Program. While it tries to please both the new and the old lefts, it has been described as being short on vision. Yet the commitment to European unity is not downgraded by tactical considerations. The program reconfirms SPD allegiance to the idea of European federalism while stressing the importance of the European Parliament:

> Federalism must also become the organizational principle of the European Community. . . . We want to develop the [EC] into the United States of Europe. By transferring sovereign rights to the EC in accordance with Article 24 of the Basic Law, the existing state structure will already have been complemented. . . . We aim for a Community Constitution which combines democracy with the principles of the constitutional and social state. . . . This requires full rights for the European Parliament, a capable government which would be answerable to the Parliament, clearly delineated fields of competence and European economic democracy. (Basic Policy Program 1991, pp. 14, 44-45)

Sassoon (1989) has characterized the new program as moving the SPD from a strategy "which is nation-based to one which is Europe-based" (433). With German labor (the DGB) tentatively supporting the single market in hopes of the economic return, the SPD now appears to see a stake in European decision-making as much more critical. Indeed, the SPD in 1990 introduced legislation in the Bundestag to create a subcommittee exclusively for EC affairs. Reconfirming the European orientation, the new SPD leader, Bjorn Engholm, stated in a recent interview that he is "a convinced federalist, I am German and happy to be so, but the national State no longer has the same meaning for me as it did for my grandfather." (*Agence-Europe,* #5477, 22 April 1991).

Finally, at the SPD Congress held in Bremen at the end of May 1991, the party adopted a resolution that, among other things, called for strengthened transnational organization among the EC social democratic parties. The document, entitled *Europapolitische Perspecktiven der SPD* (European Perspectives of the SPD), calls explicitly for the "foundation of a European Social Democratic Party" (p. 10). According to the document, the "point of departure for the European Social Democratic Party should be the Confederation of the Social Democratic Parties of the European Community" (ibid.). It specifically advocates the following: adopting majority decision-making over the present consensus principle; the "election of delegates from national member parties" to the Congress of this new European party; and the election of the executive committee of the new party at the Congress "according to a formula agreed upon by the member parties." Finally, in terms of organizational development, the resolution notes that "political impact and efficacy depend on the readiness of all national member parties to finance the joint party to the best of their ability; only in this way can it fulfill its function as an important political decision-making centre for Europe's Social Democrats" (pp. 10-11). The influence of this resolution and its timing are noteworthy beyond the confines of the party. No doubt the timing was simply fortuitous, but five days after the adoption of this resolution at the SPD Congress the party leaders of the Confederation of Socialist Parties of the EC met to discuss this very idea.

Thus, in the midst of electoral strategy concerns in the 1980s, when the SPD seemed most affected by electoral flux (some, for example, Dalton [1989], have called it dealignment), the party faced a New Left challenge together with the risk of losing centrist voters. At the same time, the economic crisis of the late 1970s and early 1980s forced a review of economic policy. New Left ideas on qualitative and environmentally conscious growth apparently reflect an apparent shift away from the SPD position of past years. This, combined with talk of labor-market flexibility, suggests that a commitment to EC-sparked growth with democratic control is a possible complementary strategy. Consequently, the turn toward a determined European presence for the SPD in the context of the rest of the social democratic group appears to reflect this new programmatic orientation.

Before turning to evidence of change at the European level, it is important to note that French Socialist-SPD links have developed quickly over the past few years, no doubt accelerated by German unification. France and Germany, by virtue of their economic and political clout, are absolutely crucial in terms of any substantive leaps in EC integration. Cooperation or common strategies by both parties to achieve the goal of a democratic European Union could be very significant. The two parties are deepening their party-to-party relations. The SPD's research center, the Friedrich Ebert Stiftung, has had an office in Paris for a number of years, recently sponsoring with its Partie Socialiste (PS) counterpart, the Institut Socialiste d'Etudes et de Recherches (ISER), major colloquia on topics such as "The Integration of Germany and Europe—The Common European Future." The ISER announced in 1990 that it would open for the first time an office in Bonn in order to improve communication and coordination between the two parties. PS leader Mauroy addressed the SPD unification congress in Berlin on 27 September 1990, emphasizing the common task of the European Social Democrats to advance a common market, develop common policies, and a monetary union. He stated that "this is, furthermore, our common task in the operation of the Confederation of Socialist Parties of the EC" (Mauroy 1990, p. 126). Finally, close collaboration among British, French, and German delegations in the EP Socialist Group is considered a hallmark of this group's parliamentary efficiency.

## TRANSNATIONAL PARTY ACTIVITY

By 1990 SPD party leaders had called for a strengthened EP and CSPEC. A strengthened EP benefits European Social Democrats in two ways. First, enhancing the principle of representative democracy, a popularly elected assembly allows influence on the formulation of EC directives and, with the right of initiative, allows members to bring certain issues to the fore of Community decision-making that might not ordinarily appear. It is in this context that an EP coequal with the Council of Ministers could presumably alter the integration dynamics from the focus on market enhancement to include social issues and regulatory development in areas such as labor (Rhodes 1991).

Second, a strengthened EP could advance positions in Brussels beyond that of purely national interests, which is not currently the case because of leverage by the Committee of Permanent Representatives (COREPER). In addition, the democratically enhanced EP would add another dimension to intergovernmental bargaining where Social Democrats do not occupy national office. Although the Socialist Group would not control a majority—nor would it likely in the near future—its size would mean that issue positions by the EP will be influenced by the need for coalitions. The Socialist Group is now large enough and, if cohesive, will play a part in any significant initiative.

Since becoming president of the Socialist Group, the French Socialist Jean-Pierre Cot has pursued a strategy of calculated confrontation in order to advance the powers of the Parliament. Commenting before the Maastricht EC summit on what he considers to be insufficient progress toward strengthening the Parliament, Cot stated: "If we want to seriously attack the problem of the democratic deficit in Europe, the Intergovernmental Conference has to change course. Otherwise, the European Parliament will be regretfully obliged to reject the results of the conference, i.e., to create an institutional crisis" (*Agence-Europe,* #5455, 20 March 1991).

This stand was reiterated only weeks before the summit by Klaus Hänsch (SPD), vice-chair of the EP Socialist Groups. He affirmed that the "EP should prove it is ready to make a reform miscarry if it does not comprise substantial enhancement of its own rights" (*Agence-Europe,* #5609, 15 November 1991). Immediately after the adoption of the Treaties on Economic and Monetary Union and Political Union, the SPD threatened to block German ratification. The party demanded "renegotiation of significant parts of the EC treaty on political union to bolster the powers of the European parliament and include 18 extra Members of the European Parliament (MEPs) for the new states of united Germany" (*Financial Times,* 13 December 1991).

The other area of transnational party activity experiencing change is the Confederation of Socialist Parties of the EC (CSPEC). CSPEC holds the potential to play a crucial coordinating role between the EP Group, the national party leaderships, and social democratic governments. It was noted earlier that transnational party federations such as CSPEC are the weakest of the party organizations operating at the European level. Since 1989, however, organizational development leading to a stronger capacity for CSPEC began. The February 1990 Berlin Congress of CSPEC adopted a report entitled "Strengthening the Confederation." Although no agreement was reached on shifting decision-making from consensus to majority voting ("representatives of *all* Member parties, however, spoke in favour of continuing the discussion on this point") (8), the report did make other useful proposals, among them programmatic renewal and secretariat upgrading.

The Kok Report on European party confederation (1990) states in its preface that only "a solid organization will enable the Confederation to become the platform where 'programmatic coordination' between the parties and those politically responsible on a European level can take place . . . before the parties and socialists in the European Institutions formulate their individual standpoints." To this end, a steering committee for policy development under direct responsibility of the Confederation Bureau has been proposed.

One initiative complementing programmatic coordination is the setting up of "networks." The report notes that member parties and the institutions, professionals, and intellectuals linked to them—for example, the SPD Friedrich Ebert Stiftung and PS ISER—regularly carry out research on European policies. It notes that these "initiatives and people are rarely brought together at a European level. Instead of the 'multiplying effect' of stimulating international contacts, more than often double work is being done. . . . [T]he Confederation could be really strengthened considerably if its own networks of specialists could be created. . . . In practice, this would mean providing the necessary organizational infrastructure for a selected group" (19).

Overall, the Kok report promotes transnational party organizational development, resulting in potential coordinating benefits for the EP group and national parties. If these benefits accrue, concerns about the single market, expressed in a national context, could be considered through a complementary, supranational avenue for action.

Adding to the pressures to bring the national parties into a common position, in December 1990 "socialist leaders met in Madrid . . . and agreed to a document which drags the more cautious parties towards federalism" (*The Economist,* 12 January 1991). This was the CSPEC Party Leaders' Declaration on the Intergovernmental Conferences, just about to begin at that time. The declaration treats economic and monetary union: "Monetary integration and cooperation and enhanced convergence of economic policies must go hand in hand with an increase of democratic legitimacy of the Community Institutions." Regarding political union, the declaration called for (a) "the development of European citizenship"; (b) "a coherent approach to Social Policy"; and (c) "a much stronger emphasis on environmental protection." To achieve these objectives, the leaders endorsed majority voting in the Council of Ministers covering legislation "defining certain fundamental social rights . . . minimal standards of environmental protection . . . and decisions where the Community level is the most appropriate." The leaders also endorsed giving the EP "the right of co-decision with the Council . . . the right of initiative over legislation vis-à-vis the Commission, and increased control over the implementation of Community legislation" (Kok Report 1990, pp. 5, 6).

In mid-July 1991, two weeks before the SPD Congress, the Socialist Group in the European Parliament called on the leaders of CSPEC to create a European Socialist Party. The motion stressed that the existing CSPEC "is still far from the Party Federation organization which is needed to meet the challenges European Democratic Socialism is facing. . . . Jean-Pierre Cot commented on the initiative . . . saying that a political union cannot be imagined without truly organized political Parties of European scale" (*Agence-Europe,* #5493, 17 May 1991). Along these lines, the new SPD chair, Bjorn Engholm expressed regret that "European social-democracy is still organized on an over[ly] national basis and said he felt it was 'urgent' that the forthcoming congress of the Union of socialist and social-democrat parties in Europe result in decisions on a more European social-democracy" (*Agence-Europe,* #5561, 6 September 1991).

To summarize, the steps taken to strengthen CSPEC, although embryonic, the potential for a more influential EP, and the commitments by all social democratic party leaders to support European Union indicate a level of activity in direct response to the accelerated pace of EC integration since the SEA went into effect. Increased regionalization and the social democratic dilemma have altered the ground rules of economic and social policy-making. This has highlighted as never before the gap between intentions and the means by which they may be attained. This fact was recognized in the opening of the Party Leaders Madrid Declaration: "The ever increasing internationalization of the economy and interdependence of our societies at every level means that it is increasingly difficult to respond on a national level to the new challenges which arise. Democratic control of the future remains possible, provided that those elements of sovereignty which can no longer be exercised in a purely national framework are pooled."

## CONCLUSION

The intensified pace of European Community integration since 1985, together with generally acknowledged growing interdependence among advanced industrial societies, should stimulate at some point a "learning process" or adaptation in strategy and expansion of horizons among national actors. The activity among business elites to build economies of scale through mergers is one sign of this adaptation. Early neofunctionalists would have termed this process functional spillover (Haas 1958, 1964). Apart from Brussels bureaucrats, the process of political spillover, or the transferring of loyalties to a central, supranational institution, is not quite evident among political actors (Streeck and Schmitter 1991). The evidence presented in this chapter has demonstrated that at the national party level, in terms of programmatic orientation and intransnational party organizational activity, Social Democrats are only now beginning to take seriously the true meaning of the absence of party political influence in EC decision-making, or what has been termed the EC's "democratic deficit."

The process by which individual social democratic parties come to this realization and their subsequent policies to come to terms with it are necessarily conditioned more importantly by national considerations. Deubner (1989) has referred to this process as the "internationalization" of socialist reform parties. This internationalization process can have as its primary source of change either internal or external factors. Deubner argues that in the case of the SPD, the primary source of promoting party internationalization was internal, such as the interest of German labor to secure and protect beneficial export conditions. Thus, the promotion of EC integration, at least in terms of economic integration, was a policy that German labor endorsed. Because of the strong ties between the SPD and the DGB, through party study groups and other channels, the SPD resembles the northern European social democratic party model with a strong labor orientation. Consequently, the promotion of EC integration was in step with the general desires of its single most important constituency.

Unlike the SPD, the French Socialist Party, lacking strong ties to organized interest groups, became "internationalized" by dealing with external factors. Although it is unnecessary to recount the story here, the experience of the first Socialist governmental term, 1981 to 1986, demonstrated the degree to which the external economic and financial environment can subvert policies intended to have a domestic impact (Cameron 1988; Hall 1987). The turnaround in economic policy was itself a process of adapting to European-generated pressures, such as prioritizing inflation reduction.

The two examples of external and internal factors promoting an internationalist attitude suggest a developed or developing policy predisposition toward controlling the environment beyond the national arena. In this sense, the resumption of European integration in the late 1980s, together with the Intergovernmental Conference negotiations, beginning in late 1990 over economic and monetary union and political union, has given social democratic parties an institutional focus more conducive to party influence, the European Parliament. Consequently, social democratic parties have adopted as a common platform the enhancement of the EP. The SPD accounts for the second largest national delegation in the EP Socialist Group, and so its explicit support for EP codecision and a European supranational party are logical extensions of its internationalist/domestic orientation. *The Economist*'s statement that the Socialist Party Leaders' Madrid document "drags the more cautious parties towards federalism" testifies to the pressure on various social democratic parties to overcome internal ideological and/or other factors precluding them from supporting EC political integration. Once attention to strengthening the European Parliament is accepted, then stronger coordination with other social democratic parties follows. Thus, growing transnational party activity and party-to-party relations, as with the French PS and German SPD, suggest that the reformulation of European social democracy may depend on the institutional development of the EC together with transnational coordination between national political actors.

## REFERENCES

*Agence-Europe* (1991). #5455, 20 March; #5477, 22 April; #5493, 17 May; #5561, 6 September; #5609, 15 November.

Attina, Fulvio (1990). "The Voting Behaviour of the European Parliament Members and the Problem of the Europarties," *European Journal of Political Research* 18, pp. 557-579.

*Basic Policy Programme of the Social Democratic Party of Germany (1989).* Adopted by the Programme Conference of the SPD at Berlin, 20 December.

Braunthal, Gerard (1989). "The Social Democratic Party: Reformism in Theory and Practice," in Peter Merkl, ed., *The Federal Republic of Germany at Forty*. New York: New York University Press.

Bulmer, Simon (1989). "The European Dimension," in Gordon Smith et al., eds., *Developments in West German Politics*. Durham, NC: Duke University Press.

Bulmer, Simon, and William Paterson (1987). *The Federal Republic of Germany and the European Community*. London: Allen & Unwin.

Cameron, David (1988). "The Colors of a Rose: On the Ambiguous Record French Socialism," *Working Paper Series* 12. Harvard University: Center for European Studies.

Cerny, Philip (1990). *The Changing Architecture of Politics: Structure, Agency, and the Future of the State*. Newbury Park, CA: Sage.

Dalton, Russell (1989). "The German Voter," in Gordon Smith et al., eds., *Developments in West German Politics*. Durham, NC: Duke University Press.

Deubner, Christian (1989). "Sozialistische Reformparteien und die Bewältigung von Internationalisierungsprozessen," in H. Elsenhans, G. Junne, G. Kiersch, and B. Pollman, eds., *Frankreich-Europa-Weltpolitik*. Opladen: Westdeutscher Verlag, 1990, pp. 314-328.

*The Economist* (1991). "Two Big Rival Families." 12 January.

*Europapolitische Perspektiven der SPD* (1991). Presseservice der SPD, 106.

Fabius, Laurent (1989). "A Left Programme for the European Community," in Piet Dankert and Ad Kooyman, eds., *Europe without Frontiers: Socialists on the Future of the European Economic Community*. London: Mansell Publishing for Cassell.

Featherstone, Kevin (1988). *Socialist Parties and European Integration*. Manchester: Manchester University Press.

*The Financial Times* (1991) 13 December.

Haas, Ernst (1958). *The Uniting of Europe: Political, Social and Economic Forces, 1950-1957*. Stanford, CA: Stanford University Press.

——— (1964). *Beyond the Nation-State: Functionalism and International Organization*. Stanford, CA: Stanford University Press.

Hall, Peter (1987). "The Evolution of Economic Policy under Mitterrand," in George Ross et al., eds., *The Mitterrand Experiment*. New York: Oxford University Press.

Howell, Chris (1991). "The Fetishism of Small Difference: French Socialism Enters the Nineties," *French Politics and Society* 9, pp. 26-39.

Lodge, Juliet (1989). "Social Europe: Fostering a People's Europe?" in Juliet Lodge, ed., *The European Community and the Challenges of the Future*. New York: St. Martin's Press.

Mauroy, Pierre (1990). "Intervention au Congres de Reunification du S.P.D.," *La Nouvelle Revue Socialiste* 11, pp. 123-129.

Nugent, Neill (1989). *The Government and Politics of the European Community*. Durham, NC: Duke University Press.

Padgett, Stephen (1989). "The Party System," in Gordon Smith et al., eds., *Developments in West German Politics*. Durham, NC: Duke University Press.

Paterson, William, and Alastair Thomas (1986). "Introduction," in William Paterson and Alastair Thomas, eds., *The Future of Social Democracy: Problems *and Prospects of Social Democratic Parties in Western Europe.* Oxford: Clarendon Press.

Pridham, Geoffrey, and Pippa Pridham (1981). *Transnational Party Co-operation and European Integration.* London: George Allen & Unwin.

Reif, Karlheinz, and Oskar Niedermayer (1987). "The European Parliament and the Political Parties," *Journal of European Integration* 10, pp. 157-172.

Rhodes, Martin (1991). "The Social Dimension of the Single European Market: National Versus Transnational Regulation," *European Journal of Political Research* 19, pp. 245-280.

Sassoon, Donald (1989). "German Social-Democracy Between a National Strategy and a European Dimension," *Il Politico* 54, pp. 425-439.

Scharpf, Fritz (1991). *Crisis and Choice in European Social Democracy.* Ithaca, NY: Cornell University Press.

"Socialist Party Leaders Declaration on the Intergovernmental Conferences." Meeting of the Leaders of CSPEC, Madrid, 10 December 1990.

Streeck, Wolfgang, and Philippe Schmitter (1991). "From National Corporatism to Transnational Pluralism: Organized Interests in the Single European Market," *Politics & Society* 19, pp. 133-164.

"Strengthening the Confederation." *Report of the Kok Working Party to the Bureau and Congress of CSPEC.* Berlin, February 1990.

Vogel, Hans Jochen (1989). "The Challenge of 1992," in Piet Dankert and Ad Kooyman, eds., *Europe without Frontiers.* London: Mansell Publishing for Cassell.

# 6

## Transnational Market Integration and the Green Project in Germany

Carl F. Lankowski

### INTRODUCTION

This chapter explores the challenges implied by the new dynamism in the European Community (EC) for one of the most remarkable features of German social development in the 1980s—its social movement sector. In the following, I seek to demonstrate the relevance of EC developments for movement aspirations. For the sake of manageability, the environmental movement will be the primary frame of reference. Still, this movement segment must be seen as part of a larger project of general social transformation. This chapter is really about the outlook for that project, and more particularly about the connections among its component parts.

Traditionally, political parties and nongovernmental organizations have been differentiated as to mission and strategy. Noting the deficiencies of the system of interest intermediation in advanced industrial, liberal parliamentary regimes, the new social movements, and the Green Party have sought to reform the traditional relationships. Some Greens went so far as to conflate the movements and the party. The Greens were to be the movements in the parliament and, as such, an antiparty party. Nevertheless, the logic of the political system created strong incentives to "normalize" the party, in the sense of providing integrating programs that aggregated and prioritized movement interests.

Despite the much broader social change aspirations of many of their activists, movements tend to produce "pointilistic" responses to situations affecting them. They are, by nature, "opportunistic" with respect to the arenas in which they operate and make their demands. Parties are oriented to the state and to the general exercise of power. The potential gap created by the different logics of parties and social movements has been convincingly demonstrated (Kitschelt 1988). This gap may be accentuated by the addition of political action arenas that can create a magnet for movement activity. There can be no doubt that the EC constitutes a major, additional point of interest aggregation for the movements. For that reason alone, the status of the green project will depend on how the party deals with the EC.

Just as the negotiations over the Single European Act were completed in late 1985 and early 1986, the Greens, complying with the programmatic imperatives of political party development, hammered out a medium-term "Reconstruction Program" (BuVo 1986). What was interesting about this "program to overcome unemployment, poverty and environmental destruction" is its attempt to relate to present-day institutions the Greens' vision of an ecological, socially just, nonviolent and decentralized society of the future. The Reconstruction Program was the Greens' most comprehensive and coherent programmatic document up to that time.

The document displayed the multidimensionality of its ecological concerns by spelling out the means by which air, water, and soil were to be decontaminated and secured against further pollution; production processes made safer, cleaner, and less resource-dependent; comprehensive recycling introduced; energy, agricultural, and transport systems transformed; urban development guided; armament industries converted to civilian use; and research and technological development brought under public control. The program also advocated measures to democratize the economy and provide for income redistribution.

In addition to the political appeal its authors hoped it would generate, it was designed to set the basic strategic coordinates of the green project for the medium term. For the purposes of this analysis what is most striking is its almost total obliviousness to the aims and strategy of the EC's 1992 single-market program. The framework was decidedly national—the Greens' internal market referred to that of Germany. Only in the area of air pollution control was there explicit recognition of the need to cooperate in a European framework. Beyond that, in 92 pages of text, the Reconstruction Program's only reference to the EC was a negative one—the failure of a determined French socialist effort to run a Keynesian-inspired reflationary policy from 1981 to 1983. And from this it drew the lesson that West

Germany, world export champion, should drastically curtail its exports, presumably leaving its market share to firms operating out of other countries, turning instead to products to be consumed domestically. The Reconstruction Program embraced a left-Keynesian strategy, in the sense that it assumed that public investments in the environmental and social spheres could be accomplished by way of fiscal manipulation and prohibitive regulations. In sum, the party simply did not acknowledge EC-Europe as a relevant arena of strategic action in 1986-1987.

Not that the party failed to recognize the necessity of cooperative international action for the environment. In January 1987 the Greens Bundestag group approved major funding for the development of a program-like document on international economic policy. The resulting working group, comprised of elected members and staff economists from the Fraktion's economics and international committees, aimed at producing the international analogue to the Reconstruction Program, that is, a reform strategy for the medium term based on Green principles[1] (Arbeitskreis ökologische Weltwirtschaft 1990, passim).

The working group strove to ground the international responsibilities of the highly industrialized, capitalist West in the Reconstruction Program, arguing that national reform made international reform attainable. An implicit economic self-containment concept animated the analysis. But there was also an important conceptual break with the Reconstruction Program. The desirable dimension of the economic space was regional and transnational, not national as in the Reconstruction Program. Significantly, the working group acknowledges that "the development of supranational structures in Europe is in principle the best response to the decreasing decision-making abilities of the old nation states." That said, the text becomes contradictory by condemning the EC's alleged incapacity to meet "the challenges of regional and global solidarity," while simultaneously pressing forward with an EC reform program. Moreover, the EC reform initiatives did not appear to be internally consistent. On the one hand, the demand was raised for democratization of existing EC institutions and "establishing multilateral EC merger controls." On the other hand, the authors called for the inclusion of what is now Russia in a transformed EC that was to have metamorphosized into a "decentralized European-wide federation." This federation was to be realized by an East European reform program based on pan-European institutions such as the Conference on Security and Cooperation in Europe (CSCE). European cooperation, in turn, was to be expanded to global fora. According to the authors, the United Nations' inclusivity made it the best framework for working out all important interregional economic issues.

The working group's schizophrenia over the EC derived from the rapidly evolving situation in Europe and the differentiation of internal party positions on foreign policy. Born during the spring of 1988, the first draft was completed by mid-1989. Between that time and the submission of the final versions one year later, reality had overtaken the program. Not only had East European neo-Stalinist regimes collapsed, but the rush to German unification also was rendering obsolete a major pillar of the Greens' foreign policy of self-containment.

The draft reflected the confusion within the party over its own identity. On the one hand, the fluid situation in Europe seemed to hold out the prospect of programmatically credible radical intervention. On the other hand, it appeared that the party was powerless to stop either the process of German unification or the process of EC integration. In this situation, the relevance of the pan-European CSCE faded. United Nations institutions alone could not respond to the European situation.

It would, however, be misleading to claim that even this EC assessment represented the Greens, since the document in question was never debated in a party forum in the way that the Reconstruction Program had been. In this situation it is appropriate to evaluate the EC as an arena for the realization of Green policies.

## THE GREENS' NONSTRATEGY

Despite the party's international economic program, the Green strategy enunciated in the 1986 Reconstruction Program continues to guide its approach to the EC. It is not unlikely that the strategy is a default position, a vector of two characteristics of the Greens: (1) lack of understanding of the relevance of the EC regional arena for policy, and (2) general foreign policy desiderata that have little to do with environmental policy. But to the extent that a positive rationale can be found, it may be derived from insights about the functioning of federal systems. In an application of collective action theory, it has been suggested that the EC resembles the German federal system of "joint decision-making" insofar as policies demanded in the constituent parts or "lower" level (Länder, EC Member States) can be provided only at the higher level (national, EC), but that the outcome is controlled by the lower level, as it is when decisions must be unanimous or nearly unanimous. A "joint decision trap" is set in which suboptimal outcomes are likely, either due to inability to reach agreement or because joint decision systems "lose the independent capabilities for action of their member governments" (Scharpf 1988, p. 258). In this light, the Reconstruction Program may be viewed as an attempt to "buck the tide" by restoring such independent capabilities for action.

Despite the apparent applicability of this interpretation to environmental decision-making in the EC, I would like to suggest that from the point of view of ecological politics, this may not be the whole story. First of all, there is no evidence to suggest that serious strategic thought had been devoted to the EC as an arena of action, especially not in 1986. Second, even if it had, policy may have been based not so much on the form, the federal like context of policies, but on their content. The joint decision trap analysis assumes a similarity of aims. Not only are national environmental regulation regimes technically heterogeneous; their scope, level of protection, and enforcement also varies over a wide range, reflecting not only different balances of social forces but also the existence of different historical projects in the member states. Even though the treaty framework, as amended, does provide an arena in which to articulate elements of a vision of an ecological reform project, these are secondary features that provide no direct avenues by which to affect historical projects. The problem is political, not technical.

Third, the collective action approach presupposes a "level playing field" for policy-making actors. From the point of view of the Greens, there might be two problems here. The first consists in the possibility that because the actors are states (ministers of national governments), the sectoral interests represented by the Greens are eliminated in all member states prior to reaching the Council of Ministers. The second and related problem arises from the possibility that the treaty framework itself, given its overwhelming orientation to economic growth, blends out significant and persistent ecological impulses. Although environmental problems are either thoroughly internationalized or highly localized, the treaty framework discourages an ecological approach. In sum, in addition to some exogenous reasons for the Greens' indifferent or negative EC posture, there are reasons that pertain to the policy-making process in environmental affairs itself.

In light of these aspirations and plans, how have the Single European Act and the (Maastricht) Treaty on European Union affected the locus of decision-making in areas of concern to the environmental movement? What policies have been promoted in the environmental area? How has EC development and policy altered the opportunity structure for the environmentalists? What strategic directions are now open to them? Specifically, is there still a rationale for a predominantly national orientation in environmental policy? Should such an orientation be neither desirable nor feasible, what is the role of national strategy in an EC frame of reference? Under what circumstances could an EC dimension actually clarify and strengthen a reconstruction strategy? What are the costs of not adopting an EC environmental strategy? How have German unification and the political-economic transformations in Eastern Europe affected this calculus?

The following sections survey developments in the institutional context of EC environmental policy and explore the energy sector in this context. The section entitled "The Greens, the Movements, and the EC" takes up the questions raised in the preceding paragraphs, and the section entitled "Outlook" offers some conclusions for the Greens' strategic posture vis-à-vis the EC.

## ENVIRONMENT

### EC Environmental Policy Authority

Whatever ultimate aims motivated their framers, the European Communities were set up to enhance economic cooperation. There is no mention of environmental aims in the Paris Treaty establishing the European Coal and Steel Community (ECSC) nor in the Rome Treaty establishing the European Economic Community (EEC) and the European Atomic Energy Community (EURATOM). Deliberate action in the environmental area commenced in 1973. Three developments combined to produce it: (1) the emergence of a policy subject from the "new middle strata" in the most affluent capitalist countries; (2) international agenda-setting by the United Nations at its 1972 environmental conference in Stockholm; and (3) the precocity of the EC as an international actor, as demonstrated by the ambitious goals set at its Hague (1969) and Paris (1972) summits.

The Paris summit explicitly mandated an environmental policy. The Commission obliged with the first of five draft multiyear environmental action programs. Originally, these programs were legally based on an expansive reading of Article 2 of the Rome Treaty (EEC), which refers to "an accelerated raising of the standard of living," albeit within the context of economic cooperation. Despite their rhetoric, it was admitted that the primary motive behind the programs was prevention of distortions in the functioning of the Common Market. The first and second programs focused on remediation, but the third program, adopted in 1983, embraced the notion of preventive action, and the fourth acknowledged the need for setting intra-EC standards at a high level. Nevertheless, even after the ratification of the Single European Act in 1987, which endowed the Communities with an independent legal basis for environmental action, the imperatives of market creation, as spelled out and further developed in the Commission's 1985 White Paper, remained the central thrust of EC action.

By its philosophy and constitution, the EC aims first and foremost at creating a uniform economic space within which markets can function to coordinate the activities of business enterprises. The Treaty of Rome equips the Council of Ministers with the means to reconcile technically differentiated systems through its articles on the harmonization of laws. Regulatory differences are treated as potential nontariff barriers to trade. A pivotal case in European law clarified this relationship in 1979. Reacting to the complaint of a German importer, the European Court of Justice decided that national differences were to be treated as technical differences only, and disallowed German customs from keeping out *Cassis de Dijon* on the grounds that the beverage did not comply with the definition of a liqueur established by West Germany's Monopoly Commission for Spiritous Beverages.

The provisions of the Single European Act, designed primarily to facilitate the market creation project, built upon the Cassis approach. In particular, Article 100A mandates qualified majority voting in the Council, in return for which the Parliament is given greater interventionary powers through a second reading of the privileged "White Paper" legislation.[2] Some of this legislation is highly relevant for any ecological reconstruction project:

- 79 of the 282 White Paper measures fall under the category "veterinary-phytosanitary controls"—many concerning hormone use, organic farming, and pesticide use.
- 5 measures refer to vehicular emissions.
- 13 measures on pharmaceuticals and biotechnology (genetic engineering) applications for medicines are included.
- 7 proposed measures concern free movement of chemicals (PCBs, asbestos, etc.).
- 12 measures cover the transport sector.

Moreover, the whole point of the market integration exercise at the heart of the SEA is to increase economic activity, the virtually inevitable result of which is to increase environmental stress. Responding to public outcries, the Commission authorized a kind of environmental impact study of the 1992 program. The taskforce concluded that, at the aggregate level, the removal of physical, technical, and fiscal barriers foreseen in the White Paper could increase the movement of waste, allow circulation of environmentally unsound products, preclude the use of fiscal measures for environmental management, increase air and road use, undermine land planning capabilities, and increase waste generation (Taskforce 1989, p. 2.27). Sectorally, energy, transport, tourism, and agriculture were likely to be significantly affected (p. 3.35). And regionally, peripheral areas were likely to suffer disproportionately from adverse environmental impacts (p. 4.19). As for the dynamic effects of 1992, the study foresees a general increase in economic growth and concludes that "in the absence of an adequate framework to stimulate the necessary further decoupling of economic growth and pollution and the use of ecological thresholds as the basic reference for policies, there is no guarantee that internal market growth is likely to be sustainable and to lead to an increase in welfare" (p. 5.16).

In coming to terms with the internal market's anticipated environmental problems, the taskforce takes a basically "communitarian" approach, offering advice within the parameters of official EC policy. The primary source of authority for proposed countermeasures is the new environmental title (Title VII) added to part three of the Rome Treaty by the Single European Act. The first of the title's three articles, Article 130-R, lays out objectives broad enough and principles penetrating enough to promise significant scope for policy intervention at the EC level. According to the Article, the EC may act "to preserve, protect, and improve the quality of the environment . . . to contribute towards protecting human health . . . to ensure a prudent and rational utilization of natural resources." When it does so act, the EC is to be guided by the principles of preventive action, correction at the source, liability of the polluter, and integration of these environmental concerns into all other policy domains. But action is to be tempered by available technology, balanced regional development, cost effectiveness, and the principle of subsidiarity.

While environmentally permissive in tone, the actual, effective setting for action at EC level is determined by the provisions of the other two articles. Taken together, Articles 130-R, -S, and -T do not move the EC environmental policy regime decisively away from the national regulatory conundrum inscribed in the basic architecture of the European Communities. In the first place, and quite aside from the qualifiers already in Article 130-R, that article does not contain one very important qualifier: that action should occur at a high level of protection. (This qualifier does apply to actions taken under Article 100-A, paragraph 3 [internal market provisions bearing on environment, health, and safety]). Therefore, the level of protection, rather than receiving "constitutional status," must be determined anew in each Council debate. Second, in contrast to the qualified majority voting procedure in Council for internal market measures, Article 130-S mandates unanimity, ensuring that market integration will be easier to achieve than environmental measures. Third, although Article 130-T allows member states to maintain or introduce more stringent environmental measures than exist in the EC, by ratifying the treaty, they agree that any such measures are "compatible with this Treaty." In the context of the Cassis ruling, with its "mutual recognition" principle involving freer circulation of commodities, more stringent environmental standards may be difficult to enforce. Finally, from an environmental point of view, some crucial sectors are perversely included in the internal market calculus (atomic power, transport) or excluded from sectoral treatment (energy).

## Maastricht

The Treaty on European Union, signed on 7 February 1992, amplified the schizophrenia between rhetoric and decision-making authority in the Community, but corrects at least some of the weaknesses of the SEA environmental articles.[3] Rhetoric, especially constitutional rhetoric, can be important. In this regard it is worth underlining that the treaty creates a union and that the EEC is to become the EC, the European *Community.* These changes are intended to signal that the European enterprise is not terminally preoccupied with market creation. The treaty framers put a political face on the EC and sought to enhance its social and environmental profile. The market continues to be the core of the integrative enterprise, but EC identity assumes social and environmental dimensionality. Hence, the union's basic objective is defined in terms of sustainability (Title I, Article B). The economic growth objective in the old Article 2 (EEC) is similarly qualified (Title II, Article G, para. 2). More to the point, the SEA environmental articles are modified (Title II, Article G, subtitle XVI). The amended policy objectives paragraph adds international cooperation. The principles paragraph in Article 130-R (#2) mandates aiming at a high level of protection. This paragraph then authorizes a "safeguard clause allowing Member States to take provisional measures, for non-economic environmental reasons, subject to a Community inspection procedure." Furthermore, the decision-making paragraphs in Article 130-S are amended so as to extend the cooperation procedure (qualified majority voting in Council and Parliamentary second reading) to all environmental matters (#1). Even greater European Parliamentary (EP) intervention under the so-called "third reading" or "negative consent" procedure (Article 189b) is assigned to adoption of environmental action programs. Unanimity is reserved for fiscal-environmental measures, town and country planning, land use (except waste matters), and management of water resources, and "measures significantly affecting a Member State's choice between different energy sources and the general structure of its energy supply."

In this latter respect the Maastricht Treaty acknowledges the strategic role of the energy sector in defining a member state's specific environmental profile. The same paragraph also allows the Council to use qualified majority voting in these areas, but only after a prior, unanimous decision to do so. Other environmentally relevant treaty articles appear as subtitles X-XII and XV of the EC reform provisions (Title II). The text gives authority to act in public health, consumer protection, transnational infrastructure projects, and research. These last two are introduced in the environmental dimension of regional development and in the "Economic and Social Cohesion" subtitle (XV). A social cohesion fund is established that can be used to help poorer areas of the Community finance environmental projects. Finally, the architecture of the union introduces a consultative "Committee of Regions" (new Articles 198 a-b-c) that parallels the text's general subsidiarity guideline written into the basic principles of the amended EC (new Article 3-b).

## Energy and the EC

Energy is a strategic sector with pronounced effects on the price system, balance of payments, foreign policy, and, last but not least, the environment. Energy systems are about the transformation of nature—for power in transportation and generation of electricity, and for heating and industrial uses—and for that reason alone are at the heart of political ecology. The fact that energy generation and use constitutes the biggest source of ambient air pollution thrusts this sector into the center of politics and policy-making. From an environmental point of view, the main issues in the field of energy come down to the mix of energy technologies and the overall level of energy use. Like monetary institutions, energy arrangements are a hieroglyph for the national system. National energy constellations represent the alignment of powerful societal interests—expressed in ownership patterns, pricing, and subsidy schemes—that politically are very difficult to disaggregate, the more so because government is everywhere actively and massively involved. On the other hand, this condensation of social forces makes national energy systems natural foci for environmental movements.

### EC Energy Policy

Thus far, not the logic of integration, but world events, and national interests have produced an EC energy policy. Energy played a key role in the schemes of early advocates of European integration, however. The central role of energy in national-level integration is precisely what led them to focus on it as a bridgehead to other efforts. Secure energy supplies and Franco-German cooperation were two benefits to be obtained by the Schuman Plan. However, national governments managed the switch to cheap imported oil, which produced surplus production and government-sponsored rationalization and subsidy schemes in coal over the course of the 1950s. At the almost single-minded insistence of Jean Monnet, the "relaunching" of the flagging integrative effort in the wake of the collapse of the European Defense Community in 1954 also focused on the energy sector. EURATOM had the same rationale as the ECSC: Supranational control over a single sector was supposed to have spilled over, producing cooperation in other sectors.

Against these expectations, there is more than sufficient warrant to consider energy as "the most spectacular failure of the process of integration" (George 1991, p. 116). On the other hand, in light of the recalibration of politics to reflect concerns about the environment, this failure is surely fortuitous. The technocratic character of the Community and the absence of any mechanisms to register social movement activity blocked competing visions of an ecologically revitalized European political economy. The "constitutional" status conferred on nuclear power by EURATOM has been particularly appalling to the movements since their emergence in the 1970s (Agenor 1975, 1976, 1976a, 1977, 1977a, 1979).

In the 1980s, two sets of EC energy goals were debated and adopted that featured targets for the optimal mix of energy technologies as well as the intensity and overall levels of energy use (Commission of the EC 1985). Although plans for creating an internal market for energy had not been written into the SEA, the commission viewed this as critical to the overall success of the 1992 program and produced a raft of proposals for directives (Palinkas 1989). During the Maastricht Treaty negotiations energy policy did come up, but action was deferred to the 1996 intergovernmental conference, which will evaluate treaty implementation. Once again, the EC improved its position in energy indirectly through the specification in the treaty of a program for "trans-European networks," which will include fuel and electricity provision, especially to peripheral areas (Treaty on European Union, Title II, Subtitle XII, Articles 129 b-c-d).

## Energy in the Action Programs

The EC launched its first environmental action program in November 1973, but it was composed prior to the Yom Kippur War and the debut of the Organization of Petroleum Exporting Countries (OPEC) as an effective international commodity cartel. Its energy provisions are restricted to studies of the forms of pollution, methods used by member states in combating them, the feasibility of doing research to improve these methods, and the cost-effectiveness of pollution control (Official Journal of the EC, Series C, p. 112, 20 December 1973). The second multiyear program (1977 to 1982) was similarly restricted to studies (OJ C 139, 13 June 1977). The political insulation of the energy sector is reflected in the fact that almost a decade later, despite the existence of active environmental and antinuclear movements, the commission reacted to public alarm over Three Mile Island with promises to improve (spend much more on) and facilitate the expansion in use of nuclear technology. Apart from this, there is no statement about the environment in the document (Commission of the EC 1983).

Organized by media, the Third Action Program covering the period 1982 to 1986 (OJ C 46, 17 February 1983), focuses on pollution remediation. There is no weighing of elements of the energy-technology mix. The reason for this is not hard to find: Member states were reacting very differently to the renewed oil shocks of 1979, at least with respect to the mix of energy technologies. While France dramatically expanded nuclear power generation, the German federal government, responding to Green Party electoral success at the Land level, called a moratorium on plant construction, pending a solution to the waste problem (Nelkin and Pollak 1983). In this context, the major theme in the energy sector continued to be the management of national political heterogeneity.

A brief look at the EC energy planning process beginning in 1984 clarifies the picture. Three factors come into play: the rising general political salience of the environmental dimension, the particular debate over nuclear power, and the internal market program itself. The major factors affecting the fate of the energy objectives shifted dramatically over the course of the 1980s. At the beginning of the period, with the oil price shocks of 1979 still fresh, the Community was preoccupied with security of supply issues. The recession, North Sea production, and interfuel substitution in favor of natural gas during the early part of the decade reduced overall demand for imported oil and is associated with declining crude prices.

Drafted in 1980, the EC's 1990 Energy Objectives[4] aimed at reducing (to 0.7 or less) the average ratio between growth in gross primary energy demand and the rate of growth of gross domestic product, reducing oil consumption to 40 percent of gross primary energy consumption, covering 70 to 75 percent of the primary electricity with solids and nuclear generation, encouraging the use of renewables sufficiently to increase their share of the overall energy budget, and working toward an energy pricing scheme that supported the other objectives. By 1983, apparent success toward fulfilling some of these objectives caused the commission to launch a much more ambitious effort to affect energy patterns in the Community.

The "New Community Energy Objectives" of May 1985 were based on major staff work that had been devoted to projecting energy market trends and reviewing policy preferences of the member states. Despite the ambitious scope of the objectives (seven "horizontal" objectives and six sectoral ones), the limitations of the exercise were defined in the document. The commission conceived of the EC role in terms of supporting research, development, and demonstration efforts for new and alternative technologies, monitoring energy developments, and coordinating policy. The objectives were intended as a device to articulate a purported Community consensus around which member states' policies could gravitate.

The energy planning process for 1995 began in 1984. These 1995 objectives were grouped in two parts. Energy policy was treated as a vector of other Community policy areas. This was acknowledged in the seven "horizontal" dimensions, which included external affairs (Mediterranean policy, Euro-Arab dialogue, etc.); internal market (especially regarding the "domestic" energy sources: coal, gas, and electricity); security of supply; energy pricing; environment; regional development; and technological innovation. Notably, environmental policy was given no special status in this listing. On the other hand, the sectoral objectives called for major reductions in the energy ratio (achieving the goal of 0.7 by 1990) and energy intensity (a 25 percent reduction by 1995, broken down by consuming sector: buildings, transport, commerce, and industry); reduction of dependence on foreign oil to 30 percent of total energy consumption; an increase in the market share of natural gas; and an increase in the share of solid fuels, even as the coal industry restructured itself. Solids and nuclear power were to be given priority in electricity generation (40 percent nuclear generation Community-wide). And finally, the objectives called for a tripling of energy use from new sources and renewables by A.D. 2000.

Even during the early part of the decade, discussion of the objectives revolved around the role nuclear power was to play. Indeed, the nuclear question became the crux of the debate between the commission, a staunch defender of the role of nuclear power, and opponents of that energy technology. The first occasion on which the division was articulated had been set up by the accident at Three Mile Island. The first directly elected European Parliament, debating the commission's updated energy strategy in June 1982,[5] was already deeply divided on this question, with the Socialist spokesperson, Mr. Helwig Petersen (Denmark) rejecting the report as "bad, biased, uncritical" and even "propagandistic," though the Socialist group had been divided itself on the advisability of the nuclear option. The Council of Ministers agreed with the commission's position, but only "on the understanding that it is for each Member State to make its own decision on this matter at national level . . . the realization of nuclear energy programmes on the necessary industrial scale firstly requires states to make a clear political choice on the objectives and means to be used; the Community provides a framework within which these states can find useful references and a grouping whose solidarity can be an effective instrument."[6] The commission's response was to mandate the writing of the third in a series of illustrative nuclear programs (PINCs) under Article 40 of the EURATOM Treaty.[7] Adopted in November 1984 by the commission and on May 1985 by the Economic and Social Committee, PINC-3 recommended that at least 40 percent of EC electricity be provided by nuclear generation by 1995 and at least 50 percent by 2000. Moreover, the EC should promote fast breeder technology and advanced reactor types, the continuation of enrichment and reprocessing services, reduced administrative barriers to transport of nuclear material in the EC (for example, at interstate borders), and movement toward a definitive resolution of the waste issue, in part by encouraging states to agree to welcome waste storage facilities on their own territory in principle. The PINC-3 objectives became the nuclear component of the 1995 integrated energy objectives.

The parliamentary response to the nuclear aspect of the 1995 objectives was determined by the activity of the energy (CERT) and the environmental committees, both of which entertained a draft resolution calling on the Community to abandon nuclear power.[8] The environmental committee, reporting its opinion to CERT in October 1985, while not endorsing the proposed ban on nuclear power, did insist on very stringent safety conditions (tantamount to a ban, perhaps) and insisted that nuclear technology was an issue that could not be decided at Community level; it had to be left to the member states.

In January 1986 CERT initially turned against its own rapporteur (the committee member charged to draft a report), a member from the Belgian Ecology Party, whose report supported the ban. The report had been rejected by the vote of 15 against; four in favor; two abstaining. Instead, the committee adopted the report of another rapporteur whose report called for a pro-nuclear position with modification of Part III of the EURATOM Treaty on health and safety procedures. A month later CERT adopted the Commission's 1995 Energy Objectives with a series of amendments.[9] Although the nuclear program still constituted an essential element of the preferred strategy, the adopted resolution proposed granting priority to solids in electricity generation for the Community as a whole.

The timing of the Chernobyl disaster (April-May 1986 for the most acute phase of the crisis) had the effect of deepening divergent national preferences regarding nuclear power (Joppke 1990). Already by August 1984 the Bundestag Greens had introduced a bill to end nuclear power generation in Germany. The installation of a Green as Hesse's minister of environment and energy in 1985 insured that the German political system reacted very differently from the French to the nuclear disaster. Information about radiation levels was shared with the German public and precautions were taken with respect to food products that might circulate in the EC (such as milk). For months, radiation reports focusing on food groups appeared daily in mass-circulation newspapers. A survey of the daily *Frankfurter Rundschau* by this author reveals continued coverage on a regular, weekly basis from the time of the disaster at least until 1991.

This situation placed the German government on the defensive and led to the creation of a national ministry for environmental affairs and reactor safety. Meanwhile, the Social Democratic Party could no longer resist demands to abandon nuclear power, a position adopted by the national party in 1986 on the basis of a study commissioned by the federal executive board in May of that year (SPD 1986). Not long thereafter, the German Trade Union Confederation (DGB) adopted a resolution with the same content. Such deep and widespread skepticism of nuclear power in Germany led to unrelenting, intense scrutiny of the industry. A major scandal involving the intra-European shipment of falsely declared nuclear waste with the complicity of public officials charged with supervision was uncovered within months of Chernobyl. Belgian complicity made the scandal a matter of hearings in the European Parliament.

Nuclear catastrophe in the Ukraine did not impede the Council from renewing the EC's commitment to nuclear power in the Fourth Action Program on the Environment (for 1987 to 1992), adopted on 19 October in the European Year of the Environment (EYE), 1987. The Fourth Program continued to emphasize the importance of combating air pollution, a priority that had been set after adoption of the Third Program by the European Council at its meeting in Stuttgart in June 1983.

The Single European Act provided a platform for a more independent environmental policy as well as an internal market for energy. It is not singled out for special treatment in the 1985 White Paper specifying the steps necessary to realize the internal market, but the commission launched initiatives in 1988 to include energy as a means of advancing the Community's 1995 energy goals. Aside from the Commission's intention of terminating the exemption of energy entities from the internal market's procurement policies, measures were promoted that were designed to increase energy price transparency, reduce subsidies, and encourage transborder energy transmission. These measures affect the German situation in two major ways. First, they challenge the special coal regime designed to sustain employment in that industry and achieve secure supplies (Lucas 1985, p. 245 *infra*). The second major implication for Germany of the measures designed to advance the internal market program for the energy sector is that they provide a potential vent for electricity generated by nuclear fission in France.

## Nuclear Power: A Case of Mistaken Subsidiarity

A directive permitting electricity supply through grids of other member states at "reasonable"—that is, nonexclusionary—charges was adopted by the Council in May 1990. This allowed "cheap" French atomic electricity to be substituted for German coal, once German coal subsidies were removed and the prices rose in consequence. A more compelling example of presumed equivalence of competing regulatory regimes in the circulation of commodities and services in a common market under the Cassis doctrine could scarcely be imagined. Indeed, the case of nuclear power epitomizes the problems of the single-market approach. After great political debate, Germany had decided to get by with much less nuclear power than France. In fact, as has been pointed out, strong forces were and are at work that are pushing German energy suppliers out of the nuclear business altogether.

A paradoxical situation has ensued between the EC and the states. At Community level, equivalence between nuclear power and every other energy source has been proclaimed by semantical fiat. Subsidiarity has also been acknowledged, in the sense that states may determine their own energy mixes. But the internal market program in energy means that economic equivalence is to be created between producers in different member states so that energy enterprises can compete. This kind of equivalence requires general agreement about the balance between the socialized and internalized costs of energy production. Only on such a common basis can competitive prices be set. But it is precisely here that equivalence cannot be established. Risk assessment includes an irreducible political core. Germany's deep divisions over nuclear power should be read in this context either as an assignment of costs to that technology that would price it out of the German market, or at the very least as an inability to reach any rational decision about the costs to be internalized at all. In this case the logical presumption should be impasse—that is, no Common Market in nuclear energy. But the commission's default position, backed up by the governments of other member states with large nuclear power capacities (indeed, relative over-capacities), is to preempt Germany's calculus by assuming what Germany has already signaled that it—or at least a large part of German society—does not accept. The commission's policy consists of an emphasis on uniform safety standards, low limit values for radiation exposure, a verifiable safeguard system for fissile materials, public access to all information, greater citizen involvement in nuclear planning, and complete cost accounting (Commission of the EC 1988; Palinkas 1989). Unfortunately, quite aside from the cost-accounting matter, already discussed, actual behavior by the nuclear power industry and its state and supranational sponsors does anything but increase confidence that these goals can be achieved. The Community's reaction to Chernobyl cast a momentary glaring light on each of these areas. Massive differences characterized public information policy in the different member states regarding radiation exposure. Those states most heavily engaged in nuclear power production provided little information and took virtually no precautions in the interest of public health. They did, however, attempt to promote measures in the interests of commodity circulation. On internal market grounds, the commission, backed by some member states, actually attempted to reduce radiation limit values in food after Chernobyl. When this step met with protest in the European Parliament, the commission threatened to circumvent that body altogether by decreeing a regulation under the EURATOM treaty. The outcome of any effort to move toward the entirely laudable goal of greater citizen participation in energy supply questions has already been prefigured by massive mobilizations against this technology wherever any openings in this direction already exist.

On a question of such political magnitude for the environmental movement and the Green Party, the Community's overruling of Germany's assessment of the costs and benefits of nuclear power, the Community has demonstrated the limits of the much-touted concept of subsidiarity. Admittedly, subsidiarity means different things to different constituencies in the EC, but for many, it is about respecting local priorities and values. Where these are emphatically held, any appearance of EC meddling may be rejected as an arrogant and antidemocratic abuse of power. In such a situation the Community runs the risk of purchasing the internal market with the legitimacy of the integration project as currently conceived and constituted.

Not surprisingly, this theme found its way into the Greens' campaign for the June 1989 European Parliamentary elections. Hearings were held by the Federal Working Group on Energy in September 1988 (BuVo 1988). German Greens in the EP Rainbow Group went on the offensive with literature designed to demonstrate the desirability and feasibility of a general and immediate nuclear shutdown (Rainbow Group 1989).

## The Road to Rio

The commission's internal market efforts with respect to energy had an environmental counterpart. Air pollution had been a focus of EC activity since the late 1970s. In bilateral discussions with the United States, the Community had taken notice of the link between chlorofluorocarbons (CFCs) and stratospheric ozone depletion. With the strong urging of Germany, the EC eventually adopted the Montreal Protocol in 1988, and went much further, staking out an international leadership position with its March 1989 ban on CFC production in the EC by 2000 (Jachtenfuchs 1990). In the energy field, initiatives for clean cars, air pollution from industrial and power plants, and air and product quality standards were adopted (Commission of the EC 1990a).

Several processes converged to quicken the pace of EC activity in modifying energy patterns on environmental grounds. First, the experience with CFCs convincingly demonstrated a compelling interest in tending to the atmosphere. Second, teams of scientists were producing credible scenarios of global warming if no corrective measures were taken. Third, the concept of sustainable development, as promoted by the Brundtland Commission, emphasized the necessity for industrialized countries to take the lead in reducing greenhouse gas emissions. Fourth, ecological politics was appealing to ever-wider circles of voters in EC countries. Green parties tripled their representation in the 1989 European Parliamentary elections. Relatedly, competition for votes in Europe's parliamentary systems led to the greening of virtually all political parties, making the council much more receptive to environmental initiatives. Finally, the commissioner responsible for environmental policy was an active champion of Green issues, and so facilitated and accentuated the Green EC agenda.

The council adopted a resolution on the greenhouse effect in June 1989, which invited the commission to propose ways of increasing energy efficiency and decreasing greenhouse gas emissions. In this context, the commission was able to repackage the 1995 energy goals in terms of global warming issues. Its concept paper of February 1990, *Energy and the Environment* (Commission of the EC 1990a), presents scenarios for reduction of fossil fuel use and announces plans to develop new policy instruments to secure the desired emission reductions. In light of stagnant or decreasing real energy prices, fiscal measures are promoted as a way of reducing use by internalizing environmental costs. Efficiency is to be bought with R&D support in the form of the JOULE, ECLAIR, SAVE, and THERMIE programs. Politically, the commission used the popular north/south global warming agenda to press forward with the nuclear option. Nuclear power heads the list of contributors to emission reductions in the commission's report. A regional dimension is introduced into the concept. Planning capacities at the municipal level are promoted.

The commission's agenda had the desired effect of integrating the green spectrum. Discussion of the commission's position led to the adoption of a resolution introduced in March 1990 by the chairman of the European Parliament's environment committee in May of the following year. Among other things, the resolution called for a 50 percent reduction of gross energy consumption by 2040, harmonization of levies on energy in the member states, introduction of a levy on nuclear power and strict legal liability for providers of such power, closure of unsafe nuclear plants, shutdown of all nuclear reprocessing facilities, and more stringent limit values for ionizing radiation. The report accompanying the resolution calls for general abandonment of nuclear power generation (European Parliament 1991). After the 1989 EP elections, the Greens parted ways with Danish rejectionists and other European regionalists to form their own EP political group. The relative national composition of that group shifted substantially; the French elected a larger delegation of Greens than did their German friends, the Italians also elected a sizable delegation, and an additional block of members came from Spain, Portugal, and the Benelux countries. Adopting a posture of critical engagement, the Euro-Greens strongly supported EC efforts to introduce an energy tax and geared their efforts to the UNCED process (Greens in the European Parliament 1991, 1992a).

For its part, once again, the commission was not acting in a political vacuum. The West German government was moving towards its decision of June 1990 to reduce carbon dioxide ($CO_2$) emissions by 25 percent of the 1990 figure by the year 2005 (Bericht 1990). Given that government's defense of nuclear power and its liberal market orientation, there existed a remarkable degree of alignment between the commission and the German government in the environmental field, especially with respect to energy. The governing coalition of Christian and Liberal Democrats used the EC as an arena to reconcile the Green policy imperatives emerging from the domestic political alignment, particularly after Chernobyl, and their own political coordinates. By staking out a leadership position at the EC level, they succeeded.

The high-water mark of this collaboration came at the European Council meeting held in Dublin in June 1990. The Dublin Council was devoted to the environment, particularly to the challenges of global warming. The German government's $CO_2$ reduction policy established the frame of reference for the Community's international profile at the United Nations' Earth Summit in Rio de Janeiro, scheduled for June 1992 (European Council 1990). The German position already anticipated the kind of market-conforming fiscal incentives, advocated in the commission's February 1990 paper, which would define the Community's position on the greenhouse gas convention in Rio. By hitching their policy to the EC negotiating star, the conservative government was spared from actually doing anything to implement it. In effect, by orienting themselves to the German position, the EC heads of state and government craftily adopted the same tactic toward the United States that the Germans had adopted toward their domestic Green constituencies. The EC environmental commissioner advocated adoption of an energy tax even if the United States and Japan refused to follow. One can only surmise that his refusal to attend the Earth Summit and his resignation shortly thereafter were only partially conditioned by U.S. behavior. My guess is that Commissioner Carlo Ripa di Meana also felt betrayed by the Community and most particularly by the German government, neither of which has actually adopted the tax.

Ripa's disillusionment also ran deeper than the Rio strategy. It was already quite visible in December 1991, at the advent of the adoption of the Maastricht Treaty. In citing the number of areas excluded from qualified majority voting in council, Ripa called the amended paragraphs "an empty shell," and went on to complain that "not a single proposal could be adopted through Qualified Majority Voting . . . it is not a system that can work" (*Europe* 1991). Commissioner Ripa di Meana was even more outspoken about the Maastricht ratification politics of commission President Jacques Delors. The British already had been granted an opt-out from the social provisions of Maastricht. During the spring of 1992, the government of Prime Minister John Major, eager to secure ratification against the "Euro-skeptics" in his own party, began to ask for a rollback of EC environmental legislation, especially in the area of drinking water standards. Delors accommodated the British in remarks in April. In June, three weeks after the Danish negative referendum outcome, Delors returned to the point in an effort to salvage the treaty. This waffling probably contributed to Ripa's abrupt resignation in June (öko Briefe, 26 August 1992).

In any event, the drama of German unification intruded to bring this phase of German EC policy to an end. That process both relieved the pressure from the Greens as the issue agenda drastically changed in the short run and brought fresh challenges from the EC.

## German Unification and the Search for a New Energy Consensus

By early 1992, Helmut Kohl was back where he was in June 1989, politically speaking. Eastern Germany's economic nightmare preoccupied the government. Gains at the Land level gave SPD governments, several with Green coalition partners, control of the Bundesrat. The significance here is that no recovery program for the East can be passed without the acquiescence of at least some SPD (-Green) Länder governments. Part of the reason that the Eastern German situation is so extreme is that unification entailed meeting the *acquis communautaire*. Derogations from EC legislation have been allowed during a transitional period, but eventually EC environmental standards must be met in the five new Länder (FNL). Moreover, the state privatization agency, the *Treuhand,* must operate within the guidelines of EC competition policy.

The German government produced its first comprehensive postunification energy concept in October 1991 (Bundesminister fur Wirtschaft 1991). There was an obvious convergence between the interests of the German minister of economics and those of the EC Commission, insofar as reduction in coal subsidies reduced the pressure on public finance (the minister staked his tenure on implementing substantial subsidy cuts) and struck a blow for market deregulation at the same time.

On the other hand, the municipalities of the FNL found it necessary to take the *Treuhand* to constitutional court over the assignment of communal energy production facilities to the West German quasi-monopolistic power producers. This was in violation of an understanding worked out prior to unification that would have sustained municipal property in municipal hands. At the time of this writing, it appears that the recommunalization of energy production so sought after by the Greens in the West will be allowed, at least in some respects. Although the EC has not been directly involved in this outcome, the willing reception of EC internal market ethos makes it difficult for the CDU/FDP government to intervene in this situation. Meanwhile, at least some parts of the German nuclear power industry appear ready to throw in the towel, though the precise financial circumstances have yet to be worked out. In the meantime, energy economists and engineers employed by institutions oriented to the Green agenda have produced scenarios for an alternative, nonnuclear energy system at the European level (Alber, Fritsche, and Kohler 1991).

## THE GREENS, THE MOVEMENTS, AND THE EC

The record of EC environmental policy just sketched out provides ample evidence for the proposition that in many areas, including those closest to the German Greens' historical identity—opposition to nuclear power—the constellation of forces and interests does not favor a level of environmental protection commensurate with even minimum Green expectations, let alone an alternative ecological society. Even worse, the energy/environment case study just developed demonstrates that the pretense of environmental responsiveness that emerges from SEA articles and the new Maastricht language can be easily instrumentalized by national governments to provide alibis for nonaction. A case can even be made that the particular characteristics of the EC construction have aided national politicians in actively subverting at least some aspects of national ecological reconstruction. Reasons enough, then, for confirming the Greens' generally negative posture toward the EC. Such a posture might be based on appreciation of the unique constellation of political forces in Germany. Or it might derive from the notion that high standards can be set in Germany, to be followed elsewhere. Alternatively, Green policies could be seen as precious achievements that ought to be realized wherever possible and defended, when necessary, with withdrawal from international associations that will not accept them. Finally, the Greens might argue that more general foreign policy desiderata involving the transcendence of Europe's continuing division after the Cold War require a non-EC but still regional and transnational approach. Despite these laudable motives, a series of considerations, some of them quite compelling, demand that the Greens start pushing in concerted fashion on the Sisyphean rock that is EC politics.

## Plaidoyer for Strategic Critical Engagement

In the first place, it has become painfully obvious that the EC is the site for settling policy issues of great moment for any Green movement. Hence, part of the cost of non-Europe for the Greens lies in the credibility gap that they will create if they continue to ignore the EC. "*Raus aus der EG*" is simply not a credible slogan. A nationally oriented, rhetorically radical program runs a great risk of falling into the "Erfurt trap"—into an untenable position like that of the Social Democrats between 1891 (adoption of the Erfurt Program) and the outbreak of World War I. Many nonparty environmental organizations and movement activists know this and have drawn the same conclusions. They are busy at the "slow boring of hard boards," which is the work of building up a Green lobby in Brussels. A bitter consequence of persisting in the national idiom may be in store. The "*Basis*" of movement constituencies may freeze into an abstraction as movement activists increasingly look elsewhere for ways of affecting important outcomes. Therefore, it is vitally important for the party to familiarize itself with EC institutions and agendas.

Relatedly, some key presumptions imputed to the framers of the Reconstruction Program, if once valid, are much less so at present. Policies adopted at EC level, with or without Green engagement, will override national legislation. The decisive point is that even if the Greens were able to preempt EC legislation, once the EC acted in the same area, German law could be vacated. Many matters are now handled by qualified majorities in council. Germany could be outvoted. Even those that require council unanimity, as in the fiscal sphere, may be passed with German ministerial assent. There is no viable alternative to using every means available to affect outcomes at EC level.

Furthermore, since most environmental problems do connect with the functioning of the economy—the fundamental insight of the Reconstruction Program—the appropriate site for tackling them is at the transnational level in line with the scope of industrial action, especially in Europe. This is obvious in the case of remediation programs for air and water. But it applies as well to waste, for example. The EC decides whether waste qualifies as a good or not, or with what qualifiers, and therefore how it might circulate in the EC economic space and between the EC and third countries. And it applies to a very sensitive point for the Greens, the commercial application of genetic technology. Attempts to solve problems at the national level may lead to the kind of "regulatory arbitrage" hinted at during the "industrial location debate" by representatives of the German chemical and auto industries.[10] Stated the other way, the more that is achieved at EC level, the greater the scope for even more ambitious measures in Germany under subsidiarity claims. The greater the gap between Germany and the other member states, the greater the incentive for regulatory arbitrage.

In 1986 it still may have been possible to presume that the political cards were stacked against the Greens in the European Parliament (EP), but this premise is no longer valid. Even in the period from 1984 to 1989 German Green European Parliamentarians took note of the receptiveness of colleagues in the other party groups to their initiatives. After the 1989 election, the German Greens are not even the largest national Green party delegation in the EP and comprise only a little over one-quarter of the Green group. If former GRAEL (Green-Alternative EP Group) affiliates are added, the Germans encounter a sizable block of sympathetic colleagues with fundamentally similar outlooks. Hence, although EP members from different countries will certainly bring different accents to the Green project, they are of the same political faith. If the Parliament lacks authority, the best solution may be to push for an increase in the powers of that body.

Progress can be made on environmental issues in the EC. True, the Greens' vision of a peaceful, just, and ecological European order will be refracted through the bizarre prism of currently existing Brussels institutions and the choking thicket of special interests. If anything coherent emerges, it is likely to be a project of environmental modernization. But when Mao was once asked how the revolution was going, he politely told his questioner that he would have to wait 100 years to begin to tell. In less than ten short years of Green participation in the European Parliament, much progress has been registered over an area encompassing 340 million inhabitants in making cars and industrial plants emit far lower levels of pollutants. Clean energy technologies have been promoted. Local water authorities have been screaming about the investments required by EC law to meet purity standards. Chemicals have been classified. Rolling multiyear plans and environmental surveillance systems have been set up to provide data, set priorities, and enable expert and public scrutiny to be trained on Community activities. The fifth environmental action program breaks new ground by projecting a comprehensive plan aimed at nudging the EC toward sustainability (Commission of the EC 1992). Remediation programs have been launched for Eastern Europe through PHARE, the Group of 24 aid program to Eastern Europe administered by the EC. Environmental consciousness and performance in the Community allowed it to take a leadership position at the Earth Summit in Rio. It is also true that implementation of EC environmental directives could be much better. Not all member states—Germany included—have adequately implemented the directive mandating environmental impact studies. The European Environmental Agency, a potentially important source of information, has yet to be established. But could a looser form of transnational cooperation be expected to achieve better results?

Governments earned the scornful and indignant public reception of the haphazard pastiche that emerged from the Maastricht summit. If this monster had applied for membership to the European Community, it would have been turned down as undemocratic. But the new amendments to the German Basic Law (Article 24) contribute to greater transparency and take an important step in constitutionalizing the status of the Länder in EC affairs, an achievement that cannot be overemphasized, given the dire challenges that confront the federal system as German unification proceeds.

The Greens carry on the great Enlightenment tradition; they stand for transnational civil society. But even if the party thinks it is representing movements everywhere, a strategy that emphasizes national measures is not easy to communicate to non-Germans. Preoccupation with national measures blunts the internationalist image of the Greens and may convey a "bunker mentality" instead.

In the post–Cold War period, the Greens see an opportunity to build a peaceful pan-European social and political order. To the extent that transnational cooperation is appropriate, should it not seek to engage the countries of Eastern Europe, including the Soviet successor states? Greens from EFTA countries as well as the Green authors of *Ecological Economics* think so (Gahrton 1991, passim; Arbeitskreis ökologische Weltwirtschaft 1990 [Group of Green Economists 1991]). The argument about the regional basis of cooperation rests on the presumption of organizational capacity. Whatever its faults, the EC has developed a legal facticity, institutional density, and a tradition of political cooperation that serves as the best achievable foundation for a process of regionalization. There is no question but that the EC is definitely in need of fundamental reform—*re*-form. But it is precisely the stability and the relative uniformity that goes with it that hold out the greatest promise for Eastern European countries (Reinicke 1992).

The precocious self-confidence implicit in the Greens' national strategy is admirable, but it is historically shortsighted. One of the lessons to be drawn from the UNCED case is Germany's flagging capability with respect both to financial resources and political attention to play its leadership role in environmental issues. As indicated earlier, the 1990 *Staatsvertrag,* which united the two Germanys, obliged the former GDR to accept the *acquis communautaire* in its entirety. They are EC environmental norms that have (yet) to be met in the FNL. Moreover, the same EC competition authority behind the detested internal market in energy is also available to help create the conditions for recommunalization of energy supply in the East. And yes, it was the EC that insisted no derogations from EC nuclear safety standards be permitted for East German reactors, a stand that facilitated their rapid closure[11] (Commission of the EC 1990b).

Finally, strategic critical engagement in the EC serves general foreign policy goals of the Greens. The Greens demonstrated their refreshing political uniqueness in being alone among the West German parties to resist the virtual annexation of East Germany by the West. They sensed the catastrophic social and economic consequences that would flow from the union and understood how disruptive a large Germany could become in the European state system. For years they had been calling for the Federal Republic to "recognize itself." When the Berlin Wall was breached, the party practiced the policy of self-containment it had been preaching and demanded massive aid for the reforming GDR in the context of a two-state federation. In this shining moment, the Greens were far better Europeans than any of the other parties in the political spectrum. More than any other party, the Greens conformed to the ideal of a united Europe beyond the nation-state. Alas! They were too early. Surely, the party that understood the need for a policy of self-containment when there were two Germanys will understand the need for a credible strategy of self-containment when there is one large one. If unification sent a dubious signal to the rest of Europe, then entertaining any dreams of dissolving Germany's thickest web of international connections would send one that is much worse. And this brings us back to the EC reform project.

## Differential Environmental Integration: *Durch Eigennutz zum Umweltschutz?*

Though there are several very good reasons for strategic critical engagement with the EC, there is still an important role to be played by precocious states in that context. The most sophisticated version of the variable-speed approach to EC environmental policy was written by Christian Hey and Jutta Jahns-Böhm for the European Environmental Bureau (EEB) in 1989. It formed the core of a White Book entitled *Concepts for an Environmental Community,* adopted in 1990 by 120 environmental nongovernmental organizations affiliated with the European Environmental Bureau (Weissbuch 1990). The differential or variable-speed concept is a response to the virtually programmed environmentally suboptimal outcome of EC intergovernmental bargaining in the Article 100A (EEC) framework. The differential strategy starts by acknowledging that the intra-EC productivity gap between regions precludes state-of-the-art harmonized standards. Therefore, a universal but ambitious minimum standard that all member states can meet is set. Those states whose political economies can stand it may apply the highest level of protection technically available. This prescription rests on a crucial finding: EC harmonization is not necessary in order to preserve international competitiveness. Even for those industries situated at the high end of the environmental investment spending spectrum, environmental costs are not prohibitive. The variable-speed geometry is to be supported by determined EC-level engagement of environmental NGOs pushing a reformist program. That program rests on three essential pillars: high standards, use of economic and fiscal instruments, and access to information (Weissbuch 1991).

There is already some evidence of the receptivity of the commission to this approach. A commission paper distinguishes between a "mandatory high standard based upon the best available techniques" and a target standard based on the "highest level of level of environmental protection which it is possible to envisage in the light of the latest scientific and technological findings." This regulatory approach is to be complemented by the introduction of an array of fiscal incentives, information provision, increased attention to enforcement, and R&D (Schneider 1991). This comprehensive approach has also found its way into the language of the EC's Fifth Environmental Programme (Commission of the EC 1992). The draft is remarkable for a commission document, insofar as, in framing the environmental question as a common endeavor involving all sectors of society and all levels of action, it amounts to an invitation to social mobilization. On the other hand, despite frequent reference to the principle of subsidiarity enshrined in the Maastricht Treaty, the document is tantalizingly vague about how it will achieve results.

## OUTLOOK

The Greens fashioned their Reconstruction Program in a process of self-discovery as a party. Despite the central strategic importance of the European arena for any ecological project, the program ignored the EC. As rafts of EC internal market legislation began to float past Green Bundestag staffers helplessly sitting on the sidelines, attitudes began to change, leading to an ambivalent statement on "foreign" economic policy. The West German Greens had been dismissed from the federal parliament for irrelevance in the December 1990 elections. They had run that campaign on global warming, focusing, in the spirit of Rio, on the contributions rich Germany should be making to planetary environment and development problems. Despite their unexpected defeat, the Greens can take at least some credit for the German government's ambitious $CO_2$ reduction goals and the precocity of the commission's agenda in the run-up to UNCED. Unfortunately, the brave words of both the commission and the German government have been nothing more than hot air up until now. Fortunately, the European Parliamentary Greens can continue to agitate on behalf of their agenda. There is more than a little irony in the fact that it was left to the East German foreign policy spokesman for Alliance 90-The Greens (*Bündnis 90/Die Grünen*), Gerd Poppe, to rise to speak in favor of the Maastricht Treaty during the Bundestag ratification debate, despite serious deficiencies in almost every area of Greens' concern (Poppe 1992). Gerd Poppe cast his vote hoping that the Maastricht Treaty was the beginning of a process of ecological reconstruction in a regional setting. Perhaps this sobering sequence of events will help the Greens and Alliance-90 relaunch their project by focusing on the pressing requirement of reconciling environment and development in the new Germany and the new Europe. As these two parties advance toward their own unification, there is room for cautious optimism that a new consensus may be emerging.

## NOTES

1. There is some irony in the fact that the fruit of their labor received wider attention in its English translation, *Ecological Economics in One World,* published by the Green Group of the European Parliament in June 1991—six months after the West German Greens were voted out of the Bundestag.
2. COM(85) 310 final.
3. The Treaty on European Union has seven titles with seventeen major subheadings (Articles A-S). It articulates its aims through an architecture based on three pillars: (1) institutional elaboration of representative and participatory mechanisms that also extend the scope of authority of the original three communities (EEC, ECSC, Euratom); (2) a common foreign and security policy; and (3) cooperation in justice and home affairs. The second and third pillars are built on the basis of intergovernmental cooperation, while the first further elaborates the supranational elements of the project of European regional integration.
4. Council of Ministers decision of 9 June 1980.
5. See Communication from the Commission to the Council on an Energy Strategy for the Community: Nuclear Aspects (EP Doc. 1-1065/81) and Energy Committee Rapporteur Pintat's report on same (EP Doc. 1-303/82). The debate occurred on June 18, 1982. See Debates of the European Parliament No 1-286/273.
6. Council 8552/F/82 (presse 109), released after the Council meeting of 13 July 1982.
7. Doc. COM(84) 653 final.
8. See "Report on the Future of Nuclear Energy" (CERT) and "Opinion from the Committee on the Environment," European Parliament, Session Documents, series A, Doc. A2-1/87 (19 March 1987).
9. See EC European Parliament Working Documents Doc A2-223/85 (4 March 1986) A Series, "Report on the Communication from the Commission of the European Communities to the Council for a Proposal for a Resolution Concerning New Community Energy Policy Objectives for 1995."
10. "Umweltpolitik lenkt Investitionen ins Ausland: Hoechst vermisst Augenmass in Bonn," *Frankfurter Rundschau,* 21 November 1991; "Die Standortentscheidungen des DIHT-Chefs Hans Peter Stihl," *Frankfurter Rundschau,* 8 February 1992; and Andrew Fisher, "Grass at Home Less Green for German Industry," *Financial Times,* 3 March 1992, reporting an Ifo survey of 500 German firms.
11. Commission Spokesman's Service, Information, August 21, 1990. "German Unification: The European Commission proposes a package of measures for the rapid integration of the GDR into the Community."

## REFERENCES


Agenor (1975). *Nuclear Power: Fuel for Debate.* Brussels: Nr. 55 (October).

——— (1976). *Nuclear Power: Stop and Think.* Brussels: Nr. 59 (June).

——— (1976a). *Nuclear Power: Hearings Report.* Brussels: Nr. 58 (June).

——— (1977). *Nuclear Power: Stop . . . Wyhl . . . Brokdorf . . . Malville.* Brussels: Nr. 65 (May).

——— (1977a). *Time to Choose, Guido! Open Letter to Mr. Energy.* Brussels: Nr. 68 (September).

——— (1979). *Jobs and Energy.* Brussels: Nr. 74 (March).

Alber, Gotelind, Uwe Fritsche, and Stephan Kohler (1991). *Energie Report Europa. Daten zur Lage. Ein Binnenmarkt für Europa? Strategien für eine europäische Energiewende.* Frankfurt/Main: S. Fischer Verlag.

Arbeitskreis ökologische Weltwirtschaft (1990). *Auf dem Weg zu einer ökologische-solidarischen Weltwirtschaft.* Bonn: Bundesvorstand der Grünen, August. Subsequently published as Group of Green Economists, *Ecological Economics: A Practical Programme for Global Reform.* London: Zed Books, 1992.

Bericht (1990). *Umweltpolitik. Bericht des Bundesministers für Umwelt, Naturschutz und Reaktorsicherheit zur Reduzierung der $CO_2$-Emissionen in der Bundesrepublik Deutschland bis zum Jahr 2005.* Bonn, November.

Bundesminister für Wirtschaft (1991). *Energiepolitik für das vereinte Deutschland.* Bonn, 22 October.

BuVo (1986). Bundesvorstand der Grünen. *Umbau der Industrie-gesellschaft. Programm zur Überwindung von Erwerbslosigkeit, Armut und Umweltzerstörung.* Bonn, February.

——— (1988). "Stromimporte aus Frankreich." Stellungnahme der Bundesarbeitsgemeinschaft Energie der GRÜNEN under Einbeziehung der Ergebnisse des Hearings der BAG-Energie v. 24.9.88 in Bonn. Bonn, November.

Commission of the European Community (1983). *The European Community and the Energy Problem* (European Documentation series). Brussels: Commission of the European Community, 3d ed.

———.(1984). "Review of Member States' Energy Policies." COM(84) 88 final. Brussels, 29 February.

——— (1985). "New Community Energy Objectives" COM(85) 245 final. Brussels, 28 May.

——— (1988). The Internal Energy Market (Commission Working Document). COM(88) 238 final. Brussels, 2 May.

——— (1990a). Communication from the Commission to the Council on Energy and the Environment COM(89)369 final. Brussels, 8 February.

——— (1990b). "The European Community and German Unification." April Supplement, *Bulletin of the European Communities* (Brussels).

——— (1992). *Towards Sustainability. A European Community Programme of Policy and Action in Relation to the Environment and Sustainable Development.* COM(92) 23 final (Fifth Programme). 3 vol. Brussels, 27 March.

*Europe* (1991). "(EU) IGC/Political Union: According to Ripa di Meana, the IGC Draft Is, in Environmental Matters, a Step Back from the Treaty of Rome," Europe: Nr. 5625 (new series), 6 December, p. 8.

European Council (1990). "The Environmental Imperative. Declaration by the European Council." Dublin, 26 June.

European Parliament (1991). "Report of the Committee on the Environment, Public Health and Consumer Protection on Energy and the Environment." PE 144.353/fin. A3-0124/91. Brussels, 6 May.

Gahrton, Per (1991). "Environmental Diplomacy: The United Regions of Europe," in Sara Parkin, ed., *Green Light on Europe.* London: Heretic Books.

George, Stephen (1991). *Politics and Policy in the European Community.* Oxford: Oxford University Press, 2nd ed.

Greens in the European Parliament (1991). "Struggling Against the Greenhouse Effect by Means of a Tax on Non-Renewable Energies. A Basic Step Towards Sustainable Development." Green Papers #3. Brussels, July.

——— (1992a). "Green Agenda. Principles and Policy Proposals on Environment and Development . . ." Green Papers #6. Brussels, April.

Hey, Christian, and Jutta Jahns-Böhm (1989). *Ecology and the Single Market.* Freiburg: for the European Environmental Bureau.

Jachtenfuchs, Jarkus (1990). "The European Community and the Protection of the Ozone Layer," *Journal of Common Market Studies* 28, no. 3 (March), pp. 261-277.

Joppke, Christian (1990). "Nuclear Power Struggles after Chernobyl: The Case of West Germany," *West European Politics* 13, no. 2 (April), pp. 179-191.

Kitschelt, Herbert (1988). *The Logics of Party Formation: Ecological Politics in Belgium and West Germany.* Ithaca, NY: Cornell University Press.

Lucas, Nigel (1985). *Western European Energy Policies: A Comparative Study of the Influence of Institutional Structure on Technical Change,* Chapter 5 on "West German Energy Policy." Oxford: Clarendon Press.

Nelkin, Dorothy, and Michael Pollak (1983). *The Atom Besieged: Anti-nuclear Movements and Nuclear Power in France and Germany.* Cambridge, MA: MIT Press.

öko Briefe (1992). "Streit um Auslegung des Subsidiaritätsprinzips der EG," *ökologische Briefe* no. 35, p. 7, 26 August.

Palinkas, Peter (1989). "The EC on the Way to an Internal Energy Market," *Intereconomics* 24, no. 5 (September/October), pp. 246-254.

Poppe, Gerd (1992). *Deutscher Bundestag. Stenographischer Bericht. 11. Wahlperiode, 126. Sitzung.* Bonn, 2 December. 10821-10823.

Rainbow Group (1989). "Nuclear Power: Immediate Shut-Down Possible! A Programme Outlining the Way." Brussels, January.

Reinicke, Wolfgang (1992). *Building a New Europe. The Challenge of System Transformation and System Reform.* Washington, D.C.: Brookings Institution.

Scharpf, Fritz W. (1988). "The Joint-Decision Trap: Lessons from German Federalism and European Integration," *Public Administration* 66 (Autumn), pp. 239-278.

Schneider, Guntor (1991). "Legislative and Policy Developments—The European Commission's Programme." Brussels: Commission of the European Community, November.

SPD (1986). "Die Lehren aus Tschernobyl: von der Empörung zur Reform. Zwischenbericht der Kommission 'Sichere Energieversorgung ohne Atomkraft.'" Bonn: SPD, August.

Taskforce (1989). *Taskforce Report on the Environment and the Internal Market.* Brussels: Commission of the European Communities, November.

van Ermen, Raymond (1991). "Gegen den nationalen Alleingang: Perspektiven für eine europäische Politik der Umweltverbände," *Politische ökologie* 9, no. 22 (June), pp. 27-29.

Weissbuch (1991). "Konzepte für eine Umweltgemeinschaft. Weissbuch der europäischen Umweltverbände für den Binnenmarkt der Europäischen Gemeinschaft." Reprinted in *Politische ökologie* 9, no. 22, Sonderheft 3 (June), pp. 6-19.

# PART IV

# EXTERNAL RELATIONS

# 7

## A Unified Germany, a Single European Economic Space, and the Prospects for the Atlantic Economy

James Sperling

The unification of Germany in 1990, the dissolution of the Warsaw Pact in 1991, and the ongoing construction of a single European economic space have accelerated the demilitarization of international affairs in the Atlantic area. An unwarranted "Europessimism" in the early 1980s generated declarations about the onset of the "Pacific Century" and encouraged an American reorientation toward the Pacific Rim nations. Today a "Euroeuphoria" has reinvigorated America's postwar preoccupation with Europe. Indeed, the prospects for a renewal and expansion of the Atlantic Community, for partnership rather than hegemony, for cooperation rather than disengagement, seem better than ever before. Yet the progress toward economic and monetary union (and political union) in the European Community (EC) has also fostered an American fear of a "Fortress Europe"; and America's loss of competitiveness in international markets and intractable budget and trade deficits have raised the specter of a "Fortress America" in Europe. The question, then, becomes which future will come to characterize Atlantic economic relations: a cooperative and reinvigorated Atlantic Community or two competitive and antagonistic trading blocs anchored by the United States and the Federal Republic?

The changed military-strategic and political maps of Europe undermined the preexisting interdependence between the containment of economic conflict among the nations of the Atlantic Community and the containment of the Soviet Union. Mutual security dependence no longer restrains the European (particularly the German) reaction to American economic policy. Moreover, American hegemony has been replaced by a more ambiguous hierarchy of power in the Atlantic economy: the combined gross national product (GNP) of the EC nations is equal to that of the United States; the yen and deutsche mark (DM) compete with the dollar as reserve and transactions currencies in the international economy; and global interest rates are set in Frankfurt and Tokyo as well as New York. The economic map of Europe has altered as well: Prior to 1990, Europe was divided into three regional trading blocs (the European Community, the European Free Trade Association [EFTA], and the Council for Mutual Economic Assistance [CMEA]) and a number of competing exchange rate relationships (ranging from the DM-dominated European Monetary System [EMS] to currencies tied informally to the DM or the dollar to currencies tied to the transferable rouble). The divide between the market economies of Western Europe and the command economies of Eastern Europe has been bridged; the nations of north-central and Eastern Europe have embarked on programs of economic and political liberalization. The prospect of a single European economic space encompassing the Atlantic to the Urals, of a single European free trade area with most (if not all) national currencies pegged to the DM or supplanted by a common European currency, most probably a convertible European Currency Unit (Ecu), seems possible if not inevitable in the not too distant future.

A unified Germany and the creation of a single European economic space raise a number of important questions about the future of the Atlantic economy and more specifically about the future of German-American relations in the 1990s: Will economic liberalization in Eastern Europe and the process of economic and monetary union in the EC create an able partner or a vexing antagonist for the United States? Is there an incentive for the Germans and the Americans to seek economic convergence in their macroeconomic policies and thereby ensure the stability of the Atlantic economy? What barriers exist to German-American economic cooperation and are they surmountable?

Answers to these questions require an examination of the structure of trade and patterns of investment in the Atlantic economy; of German unification and its ramifications for German foreign economic policy; of the creation of a single European economic space and its consequent impact on the European-American balance of power; and of the pattern of German-American cooperation and conflict over the issues of trade, exchange rates, and macroeconomic policy in the last decade.

## PATTERNS OF TRADE AND INVESTMENT IN THE ATLANTIC ECONOMY

German and American calculations of economic interest and the propensity for cooperation will reflect the current and future patterns of trade and investment in the Atlantic economy. The more tightly interwoven are the economies of Germany and the United States, the more likely is the prospect for cooperation or the emergence of a German-American "double hegemony," or duumvirate, managing the Atlantic economy. German and American investment patterns suggest common and interdependent interests facilitating a duumvirate; the structure of German and American trade suggests the opposite.

German direct foreign investment (DFI) in the United States has increased steadily over the past fifteen years. (See Table 7.1.)

Between 1976 and 1988, the American share of German DFI increased from 14 percent to 27 percent while the European share declined from 53 percent to 49 percent. Perhaps more significantly, the American share of German DFI in Western industrialized nations jumped from 18 percent to 32 percent between 1976 and 1988, while the European share dropped from 72 percent to 59 percent. During the same period, German DFI increased by 280 percent (from DM 48.4 billion to DM 184 billion): Investment in Europe increased by 252 percent (from DM 25.7 billion to DM 90.7 billion), while investment in the United States rose by 655 percent (from DM 6.5 billion to 49.7 billion). But the upward trend in German DFI in the United States has been accompanied by a sizable reduction in portfolio investment there: In 1966, almost 61 percent of net German portfolio investment (on a transactions basis) was placed in the United States (22 percent in Europe); in 1988 the American share dropped to almost 9 percent (the European share rose to 77 percent.)[1] Moreover, the Federal Republic held 14 percent of total short-term Treasury obligations held by foreigners in 1981. In 1988 that figure dropped to 0.6 percent, a shift that also represents an absolute drop in the amount held by Germans, from $8 billion in 1981 to $696 million in 1988. At the same time, the Japanese share of short-term Treasury obligations remained more or less unchanged between 1981 and 1988 (22 percent and 23 percent, respectively), although the dollar amount held by the Japanese doubled from $12 billion to $25.6 billion (U.S. Department of Treasury, 1982, 1989; see Table 7.2.)

Total DFI in the Federal Republic rose from DM 63.5 billion in 1976 to DM 109.9 billion in 1988. European DFI in Germany rose from DM

Table 7.1
**Geographic Concentration of German Direct Investment, 1976-1988 (in billions of current DM and percentage of total in brackets)**

| | 1988 | 1985 | 1980 | 1976 |
|---|---|---|---|---|
| World | 184.065 [100%] | 147.453 [100%] | 84.361 [100%] | 48.377 [100%] |
| OECD | 154.123 [83.7%] | 118.614 [80.4%] | 65.141 [77.2%] | 36.579 [74.4%] |
| Europe | 90.743 [49.3%] | 64.481 [43.7%] | 41.279 [48.9%] | 25.751 [53.2%] |
| U.S. | 49.686 [27%] | 44.348 [30.1%] | 18.234 [21.6%] | 6.577 [13.6%] |

Source: Deutsche Bundesbank 1983, 1990e. Author's own calculations.

33.5 billion to DM 69.6 billion between 1976 and 1988. American DFI in Germany rose from DM 26 billion to DM 35.5 billion, although the American share of total foreign DFI in Germany declined from 41 percent to 33 percent. (See Table 7.3.)

Between 1965 and 1988, the United States increased its direct foreign investment in Europe, while its investment position in the Americas and the Pacific Rim nations decreased. In 1965, 28 percent of American direct foreign investment was in Europe while almost 59 percent was in the Pacific Rim and the Americas; but by 1989, 47 percent of American direct foreign investment was in Europe while the share held by the nations of the Pacific Rim and Americas dropped to 49 percent. (See Table 7.4.)

However, the American DFI position in Germany ($23.1 billion) lags behind its American position in the United Kingdom ($60.8 billion) and Canada ($66.9 billion). Thus, 16 percent of total American DFI and almost 35 percent of American DFI in Europe is in the United Kingdom; the corresponding figures for Germany are 6.2 percent and 13 percent.

Table 7.2.
**Geographic Concentration of German Portfolio Investment, 1966-1988 (billions of current DM on transactions basis and percentage of total in brackets)**

| | 1988 | 1985 | 1980 | 1970 | 1966 |
|---|---|---|---|---|---|
| World | 72.855 | 31.524 | 7.712 | 2.021 | 0.810 |
| | [100%] | [100%] | [100%] | [100%] | [100%] |
| Europe | 46.971 | 13.524 | 2.727 | 0.612 | 0.183 |
| | [77.3%] | [42.9%] | [35.4%] | [30.3%] | [22.3%] |
| U.S. | 9.426 | 7.363 | 2.606 | 0.816 | 0.498 |
| | [8.8%] | [23.4%] | [33.8%] | [40.4%] | [60.8%] |

Source: Deutsche Bundesbank 1968, 1971, 1989c. Author's own calculations.

DFI in the United States is overwhelmingly European in origin (65 percent of total DFI in 1989) and has been at that level since 1965. (See Table 7.5.)

The United Kingdom and the Netherlands are the major European investors in the United States, followed by the Federal Republic and France. The German share has increased from 2 percent in 1965 to 7 percent in 1989, but lags far behind the British share of 29.7 percent. The share of DFI in the United States held by the nations of the Pacific Rim and the Americas has also been relatively stable: In 1989 the share was 33 percent as compared to 30 percent in 1965. Yet the Japanese investment position in the United States has grown from 1 percent in 1965 to 17 percent in 1989, making Japan the second largest investor in the United States after the United Kingdom.

Whereas the pattern of DFI by the United States and the Federal Republic indicates a more integrated and interdependent relationship between the two key nations of the Atlantic economy, the structure of German and American trade suggests a tendency toward regional concentration. The United States is not an important trading partner of the Federal Republic; nor is the Federal Republic important to the United States. Over the past 25 years, the United States has become progressively less important to the Federal Republic as a source of supply and as a market for German goods. (See Table 7.6.)

Table 7.3.
**Geographic Concentration of Direct Foreign Investment in Germany, 1976-1988 (in billions of current DM and percentage of total in brackets)**

| | 1988 | 1985 | 1980 | 1976 |
|---|---|---|---|---|
| World | 109.987 | 90.885 | 71.758 | 63.531 |
| | [100%] | [100%] | [100%] | [100%] |
| OECD | 104.537 | 86.462 | 68.116 | 61.499 |
| | [95.8%] | [95.1%] | [95.0%] | [96.8%] |
| Europe | 69.634 | 43.011 | 35.705 | 33.514 |
| | [57.4%] | [50.6%] | [49.8%] | [52.8%] |
| U.S. | 35.55 | 34.195 | 29.498 | 26.011 |
| | [32.6%] | [37.6%] | [41.1%] | [40.9%] |

Source: Deutsche Bundesbank 1983, 1990e. Author's own calculations.

German imports from the United States, as a percentage of total German imports, dropped from 14.3 percent in 1965 to 8.5 percent in 1989. German exports to the United States, as a percentage of total exports, have fluctuated between 11 percent and 8 percent—slightly double the export share of Eastern Europe and the Soviet Union. German imports from Europe, as a percentage of total imports, rose from 58.5 percent in 1965 to 70.6 percent in 1989. German exports to Europe, as a share of total exports, increased from 67.5 percent to 77.2 percent during the same time period.[2] Europe's position as the preferred supplier to the German market has increased between 1965 and 1988 in every sector except machinery and transport equipment, (the drop in the European share was compensated by a rise in the Japanese share from 1.7 percent in 1965 to 16.7 percent in 1988) Europe's role as a market for German goods has been enhanced during this same time period except in SITC category 04 (animal and vegetable oils, fats and waxes). The United States has lost ground as a supplier to the German market in every category; and it has become a less important market for German goods in every category except SITC category 07 (machinery and transport equipment—a category of goods where the American share of total

Table 7.4.
**Geographic Concentration of Direct Foreign Investment by the United States, 1989-1976**
**(billions of current dollars and percentage of total in brackets)**

| | 1989 | 1985 | 1981 | 1975 | 1965 |
|---|---|---|---|---|---|
| World | 373.436 | 230.250 | 226.359 | 133.168 | 49.320 |
| | [100%] | [100%] | [100%] | [100%] | [100%] |
| Europe | 176.635 | 105.224 | 101.409 | 49.670 | 14.009 |
| | [47.3%] | [45.7%] | [44.8%] | [37.3%] | [28.4%] |
| FRG | 23.059 | 16.764 | 15.840 | 8.765 | 2.431 |
| | [6%] | [7%] | [6.9%] | [6.6%] | [4.9%] |
| UK | 60.810 | 33.024 | 30.260 | 13.932 | 5.123 |
| | [16%] | [14%] | [13.4%] | [10.5%] | [10.4%] |
| Netherlands | 17.168 | 7.129 | 8.813 | 3.386 | 0.686 |
| | [4.6%] | [3.1%] | [3.9%] | [2.5%] | [1.4%] |
| Pacific Rim | 184.851 | 110.750 | 110.237 | 66.184 | 29.054 |
| | [49.5%] | [48.1%] | [48.7%] | [49.7%] | [58.9%] |
| Japan | 19.341 | 9.235 | 6.755 | 3.328 | 0.675 |
| | [5.2%] | [4%] | [2.9%] | [2.5%] | [1.4%] |

Source: U.S. Department of Commerce 1966, 1976a, 1983, 1990a. Author's own calculations.

German exports has remained around 10 percent. Germany's most important export sectors of the economy—chemicals and related products (SITC number 05), manufactured goods (SITC number 06), machinery and transport equipment (SITC number 07)—had foreign sales of over $257 billion in 1989: Europe bought approximately 74 percent of those goods ($189 billion). Moreover, the lion's share of German automobile and truck exports went to Europe—$39 billion (71.7 percent of total exports) compared to American sales of $7.6 billion (14 percent of total exports). (See Tables 7.7 and 7.8.)

Table 7.5.
**Geographic Concentration of Direct Foreign Investment in the United States, 1989-1965 (in billions of current dollars and percentage of total in brackets)**

| | 1989 | 1985 | 1980 | 1975 | 1965 |
|---|---|---|---|---|---|
| World | 400.817<br>[100%] | 184.615<br>[100%] | 68.351<br>[100%] | 26.740<br>[100%] | 8.797<br>[100%] |
| Europe | 262.134<br>[65.4%] | 121.476<br>[65.8%] | 45.731<br>[66.9%] | 15.533<br>[61.8%] | 6.076<br>[69.1%] |
| FRG | 28.233<br>[7%] | 14.816<br>[8%] | 5.402<br>[7.9%] | 1.286<br>[4%] | 0.209<br>[2.4%] |
| UK | 119.137<br>[29.7%] | 43.555<br>[24%] | 12.242<br>[18%] | 6.669<br>[25%] | 2.852<br>[32%] |
| Netherlands | 60.483<br>[15.1%] | 37.056<br>[20%] | 16.909<br>[24.7%] | 3.649<br>[13.6%] | 1.304<br>[14.8%] |
| Pacific Rim | 133.075<br>[33.7%] | 57.599<br>[31.2%] | 21.530<br>[31.5%] | 6.335<br>[24.2%] | 2.639<br>[30%] |
| Japan | 70.000<br>[17%] | 19.000<br>[11%] | 4.100<br>[6%] | 0.802<br>[3%] | 0.087<br>[1%] |

Source: U.S. Department of Commerce 1967, 1976b, 1982, 1990b. Author's own calculations.

The low American profile in the German trading ledger is reciprocated: Only 4.6 percent of total American exports and 6.6 percent of total American imports are bound for or come from the Federal Republic.

The Europeanization of German trade is matched by a corresponding concentration of American trade with the nations of the Pacific Rim and Americas: These nations' share of total American exports increased from 45.2 percent to 64.8 percent between 1960 and 1987; and their share of total imports rose from 47.5 percent to 70.1 percent. Despite these gains, however,

Table 7.6.
**German Foreign Trade by Group of Countries, 1965-1989 (in percent of total)**

| | Europe | North America | Other Industrialized | Rest of World |
|---|---|---|---|---|
| | | IMPORTS FROM | | |
| 1965 | 58.5% | 14.3% | 4.9% | 22.3% |
| 1970 | 66% | 12.8% | 3.6% | 18% |
| 1975 | 63.2% | 8.7% | 4.6% | 23.7% |
| 1980 | 68.1% | 8.6% | 4.5% | 20.6% |
| 1985 | 70.4% | 7.8% | 5.7% | 16.1% |
| 1989 | 70.6% | 8.5% | 7.0% | 13.5% |
| | | EXPORTS TO | | |
| 1965 | 67.5% | 9.1% | 3.6% | 19.4% |
| 1970 | 69.8% | 10.5% | 4.0% | 15.7% |
| 1975 | 66.5% | 6.8% | 3.4% | 23% |
| 1980 | 74.3% | 6.7% | 3.0% | 16% |
| 1985 | 71.4% | 11.3% | 3.1% | 13.6% |
| 1989 | 77.2% | 8.1% | 4.1% | 10.4% |

Source: Deutsche Bundesbank 1968, 1971, 1976, 1986, 1990d. Author's own calculations.

Europe remains an important trading partner of the United States: 23.8 percent of total American imports are from Europe, and Europe purchases 27.6 percent of total American exports.

A number of conclusions may be drawn from the structure of trade and patterns of investment in the Atlantic economy. First, there has been a regionalization of German trading interests in Europe, while American trading interests seem (more or less) evenly split between the Pacific and Atlantic economies. Second, the patterns of German and American direct foreign investment may serve to counterbalance the regionalization of trade that has evolved over the course of the postwar period[3]; DFI may

Table 7.7.
**German Imports from Europe and America by SITC Classification, 1965-1988 (as percent of world imports)**

**From Europe**

| | 00 | 01 | 02 | 03 | 04 | 05 | 06 | 07 | 08 |
|---|---|---|---|---|---|---|---|---|---|
| 1965 | 59% | 53% | 43% | 24% | 30% | 70% | 77% | 76% | 76% |
| 1975 | 68% | 71% | 42% | 37% | 55% | 84% | 81% | 77% | 71% |
| 1985 | 65% | 68% | 50% | 50% | 47% | 83% | 84% | 67% | 70% |
| 1988 | 70% | 81% | 56% | 69% | 59% | 86% | 84% | 66% | 66% |

**From United States**

| | 00 | 01 | 02 | 03 | 04 | 05 | 06 | 07 | 08 |
|---|---|---|---|---|---|---|---|---|---|
| 1965 | 8% | 25% | 13% | 7% | 20% | 24% | 6% | 20% | 7% |
| 1975 | 8% | 15% | 15% | 2% | 6% | 10% | 4% | 13% | 5% |
| 1985 | 4% | 14% | 12% | .6% | 5% | 10% | 7% | 13% | 7% |
| 1988 | 3% | 10% | 11% | .9% | 4% | 8% | 5% | 10% | 6% |

Source: OECD 1967, 1977, 1990. Author's own calculations.

weaken the need for an open trading system, however, if the investment is designed to evade barriers to trade. DFI could thus mitigate trade conflicts in the Atlantic economy and make painless the gradual disassociation of Europe and the United States in the real sector of the economy. Third, the structure of trade and the pattern of investment makes the emergence of a "Fortress America" or a "Fortress Europe" contrary to the economic (and presumably political) interests of the political leadership on either side of the Atlantic; and finally, the economic ties between Germany and the United States are not sufficiently intense to guarantee unconditional German-American cooperation in the management of the Atlantic economy.

The United States and "Europe" do have an interest in cooperating on economic affairs. But it is also the case that "Europe" exists neither as a policy-making entity nor as a negotiating partner of the United States; it

Table 7.8.
**Exports to Europe and the United States by SITC Classification, 1965-1988 (as percent of total exports)**

**To Europe**

| | 00 | 01 | 02 | 03 | 04 | 05 | 06 | 07 | 08 |
|---|---|---|---|---|---|---|---|---|---|
| 1965 | 82% | 68% | 84% | 90% | 76% | 65% | 74% | 65% | 73% |
| 1975 | 87% | 71% | 89% | 83% | 70% | 77% | 86% 6 | 3% | 80% |
| 1985 | 70% | 73% | 88% | 87% | 45% | 72% | 78% | 65% | 70% |
| 1988 | 75% | 79% | 89% | 84% | 53% | 74% | 83% | 72% | 66% |

**To the United States**

| | 00 | 01 | 02 | 03 | 04 | 05 | 06 | 07 | 08 |
|---|---|---|---|---|---|---|---|---|---|
| 1965 | 5% | 21% | 5% | .2% | 4% | 4.2% | 7.6% | 10% | 10% |
| 1975 | 2% | 15% | 2% | 3% | .6% | 4% | 4% | 8% | 6% |
| 1985 | 10% | 17% | 3% | .6% | .2% | 6% | 7% | 15% | 10% |
| 1988 | 8% | 11% | 2% | .9% | 1% | 6% | 5% | 11% | 8% |

Source: OECD 1967, 1977, 1990. Author's own calculations.

remains a geographic expression and political aspiration. Rather, the United States must now look to the leading European economy, Germany, for a partner. But the real (and politicized) sectors of the German economy depend increasingly on Europe. And Europe has expanded in geographic scope and economic promise: In June 1984 the EC decided to open talks with the EFTA nations to create a single European economic space, the EC Single European Act (SEA) mandated the creation of a single internal market by 1992, the EC and nations of the CMEA established relations in 1988 and continue to deepen them; and in 1990 the two Germanys were unified.

These economic and political developments in Europe raise an important question: Will the unification of Germany and the creation of a single European economic space hinder or facilitate the cooperation between the nations of the Atlantic economy?

## THE RECONSTRUCTION COSTS OF A UNIFIED GERMANY

Forty years of Communist rule had built what had appeared to be the most powerful and modern economy in the Soviet bloc. Europeans, east and west, anticipated the emergence of a unified Germany that was also a hegemonic Germany; Germans anticipated a relatively painless and rapid transition to a social market economy in eastern Germany and the accession of a unified Germany to a federal Europe. The economic costs and external consequences of German unification remain undetermined and uncertain (Lipschitz and McDonald 1990). Unification has complicated the task of overall economic management for the Kohl government; it has also made the Federal Republic a less pliant (and less capable) partner in Atlantic economic affairs.

Monetary, economic, and social union between the Federal Republic and the German Democratic Republic (GDR) preceded political unification and was established by treaty on 18 May 1990. The treaty committed the GDR to the principles of the social market economy and the economic objectives of price stability, a high level of employment, and external equilibrium; it created a single currency area by making the West German DM sole legal tender; and it established the Bundesbank as the sole German monetary authority. The terms of convertibility for the Ostmark into the DM were the subject of intense internal debate prior to the signing of the treaty. Many within the Federal Republic and the Bundesbank, in particular, considered the terms of exchange too generous and inflationary—a position still held by leading Bundesbank officials (*New York Times,* 20 March 1991). Nonetheless, the inflationary fear has proved unfounded so far.

High and growing unemployment has been an problem in eastern Germany since unification. In October 1990, the first month of political union, the unemployment rate in western Germany had fallen to 5.8 percent, the lowest level since 1981; and in eastern Germany, the unemployment rate had climbed from 3.1 percent in July 1990 to 6.1 percent. By January 1991, the unemployment rate in eastern Germany increased to 8.6 percent; the number of unemployed rose to 757,000 (*Bulletin,* Nr. 117 [1990], 1221; Nr. 129 [1990], 1347; Nr. 15 [1991], 103). Some expect the number of unemployed to exceed 3 million by the end of 1992, representing an unemployment rate of over 30 percent. It is possible, however, that the growing pool of unemployed may sufficiently depress wages to stimulate investment in eastern Germany. Unemployment may thus provide the basis for an economic recovery there akin to the postwar West German economic miracle. What is certain, however, is that economic collapse and growing unemployment in eastern Germany poses a formidable challenge to the Kohl government. It has also become apparent that an inability to reverse quickly the economic consequences of 40 years of Communist rule has the potential to threaten German economic stability.

The reconstruction costs of the eastern German economy were discounted by the Federal Government in early 1990: It was believed that recourse to the German, European, or global capital markets would easily finance German redevelopment. A tax increase was rejected out of hand; Finance Minister Theodor Waigel stated that "tax increases are not necessary for the financing of German unification" (Waigel, *Bulletin,* Nr. 89 [1990], 769). The need for a tax increase was denied until late January by Chancellor Helmut Kohl, who made his own "no new taxes" campaign promise prior to the all-German election in December 1990. It had been initially expected that the DM 115 billion Fonds Deutsche Einheit (the Germany Unity Fund) would serve as the primary investment fund for reconstruction; Chancellor Kohl described it as a domestic Marshall Plan (Kohl, *Bulletin,* Nr. 74 [1990], 639). But the eventual stress placed on the Federal budget reflected the enormity of the task facing Germany, the three-stage reduction of income taxes, begun in 1986 and concluded in 1990, that reduced Federal revenues by DM 50 billion, and the unanticipated $11.38 billion contribution to the allied effort in the Arabian Gulf.[4] The Federal Republic pledged $6.62 billion to the United States, $3.04 billion to members of the allied coalition, and $1.72 billion to Egypt, Turkey, and Jordan for economic stabilization measures. Tax increases and spending cuts were eventually announced in March 1991.

In his presentation of the Haushaltsgesetz 1989, Finance Minister Theodor Waigel projected that the Federal Government's net credit requirement would be DM 33.67 billion in 1990 and would decline to DM 25.6 billion in 1994 (Waigel, *Bulletin,* Nr. 108 [1989], 623, Table 1). In July 1990 he announced a modest upward revision of Federal expenditures for the years 1990 to 1994, but predicted a decline in the net borrowing requirement of the Federal government: In 1990 the government would be required to borrow DM 31 billion, but by 1994 that figure would drop to DM 11.6 billion. Moreover, the estimated cost of unification was relatively insignificant: DM 9 billion in 1991, DM 7.9 billion in 1992, 10.2 billion in 1993, and 10.7 billion in 1994 (Waigel, *Bulletin,* Nr. 89 [1989], 770, 771, Table 1). In 1989 the net credit requirement was less than 2 percent of GNP and Waigel could claim in May 1990 that the Federal deficit was at its lowest level since 1974; and that if one were to include the Länder and local authorities, that deficit would be transformed into a surplus of DM 5 billion (Waigel, *Bulletin,* Nr. 66 [1990], 571). In mid-1990 the projected Federal deficit grew to 3.5 percent of GNP, a change described by the Bundesbank as "a considerable increase."[5]

At the same time, the Bundesbank accused the Federal Government of circumventing Article 115 of the Grundgesetz, which limits net borrowing to capital expenditures. The Bundesbank took the position that the costs of unification were tied predominately to consumption items, rather than to investment (Deutsche Bundesbank 1990b, pp. 20-1). Waigel assured the Bundestag that the recalculation of the FRG's credit requirements for 1990 would "not stand in contradiction to Article 115 of the Grundgesetz" (Waigel, *Bulletin,* Nr. 120 [1990], 1260).

The third supplementary budget for 1990 (issued in October) revised expenditures upward and projected a net credit requirement in 1990 of DM 66.8 billion. Despite the radical revision in the net borrowing requirement of the German government between 1989 and October 1990, the Kohl government continued to insist that the reconstruction costs of eastern Germany would not place upward pressure on interest rates or require a tax increase. Impressive statistics were quoted to reassure the markets (and Bundesbank) that the costs of reconstruction could be financed from national sources: German capital exports are approximately DM 100 billion a year; the German capital market is worth approximately DM 300 billion; and annual German national savings amount to DM 150 billion, exclusive of eastern Germany. Moreover, monetary union ensured that German enterprises would have access to the European and global capital markets (Waigel, *Bulletin,* Nr. 39 [1990], 304; Nr. 66 [1990], 563, 571).

In late 1990, the projected 1991 budget deficit already stood at DM 65 billion and the combined budget deficit of the Federal government, the Länder, and local authorities exceeded DM 140 billion, though it was anticipated to decline to DM 100 billion in 1994. The International Monetary Fund (IMF) estimated that the net borrowing requirement of the German government in 1991 would amount to DM 189 billion, an amount equal to 6.5 percent of German GNP (Lipschitz 1990, p. 10). Moreover, the interest payments on this debt could consume 17 percent of the Federal budget by 1994 and will lead to a cumulative government debt of DM 1.5 trillion in 1994—a DM 600 billion increase over a four-year period. (*Die Zeit,* 24 January 1991). These projections produced an income tax surcharge, increased gasoline and diesel fuel taxes, and spending cuts in the *Haushaltsgesetz 1990,* which reduced the estimated net credit requirement for 1991 to DM 69.6 billion, a figure that excludes the borrowing obligations flowing from the Fonds Deutsche Einheit and the DM 28 billion credit assumed on behalf of the Treuhandanstalt (*Die Zeit,* 1 March 1991).

The budgetary costs of German unification have put the Federal government and the Bundesbank at odds with one another and have created tensions within Europe and the Atlantic economy. The Bundesbank's decision to raise the Lombard and discount rate on 31 January 1991 was interpreted as breaking the agreement of 21 January 1991 (*Wall Street Journal,* 1 February 1991). The Bundesbank has claimed that the interest rate increase responded to conditions on domestic money markets, which reflected the credit demands of German industry and the German state. It has nonetheless engendered recriminations within Europe at a time when Europe is seeking to achieve monetary union: The French, for example, charged Germany with simply compensating an expansionary budgetary policy with a too-restrictive monetary policy (*New York Times,* 24 January 1991). The process of economic reconstruction has created and will continue to create economic difficulties for the Germans and complicate Germany's relations with the United States and its European neighbors. Germany can no longer fulfill its traditional role as the "Milch Cow" for Europe and the Atlantic Alliance. The costs of reconstruction jeopardize the progress toward economic and monetary union in the EC, because the Germans are neither as capable nor as willing to "pay" for economic and monetary union with side payments to recalcitrant members of the Community. At the same time, the Germans are faced with the prospect of rising prices and a booming economy in the west and a collapsing economy and rising unemployment in the east. The Germans now have less flexibility in the conduct of macroeconomic policy at a time when the United States, France, and the United Kingdom are faced with recession and the costs of the Gulf War.

The unification of Germany was described by Chancellor Kohl as a boon to the international economy: Suppressed demand and the reconstruction needs of eastern Germany would increase demand for foreign goods and spur global growth. The integration of the two Germanys economically and politically was viewed as the model for the economic and political integration of the nations of north-central Europe into a single European economic space (Kohl, *Bulletin,* Nr. 74 [1990], 639). At this juncture it is not at all clear whether the unification of Germany will be the predicted boon to the European economy and the model for integrating Eastern and Western Europe or if it will pose a barrier to economic convergence in Europe and economic cooperation with the United States.

## THE CREATION OF A SINGLE EUROPEAN ECONOMIC SPACE

An important element of Germany's postwar foreign policy agenda in Europe—the economic and political integration of the member states of the EC—is nearing completion: the Single European Act (SEA) set 1992 as the deadline for completing a single internal market in the European Community and accelerated the institutionalization of policy coordination in issue areas ranging from the environment to foreign policy; and two intergovernmental conferences, begun in December 1990 and completed with the initialling of the Maastricht Treaty on European Union in December 1991, charted Europe's path to political union and economic and monetary union. But the transformation of the political map of Europe, particularly the unification of Germany and the trend toward democratization and market liberalization in north-central Europe, have redefined and reinvigorated Europe.

The Germans desire the integration of the north-central European nations into a pan-European framework. Chancellor Helmut Kohl, following the French lead, suggested in mid-1990 that the preferred framework would be a European confederation anchored by a federal European Community. But in the German version, a federal European Community could not exclude Austria, Sweden, Norway, or Finland; and Poland, Czechoslovakia, or Hungary could not necessarily be precluded from future membership (Kohl, *Bulletin,* Nr. 74 [1990], 640; von Weizsaeker, *Bulletin,* Nr. 74 [1990], 642). Thus the EC could envelop the majority of the EFTA states as well as select members of the moribund CMEA. The Germans, uneasy with a strategy precluding the former Soviet Union or the states of Southern Europe, have also looked to the CSCE as the architecture for pan-European economic cooperation; for the creation of a single European economic space (Genscher, *Bulletin,* Nr. 98 [1990], 834). The German preference for a single European economic space, complemented by federal and confederal political and economic institutions, is located in Germany's commercial self-interest and in its desire to allay the distrust and fear of an untethered and united Germany.

The anticipated integration of the north-central European nation—Poland, Hungary, and Czechoslovakia—into a pan-European economic, monetary, and trade regime reflects the progress those states have made toward the adoption of a market economy and democratic institutions as well as the formal dissolution of the Warsaw Pact in April 1991. CMEA member states were formally brought into the economic orbit of the EC with the EC-CMEA Joint Declaration of 25 June 1988. After the establishment of formal diplomatic relations between the two organizations, the Germans emphasized the complementary nature of the Western and Eastern European economies and then fit that observation into the broader vision of a single European economic space (Wilms, *Bulletin,* Nr. 144 [1988], 1298ff.; Kohl, *Bulletin,* Nr. 134 [1990], 1395; Nr. 140 [1990], 1483).[6]

In 1990 the process of reconciling Eastern and Western Europe took a further step with the creation of the Pentagonale, an economic (and political) group comprising Austria, Czechoslovakia, Hungary, Italy, and Yugoslavia (*Economist,* 25-31 August 1990). In early 1990, economic cooperation with the nations of the CMEA took on a new significance; it became an "important pillar of the pan-European security architecture" (Kohl, *Bulletin,* Nr. 68 [1990], 589). By the time of the Bonn CSCE economic conference in March 1990, the Germans made an automatic connection between the collapse of the Communist regimes in Eastern Europe and the future integration of the (broadly defined) European economy. The Germans envisioned the EC as the "motor of western support for the reform of the nations of central and eastern Europe"; as the core of a confederal Europe within the broader security and economic, architecture of the CSCE (Genscher, *Bulletin,* Nr. 122 [1990], 1273-4). Accordingly, the German government embraced the proposal of Jacques Delors, EC Commission president, to forge special association agreements between the EC and the nations of north-central Europe as well as Poland's near-term association with and future membership in the EC (Stavenhagen, *Bulletin,* Nr. 39 [1990], 299; Kohl, *Bulletin,* Nr. 134 [1990], 1395; Nr. 140 [1990], 1483); and in early 1991, Bundesbank President Pöhl indicated the need to keep open the door for the future participation of Hungary, Czechoslovakia, and Poland (in addition to Austria, Sweden, and Norway) in the exchange rate mechanism of the EMS (*Financial Times,* 5 February 1991).

The tentative and differentiated role assigned the members of the former CMEA (abolished in 1991) in German economic calculations differs significantly from the German assessment of the future of EC-EFTA relations. From the German perspective, the common denominators of the EC and EFTA nations—democracy and free-market economies—initially made those nations natural partners in creating a single European economic space and later in supporting the economic and political liberalization of eastern Europe. The SEA acted as a spur for the EFTA nations to gain a preferred relationship with (if not membership in) the EC. In 1989 the EFTA nations had expressed an interest in conforming to the legislation associated with the provisions of the SEA, and they suggested the expansion and deepening of the institutional fora for EC-EFTA discussions on economic and monetary issues. Likewise, the Germans have supported the membership of select

EFTA nations in the EC as full members, particularly Austria and more recently Sweden. The German desire for a tighter relationship between the nations of EFTA and the EC is in part a calculation of commercial interest: It forms the second largest trading partner of Germany after the EC (Stavenhagen, *Bulletin,* Nr. 20 [1989], 183). Closer commercial relations between the EC and EFTA would lead, inexorably, to pressures for stable exchange rates and consequently to EFTA participation in the exchange rate mechanism of the EMS—a step already taken informally by Austria and Norway. Full EFTA participation in the exchange rate mechanism would require policies of economic convergence on German terms and indirectly give the Germans the leverage over those nations' macroeconomic policies. Moreover, it would contribute to the creation of a single European monetary authority and currency capable of competing with the dollar and yen as a transactions and reserve currency.

The conformity of the EFTA nations with the legislation implementing the SEA represents a model for a future pan-European economic and political system. The Germans also have expressed the hope that EC-EFTA negotiations, begun on 19 December 1989, would be completed by 1992, the year that the internal market is to be completed. The German government has endorsed the engagement of the EFTA nations in the creation of a single internal market and view it not only as economically rational, but as politically important.

Continued progress toward economic, monetary, and political union by the EC nations is a necessary requirement for a single European economic space. The SEA and the outcome of the Maastricht negotiations are determining whether and how successfully Europe can negotiate with the United States and the Japan with equality and equal facility on trade, financial, and exchange rate issues.

The move toward a single internal market is well under way, but it is well understood that the creation of a single internal market remains incomplete so long as multiple currencies (and macroeconomic policies) compete with one another, even though, on balance, the EMS has muted that competition. The transactions costs of using a large number of currencies led the Germans, and other members of the Community with varying degrees of enthusiasm, to support the creation of a European central bank issuing a common European currency. The Germans have argued that without a single European currency, the completion of a single internal market cannot be realized (Genscher, *Bulletin,* Nr. 59 [1989], 522).

The outcome of the EMU negotiations reflects the German negotiating position in most particulars. The German government and Deutsche Bundesbank had established six general conditions for German participation in European monetary union: the completion of the internal market; price stability as the sole objective of any European central bank; a federal structure for the European central bank; the political independence of that institution from national and Community institutions; binding restrictions on the monetary financing of national or community budgets; and parallel progress the convergence of economic policies and performance (Bangemann, *Bulletin,* Nr. 149 [1988], 1339-40; Deutsche Bundesbank 1988, p. 22; Deutsche Bundesbank 1990a, 5; 1990c, p. 29ff; Kohl, *Bulletin,* Nr. 98 [1989], 907; Kohl, *Bulletin,* Nr. 69 [1989], 612; Stavenhagen, *Bulletin,* Nr. 39 [1990], 300; Voss, *Bulletin,* Nr. 30 [1990], 301). Moreover, the chancellor and the Bundesbank have assured the German public that during the transition to full monetary union (on German conditions), neither the statutory obligation of the Bundesbank to target price stability nor its political independence would be jeopardized. Both the German government and Bundesbank jealously guard the Bundesbank's domestic monetary autonomy and its informal role as the manager of Europe's money. (Kohl, *Bulletin,* Nr. 136 [1990], 1407; Deutsche Bundesbank 1990a, pp. 5-6; Kohl, *Bulletin,* Nr. 20 [1988], 1633; Deutscher Bundestag 1988, pp. 3994C, 3995C).

The Hannover Summit of 1988 mandated a report outlining the challenges, barriers, and institutional requirements for monetary and economic union. The subsequent report, named after committee chair and EC Commission President Jacques Delors, established a three-stage process for achieving economic and monetary union. Perhaps more important, it arrived at a set of principles guiding the process and end point of monetary union; and those principles conformed generally to German preferences: price stability, the independence of a federal European central bank, prohibition of the financing of public debt by central bank borrowing, and the emphasis on market solutions to economic problems. These principles were complemented by the requirements of economic union, particularly the need for coordinated macroeconomic policies and binding rules for budgetary policies (European Commission 1989). The principles of economic and monetary union, as well as the institutional outline of a European System of Central Banks (ECBS), were ratified at the Madrid meeting of June 1989.

The Germans have insisted that economic convergence among the member states of the EC—measured by price stability, the level of net public borrowing as a percentage of GNP, and external balance—precede monetary union. Although the exchange rate mechanism of the EMS established a framework for economic convergence and the convergence of national economic policies, the final stage of monetary union—the incontrovertible fixing of national currencies and the introduction of a European currency—depends on the actual convergence of national economic performances and policies; and convergence has come to mean conformity to the German preference for fiscal rectitude and price stability (Bangemann, *Bulletin,* Nr. 149 [1988], 1339; Genscher, *Statements and Speeches* [1988], p. 2; Kohl, *Bulletin,* Nr. 59 [1990], 462; Kohl, *Bulletin,* Nr. 144 [1989], 1221; Kohl, *Bulletin,* Nr. 88 [1988], 800; Nr. 40 [1985], 336).

The institutional outlines of the proposed European System of Central Banks (ESCB) had taken shape by the end of 1990: It will have a federal structure; its membership will comprise the member state central banks and a central body; ESCB Council membership will be drawn from the governors (or presidents) of the member state central banks and a smaller number from the central body; and monetary policy will be made by simple majority. Bundesbank President Karl Otto Pöhl had favored a ESCB modeled on the American Federal Reserve System: There would be a board of governors representing the "European" interest and a rotating vote among the national central banks, with the exception of the Bundesbank (parallel to the role of the New York Federal Reserve Bank in the United States) that would have a permanent seat and a privileged position in the Community (*Die Zeit,* February 2, 1990, p. 8; European Commission 1991, p. 2). The Bundesbank, jealous of its policy autonomy and political independence, has suggested that the EC member states, in anticipation of European monetary union, begin the process of monetary emancipation with the granting of statutory independence to national central banks (Deutsche Bundesbank 1990a, p. 32). The Germans are simply asking that the EC governments act upon the commitment made at the Madrid Summit, namely, the granting of political independence to their central banks. Despite EC efforts to accommodate the Germans on the principles of monetary union and the definition of economic convergence, the Germans remain fearful that stable DM may be sacrificed on the altar of European monetary union. And this fear, if not distrust, has led the Germans to propose the postponement of the decision to create the ESCB in 1997 rather than in 1994; that is, at the end of the second stage of economic and monetary union rather than at the beginning, "as proposed in the Delors Report (*Economist,* 2-8 March 1991). The Bundesbank is undoubtedly aware that once the ESCB is established and the final stage of monetary union is completed, the German capacity to manage Europe's money will be shared with the other (and less inflation averse) central banks of the Community; and the German definition of price stability may not survive.

The German government expects the completion of the single internal market in 1992 to be followed by the parallel development of economic and monetary union and political union. The German conception of European political union is both federal and confederal: The nations of the EC, EFTA, and north-central Europe will form a United States of Europe that is confederated with the remainder of Europe, including the Soviet successor states. The German conception of economic and monetary union is simply a single European economic space governed by German economic precepts; and secondarily, the aggregation of European economic power to create a pole of economic power capable of competing with the United States and Japan. The development of Europe politically and economically is contingent upon a number of variables, ranging from the German willingness (along with that of the French and the British in particular) to relinquish economic and monetary sovereignty to Community institutions to the continued demilitarization of interstate relations in Europe.

Chancellor Kohl observed that prior to progress towards a single internal market, the future was believed to be in the Pacific Rim and between the Japan and the United States. The Single European Act and all that has followed—economically, monetarily, and politically—led him to suggest that the 1990s could become the decade of Europe (Kohl, *Bulletin,* Nr. 59 [1990], 462; Nr. 68 [1990], p. 587). It may well be the decade of Europe, but where and how does the United States fit in? If the monetary and trade disputes of the 1980s foreshadow the future, Europe and the United States may find it easier to turn eastward or inward to resolve the economic challenges of the 1990s.

## A Decade of Tension in the Atlantic Economy

The impending formation of a single European economic space, the progress toward economic and monetary union within the European Community, and German economic policies caught between the demands of German unification and European union do not promise a willing or pliable partner in Germany (or Europe) for the United States. German trade is concentrated in Europe, and as income levels rise in north-central Europe and the Soviet successor states, it should become further concentrated in Europe. And even though Europe is a major trading partner for the United States, the free trade agreement between Canada and the United States and the tripartite negotiations among Canada, Mexico, and the United States promise a vast North American free trade area prejudicing European access to the American market. The emergence of the DM as the antipolar currency of the dollar and the probable role of the ECU as a direct competitor of the dollar (and the yen) as a reserve, transaction, and intervention currency reinforce the potential for a fragmentation of the Atlantic economy into two trade blocs. Moreover, the pattern of German and American direct foreign investment may consolidate rather than mitigate existing trade patterns: Direct foreign investment may make trade increasingly unimportant and depoliticize economic relations so long as there are no significant restrictions on capital flows. It is clear, however, that the economic interests and futures of the Federal Republic and the United States are not symmetrically interdependent; the trade, capital, and currency relationships between these two states do not indicate that either one has an unconditional interest in the sustained coordination of macroeconomic policies or in the convergence of economic performance required for a stable Atlantic economy.

The brief period of economic comity created after the Bonn Summit in 1978—supported by the Carter administration's subsequent rescue package for the dollar in November 1978 and the creation of the EMS as a self-help measure guaranteeing a "zone of monetary stability" in Europe—ended shortly after the Reagan administration implemented its fiscal and monetary policies. High American interest rates and a climbing dollar ultimately led to instability in the foreign exchange markets between 1981 and 1985. The steady rise of the DM against the dollar between 1981 and 1985 exasperated the Federal government and the Bundesbank; both had lost a considerable degree of control over the German economy, particularly the level of interest rates and the value of the DM. In 1983 the Bundesbank described the DM as the "antipolar" currency of the dollar; that is, the value of the DM was inversely related to the value of the dollar (a relationship reflecting both the openness of the German capital market and the growing reserve currency role of the DM). Thus, the Bundesbank complained that the DM-to-dollar exchange rate did not reflect economic fundamentals—the large German current account surplus, the consolidation of the West German Federal budget, and a modest revival of economic activity (Deutsche Bundesbank 1984, pp. 24, 28, 51, and 66). The depreciation of the DM against the dollar made West German goods more competitive on the European and global markets, but it also risked higher inflation owing to increased import prices. It was also believed within the Federal Republic that an ever-appreciating dollar and high American interest rates forced the Bundesbank to follow more restrictive policies than domestic economic conditions required (Sachverstaendigenrat 1984, section 16), because the "antipolar" role of the DM subordinated the Bundesbank's monetary policy to the requirements of external balance rather than to the requirements of domestic growth and structural unemployment.

The Reagan administration dismayed the West Germans with continued denials that there was a connection between high real interest rates, an overvalued dollar, and massive American trade deficits (Sperling 1989, pp. 388-389, Tables 17.1-17.5). Moreover, different political and economic priorities at either end of Pennsylvania Avenue ruled out any significant reduction of the budget deficit and consequently of interest rates, of the dollar's overvaluation, or of the American trade deficit. Once the administration acknowledged that a "strong" dollar did not necessarily translate into a "strong" American economy and feared that the deindustrialization of America was linked to an overvalued dollar, the United States retreated from its earlier insistence that the market determine the dollar's value. Thus when the United States turned to West Germany and Japan to reverse the dollar's climb in September 1985, it found a reluctant and suspicious partner in the Federal Republic.

In September 1985, the finance ministers of the G-5 nations met at the Plaza Hotel in New York. They agreed to effect an orderly appreciation of their currencies against the dollar with the coordinated intervention by their monetary authorities in the foreign exchange markets. The Plaza Agreement helped "correct" the overvaluation of the dollar and paved the way for a coordinated interest rate reduction in 1986, but the West Germans nonetheless resisted American pressures to adopt more expansionary fiscal and monetary policies until the United States made serious cuts in the budget deficit (Sachverstaendigenrat 1985, section 12; Stoltenberg 1986, p. 103). The Plaza meeting was heralded by many as the beginning of a new phase of monetary cooperation between the major industrialized nations. Despite the coordinated intervention by the major central banks in the foreign exchange markets, the Federal Reserve Board insisted that the Plaza meeting only "drew attention to changes already occurring in fundamental economic conditions in the world" that had not yet been reflected in the structure of exchange rates (Axilrod 1986, pp. 15ff). After the Baker-Miyazawa accord failed to stabilize the dollar-yen rate in early 1987, the dollar continued to decline and occasioned renewed turbulence in the foreign exchange markets.

At the February 1987 Louvre meeting, the major industrial nations agreed to stabilize exchange rates at the existing levels and to intervene in the exchange markets toward that end. But over the course of 1987, the West Germans voiced their concern that the United States would rely on a depreciating dollar rather than on corrective domestic economic policies to reverse the American trade deficit (Stoltenberg, *Bulletin,* Nr. 36 [1987],

309-310). After the October 1987 stock market crash, the G-7 met in late December and reaffirmed its intention to stabilize exchange rates in accordance with the Louvre Accord. The December meeting committed the United States to significant cuts in the budget deficit, the Japanese to expansionary economic policies consistent with a reduction of their trade surplus, and the West Germans to tax cuts and an interest rate reduction. The Bundesbank coordinated an interest rate reduction among the EMS countries, but it only provided limited support for the dollar (Federal Reserve Board 1987, pp. 48-53; 1988, pp. 54-59). But the Americans failed to make a significant cut in the federal budget deficit despite Gramm-Rudman-Hollings legislation.

At successive G-7 meetings and economic summits, the United States was reminded that the reduction of American budget deficits was essential for stable exchange rates, lower interest rates, and a stable global economy. The G-7 did coordinate interest rate reductions and extensive interventions in the foreign exchange markets to stabilize the dollar-yen-deutsche mark rates; at the Houston Summit, the G-7 declared that their cooperation had "improved the stability of exchange rates by concentrating attention on multilateral surveillance and close coordination of economic polices" (U.S. Department of State 1990a, section 7).

The American and European response to the problems besetting the Japanese economy and the yen in early 1990 did not yield a second Louvre Accord; the Americans redefined and diluted the criterion of successful and meaningful cooperation; it now meant "the ability of the participants to grasp more fully all the dimensions of their own situation and the situation of others and their ability to frame their own policies in a manner in which the sensitivities to the problems and perspectives of others loom larger rather than smaller" (Corrigan 1990, p. 14). Even this modest criterion was not fully met after the 21 January 1991 G-7 meeting. Prior to the meeting, the other members of the G-7 had criticized the restrictive monetary policy of the Bundesbank. The January communiqué reaffirmed G-7 "support for economic policy coordination" and the need to undertake fiscal and monetary policies that would "create conditions favorable to lower global interest rates" (*New York Times,* 22 January 1991). The other members of the G-7 believed that the Germans had agreed to refrain from an interest rate increase at a time when its partners where fighting recession. Yet ten days later the Bundesbank raised two key interest rates, an act that forced its partner nations in the EMS to choose between higher interest rates and a deeper recession or a realignment of their currencies' value against the DM.It also made it more difficult, given the DM's role in the international monetary system, for the United States to lower its interest rates to moderate the American recession without risking a flight from the dollar (*Die Zeit,* 1 February 1991; *New York Times,* February 1991; *Wall Street Journal,* 1 February 1991). The German decision to raise interest rates has been interpreted, rightly or not, as an indication that domestic economic policy takes preference over Germany's commitment to European monetary union or to the more general principle of international economic cooperation.[7] Karl Otto Pöhl, in defending the Bundesbank's action, stated that "without a stable Deutsche Mark, you can't have a stable EMS." Moreover, the blame for the interest rate rise is associated with the budgetary deficits of the Kohl government, driven by the costs of unification and the contribution to the allied effort in the Arabian Gulf (*Die Zeit,* 1 February 1991; *New York Times,* 11 February 1991).

The difficult task facing the Federal government and the Bundesbank in the 1980s has been the striking of a balance between the economic imperatives of price stability, exchange rate stability in Europe, and policy convergence among the member states of the EMS and the political imperative of economic cooperation with the United States that does not jeopardize its domestic or European policy agenda. The desire to export German preferences to Germany's European trading partners and to sustain Germany's commercial dominance of Europe with stable exchange rates cannot be struck independently of American macroeconomic policies or the relative value of the DM, dollar, and yen. The asymmetrical interdependence of German and American macroeconomic policy is all the more problematic for the Germans because American fiscal and monetary policies have been and remain inconsistent with internal and external balance. The desire to "protect" Germany from wayward American economic policies explains not only an important source of German-American conflict in the 1980s, but the German willingness to risk European monetary union.

The EMS had the stated objective of creating a "zone of monetary stability" in Europe to buttress European-American economic cooperation and to serve as a hedge against its failure. In addition to the objective of exchange rate stability, the EMS had two other objectives: price stability and policy stability among the EMS member states. These two objectives, in turn, would lead to the end point of European monetary union: policy convergence in accordance with German economic preferences and practices. The EMS has fostered greater exchange rate stability among the states participating in the exchange rate mechanism: Between March 1979 and spring 1983, the DM appreciated 27 percent against the EMS currencies; between spring of 1983 and the beginning of 1987 the DM appreciated by 8 percent; and since 1987 the value of the DM has changed against the lira only by 3.5 percent (Deutsche Bundesbank 1989b, p. 30). Moreover, the EMS has encouraged a greater degree of economic convergence in the Community, particularly with respect to price stability.[8] Between the period 1974 to 1978, the gap between the lowest inflation country (Germany) and the highest (Italy) was 11.6 percent, and in 1990, the gap between the lowest (the Netherlands) and the highest (Italy) inflation countries was 4 percent (Deutsche Bundesbank 1989b, p. 35) because the monetary authorities of EMS countries have been forced to orient their monetary policies to those of the Bundesbank to prevent realignments within the EMS (Deutsche Bundesbank 1989b, pp. 30ff; Ungerer et al. 1990). Policy convergence has not yet occurred and the Germans insist that the hardening of the European monetary area requires EMS members to follow domestic economic policies oriented around the "most stable currency in the Community"—the DM—and not the Community average (Deutsche Bundesbank 1989b, p. 35). Progress toward the completion of a single European market provides the rationale for a further tightening of the cross-rates of the European currencies, the opportunity for continued German economic leadership, and progress toward a European central bank.

The transition to a federal Europe will aggravate Atlantic economic relations: The institutional frustrations experienced by the American executive and his European counterparts will be aggravated by the principle of subsidiarity and the inevitable institutional disarray in Europe prior to the consolidation of political union. The process of institutional development in the Community runs the risk of fragmenting policy competencies and diluting responsibilities. And the Atlantic economy will find a United States without a European "partner"or addressee either for resolving economic grievances or solving common problems. Once economic and monetary union is completed, however, the United States and Europe will finally be faced with two mutually exclusive options: They can opt for autonomy and the regional segregation of the Atlantic economy into two monetary and trade blocs; or they can opt for cooperation that will lead inevitably to policy convergence. Until that time comes, however, the Germans continue to face two dilemmas. First, European monetary union runs the risk of denying Germany a European economic space tethered to German economic preferences and practices, while monetary leadership without monetary union may keep the Germans (and Europeans) too weak to negotiate successfully with the United States on global macroeconomic and exchange rate policies. Second, the gradual emergence of a German-led monetary and trade bloc may fracture the Atlantic economy, although it is certain that the status quo will ensure discord and create the context for the rancorous disintegration of the Atlantic economy.

The limited exchange rate and macroeconomic cooperation in the Atlantic economy after the Louvre Agreement has not been matched by cooperation in the area of trade. The American policy of free and fair trade has continued to coexist uneasily with the strong German preference for and interest in a protected regional trading arrangement buttressed by an open international economy. Both the United States and the Germans pushed for the reduction of tariff and nontariff barriers to trade at the Kennedy and Tokyo Rounds, but German fidelity to the discriminatory trade policies of the European Community has contributed to frictions in U.S.-German relations. This is particularly true in the area of agriculture—for example, the Chicken War in the 1960s and the Beef Hormone War in the 1980s. These mini-trade wars neither upset the general trend toward the liberalization of trade in industrial goods nor threatened to divide the Atlantic economy into two separate commercial blocs. However, an impasse over agricultural trade led to the suspension of the Uruguay Round talks in December 1990.

At the Uruguay Round, the United States and the Federal Republic supported the expansion of the domain of the General Agreement on Tariffs and Trade (GATT); both nations desired the development of rules protecting intellectual property rights and rules governing trade in services as well as the removal of restrictions on direct foreign investment. Toward the end of the 1980s, a stable but fragile community of interest arose between the Federal Republic and the United States when both nations viewed the nations of the Pacific Rim as the source of the persistent American trade deficit. The debacle over agriculture at Geneva shattered that coalition. Likewise, just as German-American disagreement over the export of sensitive technology to the nations of the Warsaw Pact was muted in 1990, the Bush administration in early 1991 modified its position on relaxing export controls in response to uncertainties about the future of the Soviet successor states. As a consequence, the United States challenged the German effort to decontrol the sale of advanced telecommunications equipment to the Soviets (*New York Times,* 4 March 1991).

The United States and the Federal Republic also favored the liberalization of capital markets. The United States had led the movement at the Uruguay Round negotiations "to impose GATT discipline of trade-related investment measures (TRIMS)" (Niehuss 1990, p. 6). The initial American position at the Uruguay Round was the removal of performance criteria on direct foreign investments. Yet during the American effort to negotiate such an agreement, the United States House of Representatives was seeking an amendment to (the now lapsed) section 721 of the Defense Production Act of 1950. Section 721 (the Exon-Florio provision) authorized the president to prohibit or suspend a foreign acquisition if the president found that it threatened an impairment of the national security. The proposed amendment to section 721 expanded the criterion for prohibiting foreign investment from a threat to the national security to a threat to the national security coming from the impairment of the industrial or technological base of the United States (Niehuss 1990, p. 6).[9]

The administration has promised the Congress to enforce the Exon-Florio criteria informally within the Committee on Foreign Investment in the United States (CFIUS) framework (Dallara 1991). It has thereby avoided a vote on a revised Exon-Florio authority that would compromise its position at the Uruguay Round and bilateral negotiations with the Japanese. The proposed amendment was a response to increased direct foreign investment in the United States, the perceived deindustrialization of the United States, and a consequence of ten years of massive trade and budget deficits. The United States has also retreated on the liberalization of services: In November 1990 the United States retreated from its earlier demand for free trade in services and announced that it could "not accept a general obligation of non-discrimination in service trade" (*Economist,* 1-7 December 1990).

German and European wariness of American trade policy has been engendered by ten years of massive trade deficits, the protectionist sentiment of the Congress, America's propensity to live beyond its collective means, the distance between announced intentions and legislative action, and the creeping bilateralization of trade by the United States—particularly the U.S.-Canadian free trade agreement, the current trilateral negotiations among the United States, Canada and Mexico, and President Bush's vision of a western hemispheric free trade area [which have been carried over into the Clinton administration-ed.] (Bangemann, *Bulletin,* Nr. 91 [1990], 849-852; Genscher, *Statements and Speeches,* X:7 [1987]; *New York Times,* 30 January 1991, 6 February 1991; Ruhfus, *Statements and Speeches,* XI:15 [1988]). German recriminations over American departures from the free trade catechism, particularly the envisioned hemispheric free trade area, have not made the Germans particularly sensitive to the prejudicial impact that the EC decision to create a single internal market, the EC-EFTA negotiations to create a single European economic space, and the inclusion of the "reforming" nations of Eastern Europe in that economic space may have on the access of American firms to European markets.[10]

The Germans and Americans entered into bilateral negotiations, the Market Access Fact Finding talks (MAFF), in an effort to increase American exports to the Federal Republic (Kohl, *Bulletin,* Nr. 48 [1989], 428) and undoubtedly to deflect criticism of Germany of the EC.

The collapse of the Uruguay Round in December 1990 posed perhaps the gravest threat to the postwar international trading system since the inception of the GATT. In American statements about the current set of trading negotiations, the United States set as a top priority an agreement on "new market-oriented rules to reduce, and ultimately eliminate, government measures that distort world agricultural trade." (U.S. Department of State 1990a, p. 277). The American position, supported by the Cairns group of 14 agricultural exporters, is aimed squarely at the discriminatory policies of the EC Common Agricultural Policy (CAP). The breakdown of the Uruguay Round was in the offing since the Montreal mid-term review in 1988. It was apparent at that time that agricultural trade could not be decoupled from the other trade issue areas on the table and that progress on agricultural trade was the sine qua non for any conclusion to the talks (*Economist,* 22-28 September 1990; *Far East Economic Review,* 22 December 1988). The Germans were unwilling to accommodate the American demands on agriculture, a position explained in large part by the CDU/CSU desire to retain the rural vote in the December 1990 all-German election and the foreign policy calculation that the CAP had functioned as the economic foundation of FrancoGerman political cooperation in Europe. It was the German position prior to the December meeting that the CAP "remain intact" internally and externally—that is, that price supports and export subsidies not be abolished drastically or in the short to medium term. Also, even if the Germans had wanted to change the EC offer prior to the December 1990 collapse of the Uruguay Round, they may have been unable to garner sufficient support: The EC offer rejected by the United States required seven internal negotiating sessions before a common negotiating position could be agreed upon (*Economist,* 10-16 November 1990; Kiechle, *Bulletin,* Nr. 108 [1990], 1149; Nr. 143 [1990], p. 1505).

Prior to the December meeting of the GATT, the U.S. Trade Representative, Carla Hills, stated that the United States would allow the Uruguay Round to fail rather than yield on agriculture to the EC (*Economist,* 22-28 September 1990). The Europeans were as determined to prevent an American-dictated reform of the CAP. The inability to reach a compromise on export subsidies and internal price supports acceptable to the EC as well as the United States and the Cairns group caused the suspension of trade talks on 7 December 1990. The initial American negotiating position (supported by the Cairns group) demanded the abolition of all agricultural supports within a ten-year time period; that maximalist position was later "weakened" to the demand for a 90 percent reduction in export subsidies and a 75 percent cut in internal price supports. The EC's counteroffer was a 30 percent overall cut in price supports beginning in 1986, which would be the equivalent of 15 percent new cuts by 1995 (*Economist,* 1-7 December 1990). The suspension of trade talks led the Community in January 1991 to improve its offer to the United States and other agricultural producers: It would reduce subsidies by 30 percent beginning in 1989 (rather than 1986) and would consider the reduction of export subsidies (*New York Times,* 16 January 1991). This offer was rejected. The Community eventually offered the Americans and the other agricultural exporters in principle what was originally demanded: a reduction in internal price supports, the abolition of export subsidies, and improved market access for non-European agricultural producers (*Economist,* 2-8 March 1991). The resumption of negotiations does not guarantee a successful conclusion of the Uruguay Round. Moreover, if a bargain is struck there is no guarantee that the American Congress will be prevented from eviscerating the trade agreement: The fast-track authority given the president in the 1988 Trade Act, a provision forcing the Congress to vote on a trade agreement without amendment, expired on 1 March 1991. The fast-track authority was extended by the Congress for a two-year period.

The agricultural dispute between the United States and Europe, the uncertain impact a free trade area in North American will have on American employment and wage levels, and the administration's dissatisfaction within direct export subsidies for European manufactures can only reinforce the investment xenophobia in the American Congress and continues to create pressures for the selective closure of the American economy. At the present time, much of the criticism outside of the issue of agriculture is aimed at Japan; but the inevitable wealth and productivity of a unified Germany (or a [con]federal Europe) will eventually become an inviting scapegoat for America's inability to put its own economic house in order.

## CONCLUSION

The future of German-American relations will be determined not only by the structure of trade and patterns of investment in the Atlantic economy but by the evolution of the political and security architectures in Europe that replace the postwar system of two opposing military alliances buttressed by ideological enmity. Today, the United States has an asymmetrical interest in the continued integration and openness of the Atlantic economy: American investment has become increasingly located in Europe, and Europe remains an important source of goods for American consumers and an important market for American manufacturers. The same cannot be said of Germany:

The structure of German trade has become increasingly concentrated in Europe, both as a source of supply and as a market. This trend can only continue as the nations of Eastern and north-central Europe increase their per-capita GNP and gain preferential access to the wealthy nations of capitalist Europe.[11]

This conclusion is based on Steffan Linder's theory of trade (Hanink 1990) and the Bundesbank observation that the level of trade between Germany and the CMEA nations does not correspond "to the customary exchange of goods among industrial countries" (Deutsche Bundesbank 1989a, p. 24). And although German investment in the United States has increased dramatically between 1976 and 1988, the American share of total German DFI remains quite low. Moreover, it is not unreasonable to assume that the costs of German reconstruction and investment opportunities in a politically stable north-central Europe will slow German investment in the United States.

The asymmetry in Atlantic economic affairs is reproduced in the German architecture for the post-postwar period. The West German foreign policy strategy consisted of two informal contracts: an American security guarantee purchased in the coin of trade and monetary concessions supporting American hegemony, and European political and economic integration purchased at the price of French leadership. The post-postwar European state system and German unification has canceled both. The Germans have demanded and been conceded a leadership role in Europe: Germany defines the principles and purpose of European economic and monetary union. In exchange the Germans have acquiesced to political union to allay fears of a hegemonial Germany without sacrificing its leadership role. The German preference for a security architecture anchored by the CSCE, for a collective security arrangement encompassing Europe from the Atlantic to the Urals, will diminish American leverage on security issues and the German need to compromise on issues of trade, exchange rates, or macroeconomic policy. Moreover, the creation of a single European economic space will support the CSCE security order and transform Europe into an economic power equal to the United States.

A different understanding of the objectives and methods of macroeconomic management was the key source of economic conflict between the United States and Germany in the 1980s, and perhaps over the entire course of the postwar period. The growing uncompetitiveness of American firms and unrelenting overconsumption of individual Americans in the 1970s and 1980s was reflected, if not encouraged, by the electoral calculus of successive American administrations. Each has opted for budget deficits rather than budget discipline; each has been prone to increase in entitlements without compensatory tax increases. The Germans have followed a more virtuous economic path: price stability and fiscal rectitude (until recently). The divergence in macroeconomic policy has been inevitably transformed into foreign policy disputes, played out in the idioms of trade, exchange rates, and interest rates. The Plaza Agreement and the Louvre Accord in the 1980s emphasized the coordination of exchange rate intervention and sought stable rates of exchange between the dollar and DM (and yen). In retrospect, this emphasis seems misplaced (de Vries 1990, pp. 9-10). Rather, exchange rate and price stability require a greater degree of macroeconomic cooperation and convergence. If the American and German governments do not achieve a greater degree of macroeconomic policy coordination and convergence, Atlantic economic relations are more likely to be characterized by divisiveness than by conciliation.

What barriers exist to macroeconomic policy coordination and convergence? Conflicts of interest, institutional disabilities (domestic and external), and dissimilar economic cultures. The Federal Republic and the United States face at least three categories of interest-based barriers to policy coordination and convergence: identifying and agreeing on the economic problem to be solved, crafting a policy that does not produce asymmetrical benefits, and ensuring that the political costs of the common policy are acceptable to both nation's electorates.

The process of economic and monetary union in Europe and the separation of powers in the United States are the primary institutional barriers to macroeconomic coordination in the Atlantic economy. In the United States, the separation of powers between the executive and Congress, the annual competition between the Office of Management and Budget and the Congressional Budget Office to craft a credible federal budget, and the independent American Federal Reserve System have made policy coordination and coherence very difficult and has reduced the credibility of American commitments made at international fora. Although the Germans do not suffer from institutional disarray domestically, the simultaneous proliferation of Community prerogatives in and institutions for the making of economic policy will probably burden any effort to coordinate the macroeconomic policies of the United States and Germany. Commitments will be harder to make and possibly harder to keep; the Germans will be forced to first strike (or impose) a policy position on partner states and have as a consequence less flexibility in negotiating with the United States. Moreover, the transition to economic and monetary union will create areas of ambiguity with respect to policy competence and responsibility. The inevitable diffusion of responsibility in Europe will make it all the more difficult to deal with an American partner already suffering institutional disorder.

The intractable barrier to macroeconomic cooperation and convergence is located in the dissimilar American and German economic cultures. Economic culture identifies the noninstitutional constraints and opportunities confronting national authorities in the formulation and execution of macroeconomic policy; it implies that macroeconomic policies frequently described as "inadequate" reflect societal values, beliefs, and customs about the conduct and content of economic policy. Moreover, it reinforces the institutional disabilities and calculations of interest that confound the coordination and convergence of economic policy in the Atlantic economy. The economic cultures of Germany and the United States have impeded the coordination and convergence of macroeconomic policy in three ways:

- The United States and the Federal Republic place different values on price stability and employment.
- The American norm of fiscal laxity clashes with the German norm of fiscal rectitude.
- The insularity endemic to the United States makes American policymakers relatively indifferent to the problems of others, while the West German fixation with the outside world generates the demand for national economic policies that correspond to German preferences.

The maximalist position adopted by the Germans for their participation in a European central bank and membership in a European Union—that it occur on German terms or not occur at all—and the acceptance of the German position by many within the Community indicate the triumph of the German economic culture in Europe. The German economic culture has become the economic culture of Europe. If the United States and a German Europe cannot reach a compromise on the objectives of macroeconomic policy, the conflicts of the 1980s only foreshadow the shape of things to come.

## NOTES

1. Moreover, the Federal Republic held 14 percent of total short-term Treasury obligations held by foreigners in 1981. In 1988 that figure dropped to 0.6 percent, a shift that also represents an absolute drop in the amount held by Germans from $8 billion in 1981 to $696 million in 1988. At the same time, the Japanese share of short-term Treasury obligations remained more or less unchanged between

1981 and 1988 (22 percent and 23 percent, respectively)—although the dollar amount held by the Japanese doubled from $12 billion to $25.6 billion (U.S. Department of State, 1989, 1982).

2. Europe's position as the preferred supplier to the German market has increased between 1965 and 1988 in every sector except machinery and transport equipment. (The drop in the European share was compensated by a rise in the Japanese share from 1.7 percent in 1965 to 16.7 percent in 1988.) Europe's role as a market for German goods has been enhanced during this same time period except in SITC category 04 (animal and vegetable oils, fats, and waxes). The United States has lost ground as a supplier to the German market in every category; and it has become a less important market for German goods in every category except SITC category 07 (machinery and transport equipment)—a category of goods where the American share of total German exports has remained around 10 percent. Germany's most important export sectors of the economy—chemicals and related products (SITC number 05), manufactured goods (SITC number 06), machinery and transport equipment (SITC number 07)—had foreign sales of over $257 billion in 1989: Europe bought approximately 74 percent of those goods ($189 billion). Moreover, the lion's share of German automobile and truck exports went to Europe—$39 billion (71.7 percent of total exports) compared to American sales of $7.6 billion (14 percent of total exports). (See Tables 7.7 and 7.8.)
3. DFI may weaken the need for an open trading system, however, if the investment is designed to evade barriers to trade. DFI could thus mitigate trade conflicts in the Atlantic economy and make painless the gradual disassociation of Europe and the United States in the real sector of the economy.
4. The Federal Republic pledged $6.62 billion to the United States, $3.04 billion to members of the allied coalition, and $1.72 billion tot Egypt, Turkey, and Jordan for economic stabilization measures.
5. At the same time, the Bundesbank accused the Federal Government of circumventing Article 115 of the Grundgesetz, which limits net borrowing to capital expenditures. The Bundesbank took the position that the costs of unification were tied predominately to consumption items, rather than to investment (Deutsche Bundesbank 1990b, pp. 20-21). Waigel assured the Bundestag that the recalculation of the FRG's credit requirements for 1990 would "not stand in contradiction to Article 115 of the Grundgesetz" (Waigel 1990, p. 1260).
6. In 1990 the process of reconciling Eastern and Western Europe took a further step with the creation of the Pentagonale, an economic (and political) group comprising Austria, Czechoslovakia, Hungary, Italy, and Yugoslavia (*Economist,* 25-31 August 1990).
7. Bundesbank president Karl Otto Pöhl, in defending the Bundesbank's action, stated that "without a stable Deutsche Mark, you can't have a stable EMS."

Moreover, the blame for the interest rate rise is associated with the budgetary deficits of the Kohl government, driven by the costs of unification and the contribution to the allied effort in the Arabian Gulf (*Die Zeit,* 1 February 1991; *New York Times,* 11 February 1991).

8. Between the period 1974-1978, the gap between the lowest inflation country (Germany) and the highest (Italy) was 11.6 percent; in 1990, the gap between the lowest (the Netherlands) and the highest (Italy) inflation countries was 4 percent (Deutsche Bundesbank 1989b, 35).
9. The administration has promised the Congress to enforce the Exon-Florio criteria informally within the Committee on Foreign Investment in the United States (CFIUS) framework (Dallara 1991). It has thereby avoided a vote on a revised Exon-Florio authority that would compromise its position at the Uruguay Round and bilateral negotiations with the Japanese.
10. The Germans and Americans entered into bilateral negotiations, the Market Access Fact Finding talks (MAFF), in an effort to increase American exports to the Federal Republic (Kohl 1989, p. 428) and undoubtedly to deflect criticism of Germany to the EC.
11. This conclusion is based on Steffan Linder's theory of trade (Hanink 1990) and the Bundesbank observation that the level of trade between Germany and the CMEA nations does not correspond "to the customary exchange of goods among industrial countries" (Deutsche Bundesbank 1989a, p. 24).

## REFERENCES

Axilrod, Stephen H. (1986). "Testimony Before the Subcommittee on Domestic Monetary Policy of the House Committee on Banking, Finance, and Urban Affairs, 7 November 1985," *Federal Reserve Bulletin* 72, p. 1.

Corrigan, E. Gerald (1990). "Reflections on the 1980s," *Federal Reserve Bank of New York, Annual Report 1989.* New York: FRBNY.

Dallara, Charles H. (1991). "Statement of the Honorable Charles H. Dallara . . . Before the Subcommittee on Commerce, Consumer Protection, and Competitiveness of the Committee on Energy and Commerce, US House of Representatives," *Treasury News. NB 1152.* Washington, D.C.: U.S. Department of the Treasury.

de Vries, Rimmer (1990). "Adam Smith: Managing the Global Capital of Nations, *World Financial Markets,* no. 2. New York: Morgan Guaranty Trust Company.

Deutsche Bundesbank (1968). "Statistiche Beihefte zu den Monatsberichten der Deutschen Bundesbank, Reihe 3," *Zahlungsbilanzstatistik.* Nov./Dec. Frankfurt: BBk.

——— (1971). "Statistiche Beihefte zu den Monatsberichten der Deutschen Bundesbank. Reihe 3," *Zahlungsbilanzstatistik,* no. 6. Frankfurt: BBk.

——— (1976). *Monthly Report of the Deutsche Bundesbank.* Statistical Appendix 28, no. 12.

——— (1982). "Statistiche Beihefte zu den Monatsberichten der Deutschen Bundesbank, Reihe 3," *Zahlungsbilanzstatistik,* no. 6. Frankfurt: BBk.

——— (1983). "Die Kapitalverflectung der Unternehmen mit dem Ausland nach Laender und Wirtschaftszweigen 1976 bis 1981," Beilage zur Statistischen Beihefte zu den Monatsberichten der Deutschen Bundesbank. Reihe 3, *Zahlungsbilanzstatistik,* no. 7. Frankfurt: BBk.

——— (1984). *Report of the Deutsche Bundesbank for the Year 1983.* Frankfurt: BBk.

—— (1985). *Report of the Deutsche Bundesbank for the Year 1984.* Frankfurt: BBk.

——— (1986). "Statistiche Beihefte zu den Monatsberichten der Deutschen Bundesbank, Reihe 3," *Zahlungsbilanzstatistik* (June 1986). Frankfurt: BBk.

——— (1988). "40 Years of the Deutsche Mark," *Monthly Report of the Deutsche Bundesbank* 40, no. 5.

——— (1989a). "Recent Trends in External Transactions with the Centrally Planned Economies," *Monthly Report of the Deutsche Bundesbank* 41, no. 7.

——— (1989b). "Exchange Rate Movements within the European Monetary System. Experience after Ten Years," *Monthly Report of the Deutsche Bundesbank* 41, no. 11.

——— (1989c). "The Balance of Payments of the Federal Republic of Germany with All Countries from 1977 to 1988 and with Individual Groups of Countries and Countries from 1985 to 1988," Appendix to the Statistical Supplements to the Monthly Report of the Deutsche Bundesbank, Series 3, *Balance of Payments Statistics,* no. 8. Frankfurt: BBk.

——— (1990a). *Report of the Deutsche Bundesbank for the Year 1989.* Frankfurt: BBk.

——— (1990b). "The Monetary Union with the German Democratic Republic," *Monthly Report of the Deutsche Bundesbank* 42, no. 7.

——— (1990c). "The First Stage of European Economic and Monetary Union," *Monthly Report of the Deutsche Bundesbank* 42, no. 7.

——— (1990d). "Statistiche Beihefte zu den Monatsberichten der Deutschen Bundesbank, Reihe 3," *Zahlungsbilanzstatistik* (June 1990). Frankfurt: BBk.

——— (1990e). "Die Kapitalverflectung der Unternehmen mit dem Ausland nach Laender und Wirtschafszweigen 1982 bis 1988," Beilage zur Statistischen Beihefte zu den Monatsberichten der Deutschen Bundesbank. Reihe 3, *Zahlungsbilanzstatistik,* no. 4. Frankfurt: BBk.

Deutsche Bundesregierung (1984). *Jahreswirtschaftsbericht 1984.* Bonn.

——— (1988). *Jahreswirtschaftsbericht 1988.* Bonn.

——— (1990). *Jahreswirtschaftsbericht 1990.* Bonn.

Deutscher Bundestag (1988). *Stenographische Berichte.* Bonn.

European Commission (1991). *Background Report: Economic and Monetary Union* (ISEC/B34/90). Brussels: Commission of the European Community.

European Commission, Committee for the Study of Economic and Monetary Union (1989). *Report on Economic and Monetary Union in the European Community (Delors Report).* Brussels: Commission of the European Community.

Federal Reserve Board (various years). "Treasury and Fedederal Reserve Exchange Operations . . ." *Federal Reserve Bulletin.* Washington, D.C.: FRB.

German Information Center (various years). *Statements and Speeches.* New York: German Information Center.

Hanink, Dean M. (1990). "Linder Again," *Weltwirtschaftliches Archiv* 126, no. 2.

International Monetary Fund (1991). *International Financial Statistics.* Washington, D.C.: IMF.

Lipschitz, Leslie (1990). "Introduction and Overview," in Leslie Lipschitz and Donogh McDonald, eds., *German Unification: Economic Issues.* Occasional Paper no. 75. Washington, D.C.: IMF.

Lipschitz, Leslie, and Donogh McDonald, eds. (1990). *German Unification: Economic Issues.* Occasional Paper no. 75. Washington, D.C.: IMF.

Niehuss, John M. (1990). "Statement of John M. Niehuss . . . before the Subcommittee on Commerce, Consumer Protection, and Competitiveness of the Committee on Energy and Commerce, U.S. House of Representatives," *Treasury News* NB 901. Washington, D.C.: U.S. Department of the Treasury.

OECD (1967). *Trade by Commodities. Detailed Analysis by Production.* Series C. January-December 1965. Paris: OECD.

——— (1977). *Trade by Commodities. Market Summaries.* Series C. January-December 1975. Paris: OECD.

——— (1990). *Foreign Trade by Commodities, 1988,* Series C, vol. 1. Paris: OECD.

Pöhl, Karl-Otto (1991). Cited in the *New York Times,* 20 March.

Presse- und Informationsamt der Bundesregierung (various years). *Bulletin.* Bonn.

Sachverstaendigenrat (1984). *Jahresgutachten 1984/1985.* Bonn.

——— (1985). "Wirtschaftspolitische Entscheidungen im Sommer 1985," *Sondergutachten vom 23 Juni 1985,* in *Jahresgutachten 1985/1986.* Bonn.

Sperling, James (1989). "The Federal Republic of Germany, the United States, and the Atlantic Economy," in Peter Merkl, ed., *The Federal Republic at Forty.* New York: New York University Press.

Stoltenberg, Gerhard (1986). "Statement," in *Summary Proceedings.* Washington, D.C.: IMF.

Ungerer, Horst, Jouko Hauvonen, Augsto Lopez-Claros, and Thomas Mayer (1990). *The European Monetary System: Developments and Perspectives.* Occasional Paper 73. Washington, D.C.: IMF.

U.S. Department of Commerce (1966). "International Investments in the United States in 1965," *Survey of Current Business* 46, no. 8.

——— (1967). "The International Investment Position of the United States in 1966," *Survey of Current Business* 47, no. 9.

——— (1976a). "Foreign Direct Investment in the United States in 1975," *Survey of Current Business* 56, no. 8.

——— (1976b). "U.S. Direct Investment Abroad in 1975," *Survey of Current Business* 56, no. 8.

——— (1982). "Foreign Direct Investment in the United States in 1981," *Survey of Current Business* 62, no. 8.

——— (1984). "U.S. Direct Investment Abroad in 1982," *Survey of Current Business* 63, no. 8.

——— (1990a). "Foreign Direct Investment in the United States for Position and Balance of Payments Flows, 1989," *Survey of Current Business* 70, no. 8.

——— (1990b). "U.S. Direct Investment Abroad: Detail for Position and Balance of Payments Flows, 1989," *Survey of Current Business* 70, no. 8.

U.S. Department of State (1990a). *Houston Economic Declaration.* Selected Documents, no. 39. Washington, D.C.: Bureau of Public Affairs.

——— (1990b). *Dispatch* 1, no. 12. Washington, D.C.: GPO.

U.S. Department of Treasury (various years). *Treasury Bulletin.* Washington, D.C.: GPO.

# Conclusion

## Beyond the Cold War: Toward the Fourth Republic?

Carl F. Lankowski

These chapters examining Germany's relationship to the European Community have been framed in the stark terms of hegemony and containment. The diplomacy surrounding the founding of the European Coal and Steel Community, European Economic Community, and European Atomic Energy Community seemed to have required it. In the aftermath of the collapse of the Soviet Union and the end of the Cold War, we have arrived at a critical point in the regional experiment launched by the French over four decades ago. It is fitting to take stock of the German-EC relationship in this light. Moreover, by proceeding in this way, the aim was to contribute to clarification of the concept of hegemony, since it has been used to describe the German position in the EC (Chap. 7; Keohane and Hoffmann 1991; Markovits and Reich 1991).

The German-EC relationship provides a fertile field to explore this question, because the size, composition, and location of the German economy impart important capabilities to affect surrounding countries. These capabilities have been magnified absolutely by unification and relatively by the dramatically transformed diplomatic situation in Eastern and East-Central Europe. The contributions to this volume have helped us understand the degree to which this potential has been actualized.

For its part, the European Community (EC) has been acknowledged by most students of international organization to be a strong regime, one that is politically cohesive and organizationally deep and flexible. Though no one would question the centrality of the intergovernmental component of Community institutions, there is no general agreement about just how enmeshed national states are in the EC matrix. Hegemony is a partly a matter of boundaries of the state. In this respect, we may register changing distributions of authority between levels of government—EC, national, regional. It is also possible to identify emerging networks that could diffuse the strength of national strategies. In this context, what can be safely evaluated is the direction in which the member-state/Community relationship is moving. What do the contributions to this volume imply about this direction with respect to Germany?

## PATTERNS OF INTEREST AGGREGATION

Germany's federal structure, its multiparty coalition governments, and its parapublic institutions give its policy-making an inclusive, therefore consensual, character (Katzenstein 1987). Some evidence has been adduced to demonstrate the resilience of this pattern in the context of the EC's internal market program. (Woolcock, Hodges, and Schreiber 1991). In this regard, Chapter 1 in this volume on business by Michael G. Huelshoff and Chapter 2 on labor by Andrei Markovits and Alexander Otto share an important finding. A major impact of the internal market has been the differentiation of interests on both sides of the labor market. *Ceteris paribus,* this implies greater difficulty in aggregating and reconciling interests by union and business peak associations and, consequently, by the national government. In this situation, the government may be tempted to "borrow authority" from the EC to maintain or restore its ability to govern. Such borrowing is a net resource for governments, providing them with "alibis" for imposing their priorities on recalcitrant bargaining partners, thereby either overriding the need for consensus or establishing such consensus through creative leadership on terms that conform to the preferences of the national government. By the same token, EC directives and policies impose real constraints on the national governments and demonstrate how dependent they have become on the EC system.

Against this background, the federal government's record in integrating various constituencies has been mixed, as can be seen by two examples of German public finance and energy policy. In the sphere of public finance, building on progress in the area of fiscal harmonization in the 1970s (Lankowski and Puchala 1977), the main goal of the White Paper was rate convergence for the value added tax (VAT). Necessitated by the Kohl government's unification strategy, high levels of financial transfers to the East placed Germany's system of public finance under great strain. While the federal government responded with proposals for tax reform and a reduction in industrial subsidies, the parliamentary opposition called for major revisions in the privatization strategy being implemented by the *Treuhand.* In this case, the Kohl government was able to cloak its policy in EC raiment. It managed to push though the Bundestag and Bundesrat (due to the defection of one SPD minister-präsident) an increase of the value added tax, which had the effect of increasing the pressure on the fiscal situations of most SPD-governed Länder. The SPD leadership admitted that an agreement on VAT convergence in the EC Council of Ministers would weaken the party's position.

The outcome in case of German subsidies to coal is more equivocal. As Huelshoff points out in Chapter 1, German electricity consumers have been paying a charge to the government through the utilities to subsidize the cost of relatively expensive German anthracite coal. This "*Kohlepfennig*" cost several hundred million deutsche marks per year. Again responding to the unprecedented costs of unification, the German economics minister announced in 1991 a program to slash German subsidies, including that for coal. The proposal was facilitated by the EC Commission's efforts to create more competition and even an internal market in energy. Despite the appeal that could be made to consumers who could be expected to benefit from "low-cost" imports of electricity from French nuclear generators, the government was unable to reduce coal subsidies by the desired amount. Announcement of revisions in the *Jahrhundertvertrag,* the social program to support employment in the mines and to promote the use of relatively expensive domestic coal, led to widespread organized protests among the affected workers.

A similar pattern is observable in macroeconomic policy-making. Germany's export orientation sets limits on the usefulness of monetary and fiscal policy instruments. Unusually high state expenditures are linked to high interest rates, which, in turn, have fragmented EC macroeconomic cohesion. Rates can come down only if taxes are raised or spending is cut. During the summer of 1993 the conservative-liberal government chose the path of spending cuts, enraging constituencies benefiting from social entitlement programs. It has advertised its action as a demonstration of solidarity with its EC partners.

In all these cases, the resource scarcity occasioned by German unification led the federal government to support its preferred solutions by using EC policy to override domestic opposition. In at least a limited sense, this represents erosion of the consensus norm at the heart of the German model.

## GERMAN UNIFICATION AND THE EC

Meanwhile, the constitutional underpinnings of the German model have been affected by the inclusion of the *Fünf neue Länder* (FNL) in the EC upon unification. The EC was necessarily in a reactive posture to the Kohl government's unification strategy. Nevertheless, the Commission was able to play an important role in establishing the basic parameters of East German development. An EC Commission plan to integrate the former German Democratic Republic into the EC without any treaty revision was adopted by the European Council in Dublin in April 1990 (Commission of the EC 1990), just before the two Germanys and the four allied occupying powers began negotiations to work out the internal and external terms of unification. Although it resembled an EC enlargement, Article 237 of the Rome Treaty was not invoked, and unification was treated as a special case. Not shying from controversial German constitutional questions, the Community expressed a preference for unification under Article 23 of West Germany's Basic Law, whereby the five eastern Länder joined the Federal Republic. Since the conservative-liberal coalition government also preferred the Article 23 solution against an active opposition that desired to create a new constitution for Germany on the basis of Basic Law Article 146, this may be yet another example of the EC's alibi role. Whatever the case, the Community was to become intimately involved in the negotiations between the two Germanys as the German economic and monetary union and the state treaty on unification were worked out.

The FNL were to adopt all EC legislation during a relatively short transition period, in light of the state of the Eastern economy and administrative structure. Derogations from EC standards were worked out on a limited, case-by-case basis, extending no later than 1998. The EC was particularly concerned that competition rules be followed. This meant that the commission was to be closely involved with the *Treuhand* (privatization agency), supervising and passing binding judgments on the its industrial restructuring tasks. In this role, the commission represented the interests of the rest of the Community: of less developed member states wary of German state aids, of the more advanced members concerned about the creation of dominant firms on the basis of West German buyouts. For example, the commission's competition directorate-general intervened several times in 1991 to tighten guidelines for state aids in the sensitive shipbuilding industry. The Community also insisted on quick application of 1992 legislation and EC environmental and social standards, which even with five- to seven-year derogations, still implied the closure of many plants.

These parameters guaranteed that unification would be enormously expensive, since they implied a shock similar in quality to that experienced in Eastern Europe after the collapse of the neo-Stalinist regimes that populated the region (Suhr 1990). Eastern Europe's woeful experience has prompted calls for a moderated, holistic adjustment strategy that is not one-dimensionally oriented to economic growth (Reinicke 1992). But the terms of integration of the former GDR into the EC do not allow for such a strategy. By the same token, no one has yet been able to outline a course of action for the western part of the country that would result in real, sustainable transfers that might buffer the economic free-fall over the medium term. The unification experience is demonstrating that it is as difficult to change the patterns of life in the West as it is in the East. In any event, it is a dubious proposition that even significant reductions in western consumption would free up a large enough pool of funds to finance the costs of unification.

Efforts to finance the necessary expenditures have put severe pressure on the financial positions of the western Länder, 8 of the 11 of which are, at the time of this writing, governed by Social Democrats alone or in combination with Greens or Liberals. In 1994 the special fund set up to finance unification at the federal level will be retired and the inter-Länder equalization mechanism will take over. Given the financial resources required to meet the responsibilities of the western Länder, a major disruption of the revenue-sharing scheme at the heart of Germany's federal system may be in the offing. To the extent that the German model relies on a robust federal system, this development is ominous. The financial "solidarity pact" worked out between Bund and Länder in March 1993 seems to have been a standoff in terms of the power of the respective actors. The western Länder were able to maintain their position in the financial system, but the overall result was a net increase in public sector debt and the lingering perception that the debt liability had been significantly underestimated.[1]

What is true for the interests of labor and capital also applies at the regional level. In subjecting firms operating at significantly different productivity levels to the logic of a single market even more integrated than that of the EC, German unification has only exacerbated the condition of interest divergence produced by internal market legislation. In this sense, workers in the Five New Länder (FNL) may have more in common with those in de-industrializing Scotland than they do with their union comrades in the older Länder. Indeed, in January 1993 the German Federal Government acknowledged as much when it applied to the EC for support from the European Regional Development Fund. The FNL have been classified as "objective 1" regions—those regions entitled to receive priority treatment because they seriously lag behind average EC gross domestic product (GDP) per capita and employment performance.

The prospect of unification also yielded a regionally differentiated picture with respect to the expected future importance of the EC. A September 1990 poll revealed that 56 percent of East Germans thought unification would make the process of European integration more important, compared to 47 percent of West Germans. Only 1 percent of the East Germans polled believed that European integration would be less important, compared to 13 percent from the West; 31 percent perceived no change, compared to 40 percent of the Western respondents (Veen 1991).

To sum up, German unification under the auspices of the EC has produced an exaggeration of already divergent interests and powerful centrifugal forces operating among the Länder and between them and the federal government.

## PARLIAMENTARY CONTROL MECHANISMS

Article 24 of Germany's Basic Law permits the federal government to delegate responsibilities to international organizations. The problem is that EC action occurs in areas assigned to the Länder, either concurrently or exclusively. The German Länder have been cognizant of the de facto erosion of their constitutional status by virtue of the regional integration process for some time (Hrbek and Thaysen 1986) For example, the Länder, in their competence in the cultural domain, are responsible for radio and television programming. The EC internal market program, meanwhile, included a directive on the same subject. Similar preemptions occur in environmental legislation, education (recognition of diplomas), and other areas. The loss of control over important policy areas was not compensated by substantially increased powers of the European Parliament, despite the introduction of the second reading (cooperation procedure) under the Single European Act.

The Maastricht Treaty improved the role of the European Parliament marginally with a new "negative consent" (third reading) provision, but not nearly enough to offset the substantial widening of the scope of Community competences (for example, in the cultural and educational area, police and home affairs), not to mention the establishment of economic and monetary union (EMU), which at the very least implies monitoring, discussion of, and action on member state budgets. In the context of the fiscal problems associated with EC-supervised unification, the Maastricht negotiations provided the occasion for a *fronde* of the Länder against both the Bund and the EC itself.

The Länder reform occurred as a Bundestag committee on EC affairs was launched in June 1991, after six months of discussions between representatives of the CDU/CSU, FDP, and SPD. The Committee on European Affairs was established as the Bundestag's 24th regular committee, possessing all the powers of any other Bundestag committees. This was an improvement, replacing a subcommittee of the Bundestag foreign affairs committee.

Article 2 under Title II of the Treaty on European Union lays down the subsidiarity principle, which, as a general principle of the European Community, provides a "constitutional" basis for action by provincial (regional) or national governments. Article 198-a-b-c under Title II establishes a consultative Committee of the Regions. The committee may issue opinions on its own initiative. Commission and council may solicit opinions, and opinions are mandated in certain policy areas. These include regional affairs; trans-European networks; economic and social cohesion; and education, vocational training, and youth affairs.

As the date set for the December 1992 Bundestag ratification debate on Maastricht approached, the Constitutional Commission, charged with drawing up amendments to the Basic Law to reflect the two unifications, developed a plan that will invest the Bundestag European Affairs Committee with strengthened oversight powers. Like the Danish parliamentary Market Committee, the new committee will be able to control German positions in the EC Council of Ministers via stringent governmental reporting requirements and directive powers. Article 24 of the Basic Law was to be amended such that any assignment of competences to the EC (or any other international organization) would require a two-thirds Bundestag vote. Furthermore, the Bundesrat demanded that Article 24 be rewritten to provide the Länder chamber with a veto power over EC legislation, a position that drew fire from the chair of the Bundestag EC committee but that was ultimately accepted in February 1993.[2]

The overall impact of these organizational responses to the latest phase of integration will be to lessen the freedom of action of German ministers in the EC Council. By making the Council behavior of ministers more transparent and accountable, the alibi function of that body presumably will decline. As for the regions, aside from Länder representatives attending Council meetings as observers, their only influence will be of a collective variety, in the context of the Bundesrat. Still, these measures promise to restore some of the balance lost in the two unifications in Germany and in Europe. In that sense, they represent at least a partial restoration of the conditions for social and political inclusivity that comprise the German model.

Despite such adjustments, opposition to Maastricht has been building across the political spectrum. The Greens rejected the entire concept of Maastricht. For them, the treaty turned the EC's back on Eastern Europe and further consolidated its economic growth priority. For the Social Democrats the central problem consisted in the deplorable failure of the government to achieve greater EC democratization during the treaty negotiations. Meanwhile, the tabloid *Bild Zeitung* caught the mood of many Germans as it attacked the government's willingness even to contemplate giving up the deutsche mark, the trade mark of Germany's postwar success. Not even the ruling parties could avoid trouble over this sentiment. A high official in the *cabinet* of one of the two German EC commissioners openly denounced the treaty and the Bavarian member of the Bundesbank Council campaigned against it. A suit was initiated against the government in the highest court in the land, the *Bundesverfassungsgericht,* challenging its validity on constitutional grounds. At core, the constitutional challenge rests on Article 20 of the German Basic Law, which guarantees that "all state power originates in the people." By the time of this writing the court had directed the government to respond to a catalogue of fifteen queries in preparation for making its finding, which was due to be released during the autumn of 1993. The questions go to the heart of the integration project as currently conceived. In particular, the court was concerned about the possible surrender of Germany's "legal and democratic independence . . . [and] its constitutional identity."[3]

## NEW VOICES: TOWARD THE FOURTH REPUBLIC?

One of the most astute students of contemporary Germany offered a résumé of German politics in the 1980s in terms of three phases of postwar development, corresponding to the faces of three republics (Katzenstein 1989). In Katzenstein's analysis, the first and second republics refer to successive phases of conservative accumulation and institutional reform from the 1950s to the advent of the 1980s, respectively. The nascent, third republic refers to patterns of social and political experimentation that reflect Germany's social movement sector since that time. Defined in this way, the analysis is designed to illuminate the continuity and flexibility of the (West) German polity. Although the effects of EC membership after the Single European Act are somewhat clouded by unification, systematic inclusion of the EC dimension in such an analysis can no longer be avoided. The continued electoral success of the Greens suggests that opportunities for Länder-based regional differentiation in a European context have never been greater. Perhaps Germany is already in its fourth postwar, republican phase.

In early 1993, 9 of 16 Länder had SPD-led governments. Four of these had Green or Alliance-90 coalition partners. Another dimension affecting the posture of Germany toward the EC is the degree of representation of voices beyond those comprising labor and capital. How conducive are EC institutional arrangements, taking the EC Bundestag/Bundesrat reforms into account, to articulation of the interests of the new social movements?

On the one hand, the movements and the Greens (the party that tries to represent them) can be viewed as one aspect of the growing heterogeneity of interests with which the government of the day must contend. This is true, but it is incomplete. Insofar as their interests are postmaterialist in orientation, they cannot be easily assimilated into traditional political coalitions oriented primarily to economic growth. On the other hand, movements and movement parties introduce important new themes into political discourse that are absorbed by competitor parties. This process has led not only to the defense of stringent environmental, health, and safety standards by Germany in Council. In view of the Community's essential market design, the Greens helped create a discourse about the architecture of Europe.

The SEA and Maastricht have not been entirely unfriendly to the Greens. On the contrary. The Single European Act was a hybrid borne of efforts organized in the European Parliament to upgrade the political dimension of Community institutions, manifested in the 1984 draft European Union Treaty (Lodge 1986), and the desire for an internal market supported by the largest member states. From 1984 onward, the movements had a voice in Brussels and Strasbourg. That voice made it both more difficult and more tempting for national governments to pursue an alibi course of action. In this respect, there is no small irony. Model Germany was a configuration organized around the labor market. The export success associated with the model made others want to emulate it (Markovits and Reich 1991). As Greens were elected to parliaments at all levels, Red-Green coalitions began to appear, challenging the electoral "market share" of the conservative-liberal government in Bonn. That government subsequently staked out ambitious ecological positions in the EC framework. Germany was out front on a number of environmental issues in comparison with the other EC member states. As such, the German position once again offers a point of orientation, now for Red-Green cooperation at the EC level in an increasingly self-confident political institution, the European Parliament. Such an ecological recalibration of the social and economic spheres may contribute to redefining the European enterprise. In that sense, *Modell Deutschland* required an organized polity at the European level to overcome its own limitations.

## GERMANY AND EUROPE'S FISCAL CONSTITUTION

Measured by its net contribution, Germany's financial liabilities to the EC have grown constantly over the past decade. In 1982, Germany paid 7.5 billion DM more into the EC than it received back. In 1987, the net payment was 10.4 billion DM. In 1991 it was estimated at 12 billion DM (Deutsche Bundesbank 1988; Finanzbericht 1991). The EC Commission drafted a financial plan that corresponded to the responsibilities the Community will be incurring as a result of the Treaty on European Union. From a total expenditure level of 51 billion ecu in 1987, spending rose to 66.5 billion in 1992 and is expected to rise to 87.5 billion ecu in 1997 (Commission of the EC 1992). Despite the fact that nearly 18.5 billion DM in Community funds could be claimed under the EC structural funds budget over the five-year period for the FNL, German budgetary pressure had become so acute by the autumn of 1992 that the federal government declined to agree to an expansion of 30 percent in EC spending. The Edinburgh European Council in November 1992 decided to spread out a 27 percent increase over seven years instead, as leaders struggled to balance recession-related declines in revenue with the need to buy political cohesion across the member states. According to the 1993 report of the German Federal Ministry of Finance (Finanzbericht 1993, p. 41), Germany's obligations to the EC for the period 1992 to 1996, are as follows:

**(Billions Of DM)**

| 1992 | 1993 | 1994 | 1995 | 1996 |
|---|---|---|---|---|
| 38.4 | 39.6 | 43.0 | 45.9 | 48.8 |

In light of Maastricht's grand plans, however, this reduction should be interpreted as a decline in the EC's capacity to achieve its goals. This prospect is disturbing, for the main surviving mechanism for coordinating the economies of the member states is the European Monetary System (EMS). Nevertheless, even though German unification is making the Federal Republic a much larger recipient of EC Objective 1 regional funds, the finance ministry estimates a growing net German transfer to the EC in coming years.

## CRISIS OF THE EMS: OVERLOADED POLICY INSTRUMENT OR STRATEGIC FAILURE?

The players in the European drama were aware of the implications of German unification well before the event. In its May 1990 report on the subject, the European Parliament foresaw the budgetary drain on the Community caused by unification. It realized that unless drastic "rationalizing" steps were taken, East German agriculture could swamp the Community with surpluses; and, most significantly, prophesied tensions in the Exchange Rate Mechanism on the basis of high German interest rates. In other words, in the absence of a real solution to the financial imperatives of unification, the task of reconciling public finance with macroeconomic goals lay with the Bundesbank.

Those chapters dealing with the EMS support the hypothesis that macroeconomic policy preferences inscribed in German policy-making institutions have been transmitted and embraced by other member states. From the point of view of the EC's "internal" development, the key problem of the EMS has always been how to balance economic convergence with cohesion of the Common Market. In practice, the issue is the Bundesbank's policy orientation.

Comparison of the French and British experiences with national reflation strategies is compelling in this regard. While the reflation effort undertaken by the French Socialist government from within the ERM in 1981 to 1983 collapsed, the Tory government in Britain has had some success in reflating outside of the ERM since September 1992. These experiences show how very difficult it will be to engineer conformity to all the Maastricht EMU convergence criteria at once in the short term, particularly in a stagnant economy. They also demonstrate that the price—measured in employment and bankruptcy rates—for EC cohesion on Bundesbank terms differs from member state to member state, and that this decision is based largely on a political calculus. This point is not new, though the analyses presented in this volume significantly extend and deepen the insights of other thoughtful scholars (Barrell 1992; Calleo and Morgenstern 1990).

The shock of the Danish narrow rejection of the Maastricht Treaty in June 1992 and the perceived closeness of the French referendum outcome triggered speculative runs on the pound and the lire in the days prior to the vote in September 1992. Both were forced into exchange rate corrections. The British government chose to withdraw from the ERM altogether. The Italian government withdrew with the stated intention of rejoining at some later date. The Spanish government was forced to devalue the peseta. Capital controls were implemented in Portugal, Spain, and Ireland. The Irish punt was finally forced to devalue in January 1993, nevertheless.

The EMS meltdown confirms the central message of chapters 3, 4, and 7 in this volume. First, it is worth noting that the turbulence did not affect Germany's three small neighbors—Denmark, the Netherlands, and Belgium. Nor, for that matter, was Austria affected by the currency storm. The economic structures of all four countries had long since adapted to that of Germany. In Chapter 4 Paulette Kurzer and Christopher S. Allen demonstrated how, on this foundation, monetary policy had been deliberately linked to the DM. Large states have not been exempted from this logic. In taking up the case of France, we return to the starting point of this chapter and this volume. Even a socialist government operating under optimal conditions with respect to public control over credit allocation and investment decisions in key industrial players considered EC political cohesion more important than its own political survival in the short term. In light of such stakes, Britain's apparent freedom to reflate after withdrawing from the ERM comprised a challenge the Community could not afford to ignore. The EC's coordinated reflation plan involving 10 billion ecus in loan guarantees for infrastructure projects and support for small and medium-size enterprises in problem regions, launched at the Edinburgh Council in November 1992, even if only a symbolic palliative, signals the limits of political tolerance of Bundesbank policy. Since, as James Sperling points out in Chapter 7, German monetary authorities also bear a major share of responsibility for regulating the transatlantic economy, this reflation-investment package has been marketed as Europe's contribution to a coordinated response to recession as well (Brittan 1993). Meanwhile, further elaboration of EC mechanisms such as the structural and cohesion funds must also be viewed in the light of German priorities, since they have been deployed quite deliberately to compensate—and thereby integrate—losers as they struggle to adjust to Europe's dominant economy.

The events of autumn and winter 1992 reveal a major flaw in the European architecture: Its policy instruments are too narrow. But, given EC complicity in Germany's all-or-nothing unification strategy, one can hardly blame that country for not doing more. That strategy programmed the monetary outcome. Could an alternative strategy—one that was incremental and holistic in approach (Reinicke 1992) with respect to East Germany and "domestically" oriented with respect to West Germany, as in the Greens' Reconstruction Program, appropriately updated to focus on cleaning up the FNL—have avoided the disintegrative outcome? Would such a strategy have arrested the immigration flow from the FNL to the western part of the country? In a looser, transitional confederation, would Germans still be willing to be taxed at high rates to support the transition? Would investors be more or less motivated to move into the FNL under this scenario? Could capital be raised nevertheless?

There can be no certain answer to these questions. That they can even be raised, however, conveys an important truth about the evolving political basis of European unification efforts. Europe's postwar generations are the stuff of new collective actors, for whom materialist values must contend with "quality of life" and political concerns. The postindustrial decentering of "work society" calls into question singleminded pursuit of markets. And the fear of a European military superpower defending far flung economic interests erodes residual credibility of the project of regional integration (Barratt Brown 1991; Galtung 1989; Lankowski forthcoming).

In light of its economic and financial prowess, there is some irony in the fact that Germany comprises the center of gravity for an alternative, "Green" Europe as well. Indeed, the German Greens have demonstrated considerable skill in exploiting Germany's federal system and electoral law. Even with its federal parliamentary representation at a nadir as a result of the December 1990 "unification election," the Greens affect policy through participation in "Red-Green" coalitions in Hesse, Bremen, and Lower Saxony. Despite the absence of a fully articulated European policy, the party effectively colors the EC policies of the other parties in the Federal Republic's multiparty system. And despite the real constraints the EC places on the alternative, Green project, there can be no doubt that it has significantly affected German behavior in the EC Council of Ministers, if for no other reasons than the German delegation has an interest in preventing environmental and social "dumping" through the adoption of ambitious standards at EC level.

As some studies have shown, these voices are "incorporated" into a German position at the national level and subsequently transmitted to the EC arena (Allen 1989). To be responsive to new voices is not the same as direct articulation of preferences associated with the movement sector, however. In this sense, German hegemonic power, defined as the capacity to determine parameters for action and to identify the major contestants in the struggle, operates in two directions: toward the EC and toward its "domestic" public. On the other hand, especially in light of the increasing role of the European Parliament as a crystallization point for political strategy, demarcation of the parameters of political discourse guarantees no specific outcome. Moreover, the parameters themselves are increasingly being contested, thereby extending the range of options within which outcomes will emerge. Out of this situation arises the defining paradox of German-EC relations: The inverse relationship between the national usefulness of the EC on policy grounds versus the risk of undermining policy consensus by broadening the basis of democratic legitimation of action taken at EC level. The continuing public uproar over Maastricht demonstrates that, even if the balance of forces still favors cooptation of the new voices, there is no gainsaying the effects the EC has already had on the role of the German state both as an arena for policy-making and as a locus of political allegiance.

The palpable disappointment over the unraveling of the EMS is not about the functioning of a monetary system in any technical sense. The EMS had attained the status of an icon, symbolizing a specific version of the project of European unity. To be sure, there were powerful political justifications for maintaining the cohesion of the EMS, since it was the most accessible way yet discovered to monitor German behavior in a key area of policy-making. But the dimensionality of Germany's EC links should make one cautious about prophesying a collapse of either the project of European unification or even the Maastricht Treaty on the basis of ERM adjustments. Rather, such adjustments point to the political, as opposed to technical, character of the EMU convergence criteria spelled out in the treaty. The debate over Maastricht has shown not only that the Community has crossed an important threshold beyond which more popular participation is required in order to secure the democratic legitimation of the project. It has also demonstrated that in order to salvage it, the fundamental design features of this Community may be in need of overhaul.

## NOTES

1. See "Schulden, Schulden, Schulden," *Der Spiegel* 12, 1993, pp. 18-20; Quentin Peel, "The Deal They Were Condemned To Do," *Financial Times,* 15 March 1993, p. 13; Otto Singer, "Der verkorkste Solidarpakt: Keinen Fehler vermieden," *Regenbogen. Bündnis 90-Die Grünen im Bundestag,* March 1993, p. 10.
2. See *Frankfurter Rundschau,* 7 February 1992, p. 5; *Financial Times* 13 October 1992, p. 2; and *Der Spiegel* 13, 1992 (March 23), pp. 68-69; *Frankfurter Rundschau,* 2 December 1992, p. 7.
3. Quoted in *Der Spiegel* 21 (1993), p. 24.

## REFERENCES

Allen, Christopher S. (1989). "Political Consequences of Change: The Chemical Industry," in Peter J. Katzenstein, ed., *Industry and Politics in West Germany: Toward the Third Republic.* Ithaca, NY: Cornell University Press.

Barratt Brown, Michael (1991). *European Union: Fortress or Democracy? Towards a Democratic Market and a New Economic Order.* Nottingham: Spokesman Press.

Barrell, Ray, ed. (1992). *Economic Convergence and Monetary Union in Europe.* Newbury Park: Sage Publications.

Brittan, Sir Leon (1993). "The World Economy in 1993: Coordination for Growth," Speech for the European Chambers of Commerce in Washington, D.C., 12 February 1993.

Calleo, David P., and Claudia Morgenstern, eds. (1990). *Recasting Europe's Economies: National Strategies in the 1980s.* Lanham, MD: University Press of America.

Commission of the EC (1990). "The European Community and German Unification," *Bulletin of the European Community.* April supplement. Brussels.

——— (1992). *From the Single Act to Maastricht and Beyond: The Means to Match Our Ambitions.* COM(92)2000 final. Brussels, 11 February.

Council (1992). Council of the European Communities. Commission of the European Communities. *Treaty on European Union.* Luxembourg: Office for Official Publications of the European Communities.

Deutsche Bundesbank (1988). "Recent Developments in the Financial Relations of the Federal Republic of Germany with the European Communities," *Monthly Report of the Deutsche Bundesbank* 40, no. 11, pp. 36-43.

European Parliament (1990). "The Impact of German Unification on the European Community," Research and Documentation Papers. Directorate-General for Research, Working Document No. 1 (6-1990). Luxembourg.

Finanzbericht (1991). *Die volkswirtschaftlichen Grundlagen und die wichtigsten finanzwirtschaftlichen Probleme des Bundeshaushaltsplans für das Haushaltsjahr 1991.* Bonn: Bundesministerium der Finanzen.

Finanzbericht (1993). *Haushaltsjahr 1993.* Bonn: Bundesministerium der Finanzen.

Galtung, Johan (1989). *Europe in the Making.* London: Crane Russak.

Hrbek, Rudolf, and Uwe Thaysen, eds. (1986). *Die Deutschen Länder und die Europäischen Gemeinschaften.* Baden Baden: Nomos Verlagsgesellschaft.

Katzenstein, Peter (1987). *Policy and Politics in West Germany: The Growth of a Semi-Sovereign State.* Philadelphia: Temple University Press.

Katzenstein, Peter, ed. (1989). *Industry and Politics in West Germany: Toward the Third Republic.* Ithaca, NY: Cornell University Press.

Keohane, Robert, and Stanley Hoffmann, eds. (1991). *The New European Community: Decisionmaking and Institutional Change.* Boulder, CO: Westview Press.

Lankowski, Carl (forthcoming). *Europe's Emerging Identity. Social Movements versus Regional Integration in EC-Europe.* Boulder, CO: Lynne Rienner Books.

Lankowski, Carl, and Donald Puchala (1977). "The Politics of Fiscal Harmonization in the European Community," *Journal of Common Market Studies* 15, no. 3 (summer).

Lodge, Juliet, ed. (1986). *European Union: The EC in Search of a Future.* London: Macmillan.

Markovits, Andrei, and Simon Reich (1991). "Should Europe Fear the Germans?" *German Politics and Society,* no. 23 (Summer), pp. 1-20.

Reinicke, Wolfgang (1992). *Building a New Europe: The Challenge of System Transformation and Systemic Reform.* Washington, D.C.: Brookings Institution.

Suhr, Heinz (1990). *Was kostet uns die ehemalige DDR?* Frankfurt/Main: Eichborn & Co. GmbH.

Veen, Hans-Joachim (1991). "Die Westbindung der Deutschen in einer Phase der Neuorientierung," *Europa-Archiv* 46, no. 2, p. 38.

Wolf, Martin (1993). "Dethronement of the D-Mark," *Financial Times,* 27 June.

Woolcock, Steven, Michael Hodges, and Kristin Schreiber (1991). *Britain, Germany, and 1992: The Limits of Deregulation.* New York: Council on Foreign Relations Press for the Royal Institute of International Affairs.

# INDEX